WHAT DO YOU MEAN A BLACK GIRL CAN'T DESIGN CARS?

EMELINE KING,

SHE DID IT!

The Autobiography of the First African American
Female Transportation Designer
for Ford Motor Company

Emeline King

Copyright © 2021 Emeline King

All rights reserved. No part of this book may be reproduced or transmitted in any form or by any means without written permission from the author.

Published by:

Claire Aldin Publications
P.O. Box 453
Southfield, MI 48037
www.clairealdin.com

All photos are from the author's private collection. Every effort has been made to ensure that all information in this book is accurate at the time of publication; however, Claire Aldin Publications neither endorses nor guarantees the content or external links referenced in this book.

All scriptures marked KJV are taken from the King James Version of the Holy Bible which is in the public domain.

Art Direction and Book Cover Design: Emeline King
Personal Artwork Photography: Eugenia Hardaway
Graphic Design: Diane Simpson
Cover Photo Photography: Wayne Norman
Cover Photo Makeup Artist: Keisha Barber at The Glam Shoppe
Hair Stylist: Weave World Wholesalers with Bonza Bracy and Raven Bracy

Library of Congress Control Number: 2020931111

ISBN: 978-1733656030 (paperback)
ISBN: 978-1733656054 (eBook)

Printed in the United States of America.

"GREAT READING! This book is a must read! *What Do You Mean a Black Girl Can't Design Cars?* is a book of courage and determination. Emeline King writes with passion, as she puts her pain and desires on the line to overcome obstacles of race, gender and intelligence. After reading this book, you will know what it means to use what God gives you and truly develop a masterpiece of design and durability. Emeline cannot only design a car for transportation, but she can teach you how to not let disappointments stop you when your destiny is not determined by man, but by God!"

~Reverend Dr. Deedee M. Coleman
President Emeritus, Council of Baptist Pastors of Detroit and Vicinity, Inc.
Pastor, Russell Street Baptist Church, Detroit, Michigan

"All of us can benefit from this story...especially young African American females. Your view of the automobile industry through the eyes of an African American female transportation designer is eye opening...the struggle for recognition and fairness needed to be told. Those who come after you will stand on your broad shoulders. Thank you for sharing."

~Deacon/Attorney Dave Benson III

"Emeline King has captured the heartbreaking, faith building struggles of African American women who dare to challenge the status quo. This book is a must read for women of all ages regardless of race, creed or color. She has illuminated the dark struggles of achievement while paving the path for the next generation of barrier breaking female transportation designers."

~Patricia A. Butler, Ed.D.
Pastor, St. Luke Tabernacle Community Church, Detroit, Michigan
Community Development Specialist, Cody Rouge Community Action Alliance
Retired Educator, Detroit Public Schools

"Ms. Emeline King is a multitalented woman of whom I am proud to know, especially after learning she has contributed to my success in the automobile business through the genius of her car designs! Thank you, Cass Tech classmate!"

~Mark O' Bryant
Sales and Leasing Representative
Bob Maxey Ford and Lincoln

"Having a strong faith in God, with dedication, determination and discipline, Emeline King shares her journey as the first African American female in the department of design at Ford Motor Company."

~Rev. Oscar R. Carter, Sr., D.D.

"But as for you, ye thought evil against me; but God meant it unto good, to bring to pass, as it is this day, to save much people alive" (Genesis 50:20 KJV).

"For a just man falleth seven times, and riseth up again: but the wicked shall fall into mischief" (Proverbs 24:16 KJV).

~Rev. Charlie Knighten
Pastor, Pilgrim Travelers Baptist Church, Inkster, MI

"As a veteran and military officer with twenty years of service in the United States Army and having received an honorable discharge, I must submit and clarify that heroes and heroines are not born, but they are made on the battlefield and on fields of life. Emeline King has proven and is proving by this noteworthy exposure, behind the curtain of masculinity, as reflected in the auto industry, and "the good old boys" playground" that she is a warrior - fit for battle! She rose through the ranks from high school to college and obtained an engineering degree as a dream fulfilled. *So, who said that only boys draw cars? Girls can, too...I did it.* Yes, indeed you did. Be proud of your successes, the knowledge you have gained, your experiences of facts, and your personal stamps as you lived them. At every opportunity, speak truth to power, and let your voice be heard through the pages of your book and beyond."

~Dr. A.J. King, Sr.
Grief Recovery Specialist and Former EEO Investigator

"This book will encourage and inspire you to keep pursuing your goals. You will get motivation to keep on going."

~Annie P. Jones
Author and Teacher

"Emeline is one multi-talented African American Trailblazer! Phenomenal!"

~Melanie Lowery
Customer Service Supervisor
United States Postal Service

"To read Emeline's story was as if I walked along with her; experiencing her joy of fulfilling a dream that perhaps, many thought impossible...from the beginning to the devastation of being told your services are no longer needed, was something I related to personally. This writing is a must read for all who dare to dream – those who dare to be encouraged. Emeline King proves beyond a shadow of a doubt how she handled the good, the bad, and the ugly. Kudos to you, Emeline! I Love you."

~Wilma McGee, Author

"Author Emeline King is a newly discovered 'hidden figure' African American heroine and former automotive designer with Ford Motor Company. For the first time in history, she gives a riveting and astonishing portrayal of her experience as an automotive designer. It is a true story about what it was like to penetrate the corporate glass ceiling within a racist and toxic environment where she was rejected, humiliated, and despised. Absolutely stunning, insightful and brilliant, this is a book that has found its time for release to the public."

~Robert B Middleton, II
President/CEO, Montford
Point Marines of America

"As the master modeler presiding over the Ford Motor Company's large and luxury car program, Ms. Emeline King had the responsibility of designing the featured threshed emblem to adorn the rear trunk area of our Lincoln designed for future production. The design Ms. King produced was exemplar and highlighted our luxury car product."

~Mr. Calvin A. Morrison, Jr.,

"Emeline King, a pioneer in the male-dominated automobile design industry and its first black female designer, shares her inspiring saga of pitfalls, perseverance and triumph."

~Garth Newberry
Designer and Art Center Colleague

"In this life, the journey we travel will have obstacles and detours…no one escapes these realities. The greater the gifts, the greater the struggles. Emeline has captured the emotions and disappointments connected to her journey. As an African American female, within a white male corporate world, she had to take her punches, but the lesson here is that her faith was stronger than the punches she took. She preserved, and God lifted her up. Trust in the Lord with all your heart and He will direct your paths."

~V. Lonnie Peeks, Jr. M.Div, MSW
CEO, eBusiness Strategies, LLC

"Emeline King has written a must-read primer for all young, black girls considering quitting or not following their dreams. Read this book - and learn from one of the best."

~Dorothy Ware
Owner/CEO, BAM Best Artist Management, LLC

"Emeline, you didn't take 'NO' for an answer. When it's said that you can't, it's time to show that you can. If it's a question of *if* you can, you've answered it with your God given talent!"

– Rev. James Wheeler,
Pastor, First Progressive Missionary Baptist Church
Detroit, Michigan

"Emeline King's book is a very interesting and inspiring story about her life. The reader who loves car designs and who loves a good book to read will not put it down until it's finished."

—Willie Williams
Retired Senior Powertrain Analysts FCA

"It's an amazing read. Ms. Emeline King educates and inspires as she shares her life's journey."

~Pastor David M. Yarber, Sr., D.Min.
Pastor, Davison Missionary Baptist Church
Detroit, MI

"Ms. King provides details of her career as an African American female in a male dominated field of automotive transportation design, specifically in the private sector. This book will be a roadmap to parents, educators, and future transportation designers."

~Evelyn B. J. Williams,
Supervisor, Department of Music
Wayne State University

"Our dreams keep us alive. We can be whatever we strive to be in life. With a positive attitude and a good frame of mind, we can conquer so many obstacles in life. We all have God's gifts and talents. If we apply ourselves and grow daily, we can reach our goal. From reading this autobiography by Emeline King, I have seen the newness of life. Let us be all that we can be and give God our very best."

~Brenda Wilson Billings, Author

"A brilliant, multi-talented gifted artist and performer…a true Detroiter with unique experiences as the first female African American automotive designer. Emeline King's artistic views are futuristic and inspiring."

~Dr. Rickie Hardaway
Medical Director, Alpha & Omega Primary Health Care

"Living in a society of division on multiple levels of differences, Emeline shares her life experiences through her career, talent, religion and family that will inspire not only little girls to become what she dreams but anyone who thinks that they cannot."

~Eugenia Hardaway,
Ford Mechanical Engineer

"Emeline King is a passionate woman with a multitude of skills. Becoming the first as a female transportation designer for Ford Motor Company is an example of her tenacity, perseverance, and ability. She is designed for greatness and this was just one step in that direction."

~Schylbea Jean Hopkins
Retired School Administrator
Licensed Realtor

"Emeline, you are truly an inspiration to me, as well as my two daughters. Your past accomplishments and current endeavors merely scratch the surface of your God given talents. You never cease to amaze me with your drive and determination to push the envelope. In summation, your life reminds me of a saying that I love to quote: 'It's never too late to become what you could've been.' Your book has also inspired me to do greater things in life."

~Errol David King,
Police Sergeant, Detroit Police Department

"Emeline King shares her story of hope, ambition, frustration and triumph that bespeaks life itself. You feel the passion of struggle against a cold reality, yet the light of hope shines through."

~Dr. E. L Branch, Senior Pastor
Third New Hope Baptist Church
Detroit, Michigan

"Ms. King's autobiography is insightful, impactful, honest, life changing and mind-blowing on her journey from the valley to the mountaintop in a male dominant industry."

~Rev. Lovejoy Johnson II, Pastor
New Bethlehem Baptist Church, Detroit, MI

"Just finished reading *What Do You Mean a Black Girl Can't Design Cars? Emeline King, She Did It!* I'm excited, outraged, disappointed, but not surprised how people of color, women of color especially, were and still are being treated in a society where equality, education and commitment should surpass sexism and discrimination. Thanks for trusting me with such an outstanding season in your life that most couldn't survive. Much success as you continue reaching heights and opening doors for future Emelines."

~Rev. Thomas F. Rutherford Sr.
Pastor, Freedom Missionary Baptist Church
Detroit, Michigan

"Ms. Kings captivating autobiography is informational and inspirational. It records the resilient, triumphant spirit of Ford Motor Company's first African American female transportation designer. Her story will inspire you to overcome your odds and obstacles."

~Dr. Samuel White, III, Pastor
Friendship Baptist Church
Detroit, Michigan

"After a brief pause, discrimination, racism and pure hatred reared its ugly head again in full force. This is a true story of how the seed of prejudice so easily embedded itself in the workplace and 'destroyed' the dreams and career of one little girl who was determined to succeed and make a difference. Not by the content of her character, creative talent or exceptional skills, she was judged solely by gender and the color of her skin. Moral leadership and moral values no longer exist. Get ready! You will experience a range of emotions with the turn of each page from start to finish. Emeline, be encouraged, stay strong."

~Jeanne Markay

"I have known Ms. Emeline King for over 10 years. I am so proud of her and her ability to write such a beautiful memoir, but also to share her gift in so many areas. Besides being a saxophonist and Zumba instructor to name a few gifts, the quote from the history of World War II to the present and the impact of the male dominated car industry hooked me from the very beginning. Her involvement opened many opportunities for women to be introduced to the car industry as designers. Emeline has shared her journey of beginnings, her determination and forthrightness to not only fulfill her dream, but to become the first. It is with utmost pleasure that I endorse "What Do You Mean A Black Girl Can't Design Cars? Emeline King, She Did It".

~Lady Gale Dalton,
First Lady of New Life Assembly Church

"This book about a powerful black woman who made her mark in the automobile industry is an added gem to African American History! It is interesting, intense, informative and inspiring as you read about Emeline's journey and recollection of that season of her life."

~Rev. Stephen L. Herrod, Pastor
Bethel Baptist Church East, Detroit, MI

"Emeline's book showcases her strength, true talent and courage to overcome any obstacle set before her. If she couldn't go over it, she chose to go around it. If she couldn't crawl under it, she simply knocked it out of her way and proudly walked through it. I'm proud of all of her endeavors and accomplishments as my sister. We share a common bond in the field of transportation. She did it! The first African American female transportation designer. My automotive design shero!"

~Earnest King, Jr.
Auto Mechanic, Detroit Department of Transportation

"Emeline King, she did it! Her empowering journey as the first black female transportation designer for Ford Motor Company is spectacular, historical, exciting, dedicating, inspirational, disciplined, inviting, talented… CLASSIC!"

~Chuck Patton
Board Member, National Automotive Historic Collection

"Emeline, your skills and talents allowed you to become the first black automotive designer at Ford Motor Company. You are a role model and trailblazer who made history."

~Earnestine Simmons
Healthcare Administrator

"This book should be read by every person who has ever experienced any type of challenges in life. Emeline King candidly shares her personal testimony of triumph over adversity and how God will help you to be victorious through a bad situation. All who desire to be encouraged and inspired to step out of the box to do great things in life must read this book!"

~Rev. Richard R. White III
Pastor, Dexter Baptist Church, Detroit, MI

FOREWORD

The day Ford gave Emeline her involuntary company separation was devastating. Although she felt it was the occasion that ended her automotive career at Ford, I assured her this wasn't the end, but rather a jump start to move her toward a more exciting and prosperous destination.

She might not have fully understood the reason why it had to happen, but it was a blessing that they let Emeline go. She was then free to focus her attention on the next chapter in her life. For years, I insisted that she keep records and document every experience and accomplishment at Ford. There would come a day when she would need material to tell her story for the entire world to hear, see, learn, and read. I told her, "Emeline, all you've accomplished, achieved, and endured in twenty-five years at Ford, some people don't do in a lifetime. You have an inspiring story to tell." So the day Emeline told me, "Daddy, Ford let me go!" the Holy Spirit revealed to me that it was time for Emeline to write her autobiography.

My name is Rev. Earnest O. King Sr., and Emeline King is my daughter. I have been the pastor of Mt. Calvary Baptist Church for 43 years and was employed with Ford Motor Company as an Exploratory Fabrication Plaster Specialist for 30 years. Beginning in kindergarten, Emeline's mother and I knew there was something special within her and that God would bring it out. We didn't know her future, but she was a persistent child. Whatever she set out to do, she gave 100 percent. We were proud of her.

We recognized that she had special gifts and a talent to draw and design. She could draw anything: portraits, cars, trucks, boats, airplanes, fashion, and architecture. She had a love for designing futuristic vehicles and products. Some designs were years ahead of her time. Collecting and assembling scale model cars and constructing things out of cardboard boxes fascinated her. Emeline always carried a sketchbook and pencil with her. She was destined to become great and valuable in the fine arts and auto industry.

Emeline was raised in a home environment that was God-fearing, Christian, loving, supportive, educational, and productive. As her parents, we were selective about

Emeline's education. We enrolled her in only the best accredited schools for the fine arts and transportation design. These institutions of learning prepared and trained her, as well as enhanced her natural gifts so that upon graduation, she would be a well-equipped, productive, and successful car designer. Her background and qualifications would open doors of unlimited opportunities locally, nationally, and abroad.

She always worked hard, even her instructors with whom I spoke observed Emeline's talent and would speak well of her. She never settled for second or last. Quality over quantity was her motto. She would always strive to make her best better. I saw how diligently she put the time and effort into projects. It was a reflection of her skill and training.

Emeline was exposed to art culture at an early age, prior to her career in the automobile industry. She was introduced to my friends and colleagues. Their specialties had a major influence and impact on her life. Our daddy-daughter trips to the studio of Oscar Graves, a famous Detroit African American sculptor, were the beginning of her first mentorship. I made plaster casts for his commissioned art sculptures. Mr. Graves gave Emeline her first encounter with clay, a material that was essential in the design process in the car industry.

Emeline had hands-on experience working with clay and designing three-dimensional relief sculptures with her mentor, Mr. Graves. Little did we know that the aroma from the clay and what she took in at the studio would have such a profound effect on Emeline. It was influential in her decision to want to be a transportation designer and design cars for Ford. Her curiosity was already sparked on her first visit to my job at the Design Center.

Exposing my little girl to the design process—how cars were made, my job's role, and most important, the men who are the transportation designers that created the vehicles we purchase and drive—all made an impact on and motivated Emeline to become a transportation designer at Ford, working with her father. Emeline's passion to design cars led her to enter a technical field dominated by men, one uncharted by women, especially an African American female. Most inspiring for her was meeting my Ford colleagues. A select group of African American males who were "firsts" in their design specialties—transportation design, clay modeling, interior & exterior trim, wood craftsmanship, paint and engineering—became her mentors too.

Her success was only achievable through God's blessings, her talents, gifts, parental guidance, family upbringing, and education, along with Emeline's determination and will power. She stood on the shoulders of her mentors who provided a strong foundation. All these skills equipped her to become the first African American female car designer for Ford, applying her creative abilities to design popular cars for the buying public.

It wasn't an easy or smooth ride for my daughter. Within those twenty-five years, Emeline encountered many detours, stoplights, caution signs, potholes, speed bumps, pit stops, setbacks and turn-arounds. There were times when she was passed over for managerial promotions and treated unfairly, but she overcame this obstacle course. Strong-natured, dedicated, and determined, Emeline shifted into first gear to cross many finish lines. She achieved her victory lap and left marks of her creative and profitable design contributions.

In addition to having a successful career in the auto industry, my daughter is blessed with other gifts and talents: a vocalist, directress, musician, and motivational speaker. She mentors youth and is faithful in her church activities. She conquered her impossible dream. It happened for a little black girl growing up in the automobile capital who dreamt of one day designing cars for Ford with her father. Emeline King—she did it!

So, I invite you to follow along on Emeline's journey. Hop in, you'll enjoy the ride. This autobiography is a must-read. A black female from Detroit, the capital of the auto industry, accomplished success and triumph in a male-dominated field at Ford Motor Company Design Center.

"Motivating and inspiring everyone who dreams and desires to shift into reality."
What do you mean a black girl can't design cars?
My Daughter, Emeline King...She Did It!

~Pastor Rev. Earnest O. King, Sr.
Father of Emeline King
Retired Exploratory Fabrication Plaster Specialist, Ford Motor Company

CONTENTS

Preface	How It All Began	17
Introduction	Is This A Dream?	19
Chapter One	She Was Born With It	29
Chapter Two	She Was Exposed To It	71
Chapter Three	She Dreamed It	95
Chapter Four	She Learned It	111
Chapter Five	She Applied It	121
Chapter Six	She Designed It	147
Chapter Seven	She Accomplished It	175
Chapter Eight	She Explored It	213
Chapter Nine	She Experienced It	221
Chapter Ten	She Did It	307

PREFACE
HOW IT ALL BEGAN

FORD'S FEMALE CAR DESIGNERS

The continuation of World War II opened the door for women to join Ford Motor Company's design team. With men still fighting at war, and automobile manufacturing beginning to ramp up again, all passenger car manufacturing had to come to a halt during the war. As factories were retooled for military purposes, women filled an important gap. Illustrator Leota Carroll was the first woman designer hired, followed by a handful of others, including Beth O'Rourke and Doris Dickerson (who designed steering wheels and instrument panels), Florence Henderson (ornamentation), Elre Campbell and Letha Allen (color and trim). Their tenure at Ford was short lived. By 1948, all female designers had departed, replaced by men returning home from the front lines. Ford's Design Studio wouldn't hire another full-time female designer until 1970, when Mimi Vandermolen joined the team. As the first female car transportation designer, Vandermolen became part of a very small minority of female designers worldwide.

THIRTY-EIGHT YEARS LATER

Another female designer's dream became a reality on October 24, 1983. Thirty-eight years after World War II ended, Ford hired Emeline King, their first African American female car transportation designer. King was hired in at the Ford Motor Company Design Center in Dearborn, Michigan. Little did she know that she was making history being the first African American female transportation designer ever employed at Ford. There is no record that Ford Motor Company ever hired another African American female car designer.

INTRODUCTION
IS THIS A DREAM?

THE POSTER CHILD HAS LEFT THE BUILDING

Friday, July 31, 2008, at 1:00 p.m. was a day that, instead of shattering the glass ceiling, it sent me straight through the cement floor. I'd just returned from vacationing in Little Rock, Arkansas for the King/Scott Family Reunion. I was feeling eager to get back to work.

I had recently been transferred from out of the creative design phase of the auto industry over to the marketing side. I guess this move was management's way to get me out of the spotlight and less of an opportunity to perform in the area which I was trained and well equipped to do—to design cars.

I had no problem expressing my concerns in a professional way to Human Resources. I would be more valuable contributing to the creative side, which was proven with the successful car design projects I worked on, such as the 1989 Thunderbird, Wheel Program and 1994 Mustang. My creative side in designing outweighed applying my talents and skills to data entry, assembling competitive boards, ordering and setting up for vehicles in the showroom.

All my coworkers were in good spirits and heavily engaged in their work. We had few conversations that morning, which seemed unusual. I hadn't seen my supervisor for most of the morning, assuming he must have been in meetings. I noticed the clock on the wall said 11:30 a.m.; it was time to go to lunch. I decided to go to one of the restaurants not far from the job. After I finished lunch, I came back to work to complete my assignment. What took place in the next two hours was the catalyst that altered my career path.

There was a change in the atmosphere upon entering the studio. The coldness in the room suddenly left me feeling empty. Pushing through that unnerving feeling, I started working on my computer, putting together a list of competitive brand vehicles. It was going on 1:30 p.m., but none of my coworkers had returned from lunch. *So strange*, I thought. *They should have been back from lunch by now.* I started to get a little worried.

That unsettling feeling was the same emotion I felt on September 11, 2001. My coworkers and I were in a meeting when the studio's TV monitors switched over to breaking news. In disarray, we all watched as Flight 175 crashed into the Twin Towers, followed by the Towers descending one by one. That moment left us all speechless. We were in disbelief, totally shocked and numb—an aura of sudden emptiness and coldness.

Not knowing what was in store for me, I continued working on my computer when I noticed my supervisor. Standing halfway between the doorway of my cubicle and the studio, he asked if he could talk to me for a moment. My world at Ford was about to spiral downward.

"Sure, Tom," I replied. He held a manila envelope, which he flickered back and forth. I followed him to another area in the studio and sat down at a long black conference table. Tom was on the opposite side of the table. I thought, *maybe I'm finally getting a promotion*. As he began to talk, his words sounded slow and distant. At first, I thought I was dreaming, but it was reality awakening, especially when I heard the nervous, faint sound of my supervisor's voice telling me,

"Emeline, I'm sorry. The company has to downsize, and it is management's decision to let you go. We are offering you an involuntary company separation." He handed me the manila envelope and told me that I needed to sign the papers within.

"You have a few minutes to go back to your desk, gather your personal belongings and leave the premises," Tom said, glancing at his watch. "There's a box on your desk for you to put your personal things in. If you prefer, we can mail the rest to you." He then asked me, "Where's your car? Is it in the parking lot?"

At that moment, I had a flashback. Twenty-five years of service at Ford and here's the final thanks I get? Involuntary company separation? Well, I'll be damned! Somebody slap me in the face and wake me up! This wasn't a dream. I realized my career with Ford Motor Company was *over*! *Done!* I was still in shock.

Next thing I knew, my supervisor and I were back in my cubicle. None of my coworkers were there. I gathered up all my personal belongings and placed all I could fit inside this one brown, 12x12 cardboard box. Suddenly, my mind reflected on the times when previous supervisors called me in their office to inform me I had been assigned to work on a new program and would be moving to another design studio. I would have to call the movers to schedule my moving date and order those same brown 12x12 cardboard boxes for my belongings. I would have to assemble, label, and leave the boxes in my cubicle for the movers to come and take them to my new studio location.

I was always excited about moving on for new and better challenges, but this time it was different. This time was devastating, humiliating, unbelievable and permanent. There was news circulating that Ford was downsizing, ultimately resulting in the layoff of some executives, managers and designers. A lot of my coworkers were on edge and nervous. I thought, *something like this could never happen to Emeline King*! I was the "golden poster child." I was safe because I was the first *and* only black female transportation designer. Ford hadn't hired another one in the 24.9 years that I had been there. I thought I would be protected. Involuntary company separation was the final straw.

This black girl had drawn her last car sketch for Ford and the fat lady sang her last song. I won't ever be returning back to Ford Motor Company. My career at Ford had come to an end. It felt like the rug had been snatched right out from under me. Wow! They could have at least waited two more months to let me go. That way, I would have made 25 years of service with Ford Motor Company instead of 24.9 years.

There will be no more opportunities for me to make major design contributions for Ford Motor Company in the auto industry. No more staff meetings. No more trying to prove my leadership qualities as a talented designer to be a part of middle or upper management. No more being passed over for promotions, not that I wasn't qualified for it. The one thing that stuck out in comparison to my other Ford designers was that I was the only female African American transportation designer. No more watching those other Ford designers — who started at the bottom along with me only to see those other designers climb past me straight to the top. I can be proud of my designs that made it into production and were there for the public to purchase. No more making presentations. Not even a chance to look forward to planning a big retirement party.

You could hear a pin drop; it was so quiet in the studio. My supervisor waited until I cleared off my desk. He asked for my badge, which I removed and handed over to him. I picked up my box and walked toward the door. A security guard, who was waiting at the door, started walking beside me with my boss on the other side. We walked down the long corridor towards the parking lot where my black Ford Escape was parked. I could feel my eyes watering as one little tear slowly graced its way down my left cheek. That walk seemed like eternity.

I was still in a daze. My mind reflected on a scene from the movie, *The Green Mile*, featuring Michael Clarke Duncan. As he took his final walk down death row, you could hear the prisoners yelling, "Dead Man Walking!" from behind their cells. For me, it sounded like they were chanting, "Black Female Car Designer Walking! You might have been the first, but now you're the last."

We took the back hallway out to leave the building. My supervisor opened the blue door for me. That's when I turned around to take one final look at the door that first caught the attention of a little black girl who went with her father to his Christmas party at the design center. Amidst the aroma of clay and inquisition, he introduced me to an uncharted world in the auto industry.

As we headed to the parking lot, I glanced over and saw all my coworkers returning back together. They must have known something was about to go down because they never would have returned from lunch this late.

"I'm sorry Emeline…that this happened to you," my supervisor said again as I approached my truck. From his emotion, I could tell he was sincere. Ford had to do what it did. Nothing personal. Business was business. I can be proud that I made contributions and witnessed cars I designed driven on the roads.

I sat down in the driver's seat and before I could shut the door, the passenger side door opened. A lady from Human Resources got in and sat on the seat.

"Are you okay, Emeline?" she turned to me and asked.

"No, right now, I'm not okay. So will you please get the hell out of my truck?" I took out my phone and called my oldest sister, Am.

"Am, they let me go," I spoke into the phone. She got my other sister, Eugenia, on the other end of the phone and asked where I was.

"I'm just sitting here—numb—in my truck, in the parking lot."

My sisters told me to meet them at Starters Restaurant at Fairlane Mall. After I got there, I shared with them what had happened. My parents were out of town for the National Baptist Convention, and I was even more hurt because I didn't want to tell them that Ford let me go. My sisters reassured me, telling me that it was going to be okay and that I needed to tell Mom and Dad.

After about a week and a half, I'd mustered up enough strength to tell my parents. I drove to West Bloomfield to my parent's home. When I walked into the kitchen, Dad was preparing breakfast on the stove.

"Daddy, Ford let me go."

At first, Dad didn't say a word. He stood totally silent. I mentioned it to him again.

"Go tell your mother; she's on the porch," Dad instructed. "Then come and have a seat in the family room."

After I told Mom, she gave me some words of encouragement.

"Don't worry; you'll have another job soon," Mom encouraged. "God is going to bless you and open another door for you." After she finished, I stood there for a moment with flashback of how supportive Mama has been throughout my career. From sharing her wisdom, to traveling with me to hear my speeches and presentations at different schools and Ford events, she has been consistent. She displayed her motherly pride of my career and achievements to everyone she met. I remembered the time Mama stayed up all night with me to help me finish an art project which was due in one hour. I kissed her and thanked her for her love, wisdom and support. I went back in the house and listened to what Dad had to tell me.

"Emeline, have you been keeping a record down through the years, like I asked you to do?" Dad inquired. "Documenting everything – all that you've been through, every project you designed, every meeting with HR about your career path, every award, every magazine, newspaper, radio and television ad you were featured in, every promotion, merit and accomplishment at Ford…the good, the bad, and the ugly?"

I told him that I had thorough documentation from day one until my last day employed at Ford Motor Company. Dad began to encourage me, letting me know that God has always been with me throughout my entire years with Ford.

"He's certainly not leaving you now," Dad said. "God has more in store for you now, more than you will ever imagine or dream. With your all talent and success, you need to write a book. The world needs to hear and learn about your entire story. But first, you're going to have to release Ford, bury those hurt feelings and move forward."

I will admit; it wasn't an easy task. I was embarrassed, angry, and bottled up with a lot of emotions. It took me years to get over it, but on that special day, I reached deep down inside of me, grabbed a hold of that same ounce of determination that I had as a child who wanted to be a transportation designer designing cars for Ford with my dad. I refused to let involuntary company separation destroy or break me. I would only allow it to move me over to a higher direction. I made several accomplishments, including traveling the world and being exposed to wonderful experiences. I decided to let go of Ford, I had the will power and strength to forgive and release all negativity. So I picked up my pen, designed my story and now it begins.

EMELINE IS GOING TO DRAW CARS

Due to lack of exposure, the career choices were limited when I was growing up. I attended Harry B. Keidan Elementary School, which was located on Collingwood just a few blocks in walking distance from my home on Quincy Street. I was in the fifth grade when my social studies teacher, Mr. Calvin Summers, asked each student to stand up, state their name, and tell the class what they wanted to be.

"I'm going to be a policeman like my daddy. I want to be a fireman or I'm going to be basketball player," all the boys boasted.

The majority of the girls would softly say, "I would like to be a nurse. When I grow up I'm gonna be a teacher and a model." When it was my turn, I stood up and proudly shouted out loud, *"Good morning, Class! My name is Emeline King, and I'm gonna draw cars, just like my daddy! He works for Ford Motor Company!"* My response was greeted with snickers from my classmates.

Mr. Summers, who stood six feet tall, was a slender black man who spoke proper English. He approached me and tried to steer me in another direction by suggesting a few *feminine* occupations.

"Emeline, since you like using your hands, why don't you become a seamstress, a cook, a secretary, or a nurse?" Little did Mr. Summers and my classmates know that my daddy exposed me to a new and unique career: the world of designing cars for the auto industry. I found that career more interesting and exciting than following the standard norm of careers typically set for girls—domestic and nursing.

I was seven years old when I dreamed about becoming a transportation designer. It all started the first day my father took me to his job for their Annual Design Center Family Christmas Party. He worked at the Ford Design Center, located on 21175 Oakwood Boulevard in Dearborn, Michigan. That experience immediately triggered three strong reasons why I wanted to fulfill my destiny. First, we walked down the long hallway of the Design Center. To my right, a blue door caught my attention. My curiosity fueled my desire to find out exactly what was behind it. My impatience was relieved when my father told me that men who designed cars work behind the blue door. They are called "transportation designers."

"Lenny Girl, every car you see on the road had its start in a design studio and was created in the mind of a transportation designer."

Second, I visualized working alongside my father at the Ford Motor Company Design Center. We would be that Daddy-Daughter design team. Dad would work in one of the fabrication studios as an exploratory fabrication plaster specialist, making molds off the clay model cars, and I would work in a design studio creating concepts that turned into production models available for the buying market.

Third, I had a strong determination to overcome obstacles while acknowledging my accomplishments, struggles and failures. I had a strong passion to be a transportation designer, but it never crossed my mind that I was about to break down a gender barrier. This career hadn't been chartered by females, especially black females. A female car designer wasn't the norm in that day. I could count on my hands and feet the number of times I've heard some of my male teachers tell me, "Girls can't design cars. Emeline, you need to go into an easier and domestic field, something like teaching, nursing, or cooking. Why don't you choose a career that would be more suitable for a girl, like a secretary or librarian?"

Hearing remarks like this didn't discourage me one bit. In fact, it only increased my desire to go into the field of designing cars. I decided to pursue a career in transportation design and was determined not to let anyone or anything deter me. I refused to let my gender dictate my dream. I believed I had something to offer, precisely because I was a female. I would see things from a different perspective than a male, perhaps by bringing a softer touch, a more feminine approach. Cars weren't only a male buying market. Females bought them, too.

Working in corporate America in a field that was highly saturated by Caucasian men didn't make my journey easy. Within those 25 years of service with the Ford Motor Company Design Center, I experienced the ugly side of discrimination and affirmative action in my workplace. Through perseverance, I reached heights that others would believe impossible for a black girl. I obtained achievements and accomplishments that, with God's direction, made it possible for me to reach. I truly believe that God placed the right people in my life at the right time to assist, nurture and develop me into a successful car designer.

There were other female employees who worked in the administration department; however, I was the first and only African American female hired as a car designer at that time. With no advancement during my career, I constantly felt myself being pushed further down the corporate ladder. I longed for the day to be promoted into middle and upper management. When it came time for upper management to select candidates for promotions, I assumed my name would be on the list. As I watched over the years, my name must have never been suggested.

Many designers—both males and females who were hired in after me and worked on the same design projects often got the promotion. Each time I asked why I wasn't getting a promotion after I met all the requirements necessary to be considered. Every time I met with upper management and Human Resources, they told me I needed this and that to get into management.

When the term "diversity" was the blueprint to follow, Ford Design Center wanted to show they were a company that valued diversity, especially in management. This only made matters worse for me. Not only was I being overlooked for Caucasian males to fill those management roles, but in 1990, Ford also started hiring other ethnic minority female car designers (Asian, Hispanic, Caucasian, Filipino, Chinese and Korean) who immediately benefited from affirmative action and were promoted into middle and upper management positions. It was an uphill battle. Although we worked on the same projects and received the same performance ratings of (E) excellent or (EP) excellent plus, there was still no advancement.

I was doing the work of a manager, lead designer and was the face connected with an iconic car project: the 1994 Mustang; yet, I was never promoted to the title "manager". There was a representative of every ethnic group in management, including an African American male, with the exception of me, the only African American Female. I had the most seniority among the male and female coworker designers. I felt like I was the poster child for design in face only because I graced the covers of many magazines: *Smithsonian, Ebony, Essence, Ebony Man* and several others, and represented Ford on television and radio. However, I never gave up trying to remove the glass gender ceiling. I persevered.

Yes, this journey was major for a little black girl growing up on the west side of Detroit. I was nurtured and groomed by my father to enter into an uncharted male-dominated industry. So, who said that only boys draw cars? Girls can, too. Because I'm a girl, I can't design cars? I did it.

CHAPTER ONE
SHE WAS BORN WITH IT

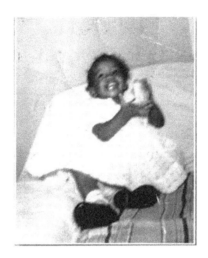

Born in Detroit, Michigan, the "automotive capital of the world" and home to legendary Motown Records founder, Mr. Berry Gordy Jr., Dr. James F. Fitzgerald delivered me on a cold winter Tuesday morning, December 16, 1957. God's appointed arrival time for me was 6:00 a.m. at the Burton Mercy Hospital, 3019 West Warren Avenue. The world was introduced to a beautiful, bubbly-eyed, caramel complexioned, six-pound baby girl with a smile that lit up the world, "Lil Miss Emeline King."

I'm the proud daughter of Reverend Earnest Ovell King, Sr. and Mrs. Emogene King. My mother told me that the umbilical cord was wrapped around my little neck three times. I guess I was determined to come out a strong fighter, determined to beat the odds. Mama said I was a stubborn child, too. When I was five years old, I was the only one of her children to get a whipping by her father, Reverend James Marshall Randall. If there was something I wanted to do or say, I wouldn't let anything, or anybody get in my way.

HOW DADDY MET MAMA

Earnest and Emogene King, 1954

Both of my parents were born in Arkansas. Mama grew up in Buena Vista; Daddy was from a small town called Amy, which was about 12.4 miles from Buena Vista. My father worked as carpenter with his best friend, Earl Jr. They worked throughout Amy repairing houses. My dad didn't have transportation, so he relied upon Earl Jr. to drive him to the different job sites. Sometimes, this ended up as a one-way trip for Dad because Earl Jr. would drop him off early in the morning and forgot to come back to pick him up.

One day, my father was informed about doing some work for a Mr. James Marshall Randall who lived in Buena Vista. Upon his arrival, my father met Mr. Randall at the door. Grandpa Randall stood six feet tall and weighed about 190 pounds. He was dark skinned and spoke in a deep, authoritarian voice. He opened the screen door, sized my father up and down before giving him a verbal warning.

"I've got plenty of work for you to do son, but I'm telling you now; I've got a daughter inside here, and I don't want no stuff from you. Don't you even think about messing with my daughter, Emogene!"

My dad, who had a smart mouth, murmured under his breath, "Sir, if she looks anything like you, you won't ever have to worry about me messing with her." However, my father's perspective changed once he finally laid eyes on my mother.

Emogene Randall was an attractive looking young lady. She stood 5'7, slim with a caramel skin complexion. Besides her beauty, what really captured his attention and made him fall in love with Mama was when he tasted her homemade biscuits, which she prepared every day for the family meal. Ultimately, they fell in love, got married by the justice of peace, and the rest was smooth history.

Dad found out that there were better opportunities in Detroit for raising a family and finding employment. My parents left Arkansas in the early 1950's and migrated to Detroit. Once they arrived, they needed to find a place to stay. That's when they met Mr. George Guiden and Mrs. Beverly Guiden. They rented a two-story flat from them on Tireman Street. The Guidens became close friends to my parents. When my parents were expecting their first born, who was my oldest sister, they asked the Guidens to be godparents.

My daddy wanted to name her Evelyn, and my mom wanted to name her Jean because it was similar to Emogene. Since Evelyn was the apple of Mrs. Guiden's eye, she wanted her to be named Beverly. Daddy ended up giving her all three names: Evelyn Beverly Jeanette King. She's the only one of us who has three names.

DADDY NAMED ME

Leonia Randall (grandmother), Horace Gene (cousin), Mama, Evelyn, Daddy and Emeline

Each of my parent's names started with the letter "E." My father's name is Earnest, and my mother's name is Emogene. It was Dad's plan to start a family tradition by having all of his children's names begin with the letter "E." One day I asked my dad, "Was there a special reason why you chose to name me Emeline?" Anxiously awaiting his answer, he just looked at me and chuckled.

"No, I just knew it was going to start with the letter 'E.' I looked in the name book, saw the name Emeline, pointed to it, and that's about it." I admit I was waiting to hear something more exciting and spectacular than what he told me. Seeing how disappointed I was, Dad later told me that on the day I was to be born, the Holy Spirit revealed to him that my name should be Emeline and that I would be a *special person*. With joy and laughter, Daddy said he was so excited that he didn't even realize he beat Mama to the hospital. I will always cherish Dad's reason for naming me Emeline.

I have three sisters and two brothers: Evelyn Beverly Jeanette, Earnestine, Eugenia, Earnest Jr. and Errol David King. My oldest sister, Evelyn, would always tell me, "Emeline, I'm the reason for you being here. I asked Mom and Dad for a little baby sister, and you were what I got!"

NICKNAMING MY SIBLINGS

My dad nicknamed me, "Lenny Girl." I felt special because out of all my siblings, I'm the only one Dad nicknamed. So, I wanted to pass nicknaming onto my siblings. Evelyn's name was too long for me to remember as a child, let alone pronounce. So, I condensed it to one word: "Am." Earnestine, another older sister of mine, received the nickname, "Tine." Eugenia, my baby sister, got two nicknames: Kizzy and Kiddo. After seeing the television series, *Roots,* I was inspired by the performance of "Kizzy," a slave in the series played by lead actress, Leslie Uggams. As the youngest of the King girls, she was always bossy and acted like she was the oldest over all her siblings. That's how she got her second nickname, "Kiddo."

I remember the time she used my oldest brother, Earnest Jr. for her scientific experiment. She took a whole jar of my mother's Royal Crown Hairdressing and greased him up from head to toe. He just sat innocently on the bathroom floor with those big, beautiful silver dollar brown eyes, and let her do that to him. He was so shiny, if humans lived on Mars, they would see him shining from Earth. Because my brother, Earnest Lonell King, Jr., was the first-born male child, Dad and Mom would always let him have his way. He was spoiled rotten but, I looked up to him. I just called him, "Brother."

MY BROTHER BOBBIE

The youngest sibling in the family was my little brother, Errol David, who was a force to be reckoned with. I nicknamed him "Bobbie" because he acted like the cartoon character "Bobby" from *Bobby's World*. Just like my little brother, the cartoon character was outspoken and mischievous.

At six years of age, Bobbie loved to showboat his favorite toy, a red and yellow big wheel, in front of his friends. He would take his red and yellow toy big wheel from out the side door, jump inside and head down the side of the house onto the sidewalk. He'd make a quick left and start peddling as fast as he could and skid into his signature abrupt stop right in front of the next-door neighbor's house, where his best friends, the Williams brothers stayed. Charlie, Dwayne, Michael and Anthony Williams would all stand on their porch, waiting patiently for Bobbie's arrival. In their eyes, Bobbie was everything and two bags of potato chips. Their world revolved around him. He was the leader of the pack. If things didn't go Bobbie's way, he had no problem calling his friends or anybody else, "monkey ass."

I think he picked up this bad habit of name calling after seeing the chimpanzee show at the Belle Isle Zoo. The zoo was a special trip for Mama to treat her children on Saturday. We watched the chimpanzees come out riding on their tricycles and do mischievous tricks to each other. When they finished performing, they would get off their bikes, scurry off to the side of the stage, climb up to the top and jump from rock to rock. From where we sat, we could see their hairy bottoms which were red, torn and swollen. It looked like they must have injured their butts on the rough rocks. Seeing the chimpanzees' back sides caused Bobbie to stand up, point at them and yell, "Owweee! Monkey ass!" Everybody started laughing except Mama who popped Bobbie on his legs with a small belt and told him, "Sit down, Errol! That's not funny, don't you say that bad word ever again."

Embarrassed, Errol sat down, folded his little arms together and scowled, poking out his lips.

TOY MUSTANG PRELUDES MY DREAM CAREER

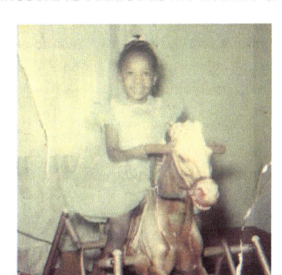

When I turned five years old, my parents gave me a birthday party and surprised me with a toy, "Wonder Rocking Horse." It was a replica of a Mustang horse. I rode my toy horse every day. It's been over 50 years, but I still have it today as a keepsake.

As I previously stated, I could never have imagined that in the near future, a black girl from the city of Detroit would one day fulfill her dreams of becoming a car designer, working with her father at Ford, and making a major contribution by designing the interior of such an iconic American car as the 1994 Ford Mustang. The Mustang project, code named SN95, would be the catalyst that launched a successful career for me as a car designer at Ford Motor Company. I was fortunate to be selected by upper management to be given the opportunity to display my gifts and talents. Little did I know that I was making history by becoming the first African American female transportation designer to ever work at Ford Motor Company.

MY FIRST DRIVING LESSON

What a coincidence it was when I noticed the year that my daddy was born, 1933, and my birth year, 1957, was the same address as the street we lived on – 3357 Columbus Street in Detroit. It was a brown brick duplex adjacent to an alley where I had my fondest childhood memories and experienced my first driving lesson.

Our neighbors were the Early family – Mr. Ernest and Daisy Early and their three children: Eula, Ardell and Al. Their house was located on Dexter Avenue. It was a bright yellow stucco framed house, the largest and most noticeable in our neighborhood. Their backyard was so large that we shared one third of their property which was separated by a thin wired fence. My parents and the Early's established a longtime friendship, along with their children.

The Early's were entrepreneurs. Mr. Ernest Early was an alley mechanic and just like my dad, Earnest King, they shared the same pronunciation in their name and loved cars. Mr. Early repaired transmissions in his garage. His shop was next to the alley by our duplex. Both he and my dad would spend hours repairing cars together and enjoying each other's camaraderie. Mrs. Early was in the business retail industry. She and my mom attended the same church, Antietam Baptist. Mom was the church's pianist and Mrs. Early sung in the choir. Am and I played with the children. Eula and Am were just five years old when they first met each other after a conversation at the backyard fence. Afterwards, they became the best of friends. I played with Ardell and her little brother Al. We were the best of friends. I give credit to Al because he gave me my first driving lesson in a go-kart. We both were seven years old and adventurous kids when Al's father built Al his own motorized go-kart. It was powered by a small Honda motorcycle engine. The interior had two small, black jump seats side by side, housed inside a black aluminum tube cage. To get the engine started, Al would pull on the engine's lever just like he was starting a lawn mower. The engine sounded something like this: *"putt...putt ...brummmmmm..."*

One day, Al drove around the corner with his go-kart and stopped in front of my house.

"Lean, you wanna go for a ride?" Al asked me.

"Sure, if you teach me how to drive it," I replied. So I hopped in, and off we went with Al in the driver's seat, and I was strapped in on the passenger side. After we rode several times around the block, I had enough of Al chauffeuring me around. I asked him to let me take the wheel and drive this thang.

"Lean, I'll let you drive; but you betta not go in that street, you gonna get me in trouble." Al warned. I said to myself, *Hmmm, now why did he tell me what I betta not do?* This was all I needed to peak my curiosity. Sarcastically, I told him, "All right Al, just let me drive." We traded places, and I took the wheel and started driving on the sidewalk.

Once I passed our house and before Al could say the word, "Don't," I was heading down the curb onto Dexter Street. Dexter was a major street, and traffic was always busy with cars. It was only by the grace of God that a car didn't come along and flatten both me and Al.

I was having the time of my life behind the wheel. My adrenaline was sky high; I had totally forgotten my promise to Al not to go into the street. I wasn't paying any attention to where I was going. We ended up in the street towards oncoming traffic. Al was on the other side having a fit.

"Leeeeean Stop! Get back on the sidewalk!" Al screamed at the top of his lungs. He grabbed the wheel and steered it back on the sidewalk.

"I told you not to go in the street, I ain't never gonna let you drive!" Al yelled. He was absolutely right, because that ended all driving lessons with my friend for a long time.

JILL OF ALL TRADES

There must be some truth behind the saying that left-handed people are highly creative. I'm the only left-handed person in my immediate family and I always had a talent for creating and designing things. I could draw just about anything I saw. I looked up to my dad. I'm so much like him—multi-talented, and a "chip off the old block." He said that I was the "Jill of all trades". He was right; I wanted to do it all, no matter what skill it was. I could sing, act, do public speaking, tap dance and do martial arts. I could also play piano, organ, soprano, tenor and alto saxophone, as well as portrait and abstract painting, graphic design, and of course, design cars.

I wanted to be the first and best in just about everything. I enjoyed collecting fifth scale model cars and making model toy cars. Sometimes, Dad and I would compete against each other just to see who could collect the most model cars. I ended up with at least, if not over, 100 models.

I was extremely competitive—a little tomboy at heart, competing with the boys in my neighborhood like Tyrone and Al. I would always beat them in running, climbing or playing sports. I was intrigued with reading about people who were the first to break historic barriers: Bessie Coleman, Dr. Mae Jamison, Marian Anderson, Bruce Lee, The Jackson Five, Aretha Franklin, Dr. Martin Luther King, Jr., Rosa Parks, Kareem Abdul-Jabber (Lewis Alcindo) and NASCAR Driver Danica Patrick.

GROWING UP ON 10023 QUINCY STREET

Am and I were excited when Mom and Dad told us we were moving to our new home at 10023 Quincy Street. It was a wood-framed structure with white aluminum siding and pink trim. We finally had our own fenced-in backyard to play in, and a two-car garage. The house was a bungalow which had a living room with a fireplace, dining room, kitchen, basement and one bathroom. My parents slept downstairs, while my siblings and I slept upstairs. Our basement was quite large, which is where I spent a lot of time riding my bike, building cars out of cardboard boxes and roller skating.

We lived in a diverse neighborhood with nice-looking houses. Our next-door neighbor, Mr. Roth, was an elderly Polish man. Three doors down from him lived an African American couple, Mr. and Ms. Bob. Mr. Bob was a tall, slender, African American man who loved cats. One day, Mr. Bob knocked on our side door and told us he had been looking for his cat. Unfortunately, he found it under a large rock on the side of our house where somebody had killed it. When Ms. Bob passed away, everyone was shocked to discover that Mr. and Ms. Bob weren't married. All those years they were living together, we assumed they were husband and wife.

LITTLE KEIDAN SCHOOL DAYS

During my preschool days at Little Keidan prior to enrolling in Keidan Elementary, we had to go to the school's nurse station where she would administer us our pink sugar cube to take for polio. Unfortunately, students who grew up in the fifties had to get our vaccination shots. This injection left a terrible scar on your arm. We practiced the emergency drills in class whenever we heard the Emergency Broadcast System siren at 1:00 p.m. Each student stopped what they we were doing, sat under their desks and covered their heads for protection.

MY CHILDHOOD PLAYTIME

I never was bored as a child. I always found something to do to keep myself busy. My siblings and I spent a lot of time playing childhood games. We enjoyed sitting on our front porch steps playing rock teacher, "Simon Says," hopscotch, jump rope, jacks, dodge ball in the alley, relay races, volleyball and hula hooping. On days when the weather was bad, I'd play schoolteacher in my room with my toy cars, trucks and a few dolls. I'd line them up in a row and if they were good students, I'd reward them with a ride in my make-believe train which I built out of several cardboard boxes and crates. One afternoon, Am and I were upstairs playing in our bedroom when she noticed outside the window something was moving slowly in the bushes.

"Emeline, you go outside and see what's in the bushes." Am always picked me to be "Lil' Miss Sherlock Holmes" to investigate. So, I went outside and pushed back the leaves on the bushes. Inside the bushes was a giant turtle the size of a large cantaloupe. Somebody must have lost their pet. I picked it up and made a little shelter out of bricks and placed a Styrofoam cup filled with water inside. The next morning, when I went to check the shelter, the turtle was gone.

On Election Day, my parents left us home alone. Mom would tell us they were going to vote and would be gone for a couple of hours. Hearing this as a young child, I literally thought they were going to get on a boat and sail off in the Detroit River for a couple of hours. With our parents gone, Am and I had plenty of time to enjoy watching television. Some of my favorite shows were the late-night cartoons like *The Flintstones, Top Cat*, and *The Tom and Jerry Show*. I also enjoyed action movies like *Lost in Space, Batman*, and *The Green Hornet*.

STOP BULLYING ME

One would think something easy as sneaking down to the neighborhood store to buy a $0.25 *Big Time* candy bar before your mother found out would be a simple task, but it wasn't. It ended up being a lesson in disobedience and bullying for me.

It was a hot summer day in July. Mom was in the living room reading the Detroit newspaper. I asked her could Am and I go play outside.

"Yes, don't go anywhere; stay on the front porch," Mom instructed. We said okay and headed outside to play hopscotch. We started to have a craving for our favorite candy bar, *Big Time*. Am gave me a quarter and told me to go to the store and buy one.

I knew we didn't have permission from Mom to go, but I decided to go anyway. Besides, I could run down to the store fast enough and get back before Mama knew I had left.

When the coast was clear, Am told me to go. I took off and made my way to the neighborhood black-owned store, the Johnson's. It was owned by Mr. and Mrs. Johnson, who were a friendly African American couple. Their store was filled with an assortment of candy, meat products and groceries.

"I like to buy one Big Time candy bar, please," I told Mrs. Johnson.

"That will be one quarter, young lady."

I handed her the money and left. Just in case I got caught by Mama, I decided to hide the candy bar inside my white ankle socks. She wouldn't notice it because my skinny legs would hide it. I was looking forward to getting back and sharing the candy with

Am. I took off running. I was only ten houses away from my house when all of a sudden something hit me hard across my back.

"Ouch, who did that?" I cried out. The pain was so excruciating, I stopped dead in my tracks. After I got enough strength to turn around to see who hit me, there he was. Wayne, the neighborhood bully and my nemesis, was standing in front of me looking like a big black roach. He was waving a big stick in the air, laughing at me with those yellow stained teeth. He had a habit of bullying me every time he saw me pass his house.

Well, he picked the wrong day. I was done being afraid of his antics. I wasn't going to stand for it anymore. Although he was bigger than me and had that stick, I didn't care. Before I knew it, I had balled up my fist and started throwing punches, landing them everywhere on Wayne's body. My skinny legs and arms were flying around like an out-of-control windmill blade. By the time I finished kicking his butt, he barely had enough strength in his body to limp back. He crawled on his porch on all fours. The bullying ceased that day.

I thought all of this could have been avoided had I obeyed Mama in the first place, and asked permission for us both to go to the store together. Wayne probably never would have jumped me if he knew my big sister was with me. Then again, it was time somebody taught him a lesson about bullying and that day was my day to teach him.

I made it back in time without Mama ever finding out I had left. I told Am what Wayne did to me and that he got the worst end of the stick. We sat on our front porch steps and made a promise that if we plan on going anywhere, first get permission from Mama and go together.

I slid my hand down inside my sock and pulled out the Big Time candy bar. It was a little soft. I broke off half a piece and shared it with Am.

"Thanks. Sorry that happened to you," Am said. She then looked at me sarcastically and asked, "Emeline, you really kicked his butt?"

"Yeah, Am. I left him crawling on all fours."

KING FAMILY PRAYS TOGETHER AND STAYS TOGETHER

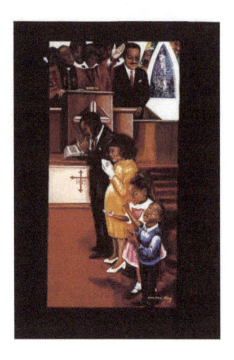

My parents were God-fearing Christians with strong values. We were raised Baptist and had a solid Christian foundation. Sunday mornings in the King household began with roll call and family prayer. Daddy would stand at the bottom of the stairs and call us one by one.

"Evelyn, Earnestine, Emeline, Eugenia, Earnest, Jr. and Errol! Y'all get on up, come on down for prayer." "Okay, Daddy I'm up. Coming!" we all responded one by one. Mom would be in the kitchen preparing breakfast: homemade biscuits, grits, bacon, eggs and orange juice. We would all rush downstairs into the kitchen and took our places around the kitchen table. Dad always sat at the head of the table; Mom sat to his right and I sat next to Dad to his left. Next to me would be Evelyn, Earnestine then Eugenia, Earnest Jr. and Errol sat at the opposite end of the table in his highchair. Our white metal frame kitchen table was small, but we managed to fit around it comfortably. We had bowed our heads while Daddy said the family prayer; however, the tempting aroma from Mama's Sunday morning breakfast made it hard for the King children to concentrate with our stomachs growling loudly against Daddy's long-winded prayers. Those prayers always included thanking God for watching over us while we slept last night and for waking us up, blessing us with food, transportation, good health and shelter. He went on to thank God for protecting his family, relatives, and church members. He remembered the sick, poor, hungry, needy, the lost, the people in prison, the homeless, the entire nation, everybody in the world *and* their circumstances. *Now dear Lawd, bless this food for which we are about to eat for the nourishment of our bodies, in Jesus' name we ask and pray…now let everyone say AMEN!*

After enjoying a good breakfast, we would take our turns using the bathroom, getting dressed and then all head to Morning View Baptist Church.

My parents took us to church every Sunday and we participated in every church function. We were not there to be "little church pew warmers." Sundays begun with Sunday School, which started at 9:30 a.m., followed by 11:00 a.m. worship service. At 6:00 p.m. we had Baptist Training Union (BTU).

Vacation Bible School was the third week in August. Bible Study was held every Wednesday night at 6 p.m., and choir rehearsal was on Thursdays at 6 p.m. Spring Revivals would last a week. The old saying was true, "The King Family was in church from sunup to sundown." My family prayed, ate, worked and traveled together. Every now and then, Dad would call us together for a King family meeting in the living room. The purpose of the meetings was to hear what was on our minds, our future plans, and if there were any concerns, issues or problems we needed to discuss as a family.

Mama always prepared healthy, nutritious home cooked meals and surprised us with her mouthwatering, succulent desserts like peach cobbler, chocolate cake, coconut cake, homemade vanilla ice cream and raisin bread pudding. We'd have exciting discussions around the dinner table, laughing and enjoying each other's company as we shared current events and our day-to-day activities.

THE KING'S HOUSE RULES

Mom and Dad had rules for all the King children to follow. We couldn't run the streets and couldn't hang out with any bad kids in the neighborhood. We had to be in the house by the time the streetlights flickered. Our bike route was already mapped out— from my house's front porch to the next-door neighbor's front porch. We had to get off our bike, turn it around on the sidewalk and head back home. Riding our bikes in the street was forbidden and would result in punishment.

That punishment was a whipping with switches we had to go get off a tree, and they better not be little twigs. I was 16 when my parents finally let me ride to the corner, which was only five houses away.

One day, I decided to be brave enough to venture out further and ride my bike around the block, knowing Mama didn't allow this. I assumed it wouldn't take me that long to get back around the corner without Mama ever knowing. Oh boy, was I wrong. Peddling really fast, trying to get back home and praying Mama wouldn't see me, when I turned the corner, there she was, standing on the porch, calling my name. She wasn't pleased to see me.

Thursdays were the days Mom would take us to the Richard Branch Library located on Grand River. We spent a couple of hours reading and checking out books. I was most interested in checking out the big illustration books on all types of automobiles: antique, racing, trucks, airplanes, boats, etc. I took my sketch book and would redraw them. I enjoyed reading autobiographies on people who made great accomplishments and differences in the world. Trailblazers.

When it came to education, there was one rule that stood firm with Mama. After we got home from school, we started on our homework. Mama would sit down at the dining table and mentor us. Art was my favorite subject, and Math was my least favorite. Whenever I ran into an algebra problem, Mom would jokingly yet sternly tell me, "Emeline, you can't slide pass and get around math; it requires thinking and repetition. You're going to have to rely up on your brain. You don't have enough fingers and toes to count out these problems. It's going to take practice, writing it down, memorization, practice, memorization, and more practice to get a good understanding about Math."

If we didn't know the meaning of a word, you better not ask Mom the meaning of that word. Mama would straight up say, "Go get the dictionary and look it up, Emeline."

KING FAMILY WEEKEND CHORES

Friday afternoons were spent cleaning and doing yard work. Mom didn't have to go buy weed killer spray because she had our little hands available to pull up dandelions and weeds. We mowed the lawn, trimmed the edges, picked up trash, cleaned the windows and swept the sidewalk clean. After we finished, later that evening Dad would surprise us and drive us to Belle Isle in his 1976 antique gold colored Cadillac Seville. I enjoyed seeing the Scott Fountain especially at night when it's all lit up and seeing the water change different colors of the rainbow. I was most intrigued with the sculptured plaster figurines surrounding the fountain.

After our excursion ended, we went home to enjoy an evening of watching a variety of television shows like *Sanford and Son*, *Julia* and *The Flip Wilson Show*. We snacked on fresh popcorn which Mom popped on the stove with her favorite silver pot. The dents and browning of the pot showed how much it had been through the ringer. Even the popcorn you purchase at the movies doesn't come close to Mom's stove-top popcorn with a little melted butter.

On Saturday mornings, Mama got us up early to do house chores. We started by making sure our beds were made, no clothes were on the floor and the rooms were clean. Then, we went downstairs to wash spots off the walls and polished the furniture with Lemon Pledge. We mopped both kitchen and bathroom floors on our hands and knees. One day, Mama was in the living room watching a television commercial about this new type of mop that could both clean and shine floors. Luckily it caught Mama's attention. Thank you, Jesus, my prayers were answered.

PREPARING FOR A KING FAMILY VACATION

Mr. and Mrs. Porchia, Emeline, Earnest Jr., Daddy

I looked forward to our family summer vacation. Every second week in August, we traveled down south for homecoming, family reunion and to visit Grandpa and Grandma Randall in Camden, Arkansas. The ride down there alone was enough to make you think we were on a cruise ship with all accommodations. The King Family would wake up early Friday morning around 5 o'clock to the smell of seasoned fried chicken that Mama prepared. Dad bought sweet, glazed donuts and windmill molasses cookies from the Hostess Bakery on 14th Street. My siblings and I would stand in formation in front of our house with our luggage, waiting for Dad to call us over. He would load our luggage in the back trunk of his black and white Ford.

The car's interior at that time were quite spacious. Three people could sit abreast on the front seat; four to five people could sit comfortably in the rear. Dad would have his 8-track player on the floor next to it the big brown bag filled with a king-sized bag of Better Made potato chips, paper towel, donuts, chicken wrapped in aluminum foil and a white plastic gallon of water. Mom was the gatekeeper to all these snacks.

The sweet potato pies would be placed in corner of the back rear window. The front middle seat was occupied by none other than my little brother and first-born male child, Earnest Lonell King, Jr. Mom and Dad treated that little booger like he was the Prince of Sudan. Brother was spoiled rotten. All he had to do was flash those big beautiful brown silver dollar-sized eyes and smile at you. He would win you over ever time. When my youngest brother, Errol David ("Bobbie") was born, "Prince Earnest Jr." had to give up his throne and ride in the back seat with us peasants, Am, Kizzy and me.

I always enjoyed our road trips with one exception. I would always experience car sickness. We hadn't left the state of Michigan before I started feeling nauseous. I don't know if riding in the back seat caused it or what. Throughout the duration of the trip, Am would be fussing at me.

"Emeline, you better get a bag. Don't throw up on me."

Mama would hand me a peppermint and tell me, "Emeline, here, suck on this peppermint. Turn your head to the side and look out the window. Hopefully, that should help you feel better." Somehow the candy would help for a moment, that is, until the next road trip when I'd get sick all over again.

Arkansas was 900 miles from Detroit. The drive was about a good 19 hours. Ever since Dad was called to preach the gospel, we had to listen to three songs which played constantly during our ride down to Arkansas and back: *Dominico by the Singing Nun*, *Rock the Boat* by Hues Corporation and Dad's favorite, *This is a Man's World* by James Brown. We almost never stopped at restaurants to eat. The evilness of racism and discrimination was still rampant in the southern states during the 1960s. I can only assume that Mama and Dad didn't want us to experience the vile and toxic treatment at some of the restaurants we passed. Besides, we had enough food and snacks to last for the whole trip. Fried chicken, wheat bread, assorted Faygo pop…my favorite was Root Beer, sweet potato pies and pound cake. We only stopped at rest stops to use the bathroom and get gas. Every gas station where we stopped, the gas attendant showed a friendly gesture to come outside and clean the windshield.

Dad packed all our luggage in the trunk with the large, white cooler chest, plus an extra empty large container to carry the bushel of speckled hull peas that we would have to shell when we got down there. This was an annual chore for the King children. We hated doing this because Dad would buy enough bushels to last us through winter. All of that shelling would turn our little fingers purple. There were a few times when our cousin Horace Gene, being mischievous, would take some of those unshelled peas and toss them over in Grandpa's wooden pigpen and serve them to the hogs. We knew that what was left of the peas we shelled would be seen again on the table for our dinner during our stay in Arkansas. Grandma Leonia and Mama prepared meals for us every day, along with the fresh chickens. I watched Grandma chase one of those chickens that I saw running around in her backyard. She caught it and swung it in the air until its neck broke. She plucked the feathers off, cleaned and seasoned it. She then placed it in one of those black cast iron skillets and served it with onions and gravy. "Umm, it tasted so good", along with those peas we shelled. Grandma taught me how to milk a cow and churn buttermilk.

Grandma would take us to The Cow Bell for an ice cream treat in her light blue 1962 Chevy Impala. All of the King kids sat in the back seat. Grandma drove with her hands on the steering wheel at "Ten and Two." I would look out the window and noticed how all the little animals hurried to get out of Grandma's pathway when she drove down the dirt road. If they didn't—roadkill.

KING/SCOTT FAMILY REUNION

There would be over 100 relatives gathered at our King/Scott Family Reunion. It was held on the estate of my great-great grandfather, Dave King, Sr. in Amy, Arkansas. He was born in the late 1800's. He was an entrepreneur and well respected throughout the neighborhood. Dad used to tell the story about his Grandfather Dave who owned a General Store uptown in Amy. One day, Dad stopped by to purchase some candy. When he got up to the counter, he discovered he didn't have any money. The store clerk knew my Dad and told the cashier, "That's Dave King's grandson. Let that boy have want ever he wants. He comes from good blood, the King family. "Dad told me, "Lenny Girl, a good, respected name will go a long way."

We had a great time at the picnic. I always carried my pencil and sketch book so I could draw portraits of my relatives and capture memorable moments. The men sat around talking, playing checkers and horseshoes. The women would prepare the long wooden picnic tables with every food imaginable. There was a whole pig roasting on a homemade wooden spit. Uncle Shed owned Arabian horses and all the children would stand in line, waiting anxiously to pet and ride one.

Am and I always looked forward to go over to Aunt Gert's house. Aunt Gert was my Dad's oldest sister. She would prepare her famous succulent homemade hamburgers especially for us. Aunt Gert would have us sit in the living room and she quietly disappeared into the back room. To us it was a mystery how she made these burgers. She would soon return carrying two plates with an enormous size cheeseburger on a toasted bun with all the sides: lettuce, pickles and onions that she grew in her garden piled high. There were so many condiments piled high on the burgers that you needed an extra pair of hands to eat it. Aunt Gert later told us she used a cold stove oven in the back to cook the cheeseburgers on.

I STOLE AUNTIE ETHEL'S HAIR

I recall the first and last time I was tempted to steal something. It was during one of our family trips to Arkansas. We were staying over my Dad's older sister's house, Aunt Ethel. We were in the living room relaxing before it was time to go to an afternoon program at Auntie's church, Saint Mary's. Each day, I passed by Auntie's room and admired her beautiful black curly wig mounted on a white Styrofoam mannequin sitting on her tall dresser.

In conversation I overheard Dad mention to Auntie that he planned on leaving in the morning heading back to Detroit. I figured that now was my chance to get up, go the bathroom and make my final stop by Auntie's room. I peeked in her room and noticed the wig wasn't on the drawer, but by her bed's nightstand. I had an epiphany; I could add some length to my short hair. So, I took a pair of scissors from off her nightstand, and I cut off a handful of hair and quickly braided them into my hair. Wow! What a difference that made. I glanced in the mirror and my braid went past my shoulder. I started swinging my head from side to side watching my long braid go *Swoosh! Swoosh! Swoosh!*

After using the bathroom, I headed outside to the car where everyone was waiting to go to church. It was almost time for Auntie's program. I made sure I kept my distance from Auntie. I sat in the back because I didn't want anyone to notice the dramatic change in my hair length.

When we got to Saint Mary's Church, I sat in the pew behind Auntie. I couldn't help but notice the back of her wig had a large section of missing hair. *Oh my God! It was the area where I had cut off the pieces of hair.* I could only pray that she didn't notice it when she put the wig on.

The program was beautiful. The choir was singing and I was having a good time clapping my hands, moving to the music, singing out loud and praising God. When I went to turn my head to swing my long braid, I noticed that it didn't move. It was gone!

I didn't know where it went. I looked down to see if it had fallen on the floor and it wasn't there. From my peripheral view, there was Auntie sitting next to me with my homemade braid in her hand. She had the meanest expression on her face with one eye squinted and the other one pierced straight through my soul. I started crying. I apologized to Auntie and begged her, "Please don't tell Mama!" I promised that I will never steal or take anything that wasn't mine ever again. I never took anything else.

MAMA'S WORDS OF WISDOM

Two things my mom hated the most was a liar and a thief. She definitely had no time for foolishness. I spent a lot of time in my bedroom standing in front of the mirror before all my toy stuff animals with a hair brush in my hand, lip syncing and listening to my favorite albums: The Jackson Five, "ABC," Aretha Franklin's "Got To Find Me An Angel" and Al Green, "Let's Stay Together." I would be imitating that I was giving a performance at Carnegie Hall. From my bedroom window I heard my mother's voice on the porch giving somebody a good old tongue lashing.
As a child I'd rather get a whooping with frozen tree branches instead of hearing choice words coming from my mother. I listened closely from my bedroom window and heard Mama talking to somebody.

"Oh no, honey; you're not going to stand in the middle of the street, call out to me and ask, 'Is Emeline home? Can she come play with you outside?' Young ladies, you come up here on this porch and address me as an adult, properly."

To my surprise, I found out it was my classmates Barbara Edens, Anita Baker and Sharon Reddin. I was embarrassed, but happy that Mom taught them the right way to speak to an adult.

DADDY'S HOME REMEDIES AND REPAIRS

I grew up on Dad's homemade remedies which could cure any ailment. Whenever I came down with a bad cold, he mixed up his special "Hot Toddy," which consisted of *Jack Daniel's* whiskey, lemons and honey. If I was congested, he told me, "Lenny Girl, go in there and rub some Vick's on your chest and put some in your nose, too." I was always singing and occasionally would come down with a sore throat. To cure this, he had me to gargle with warm salt water.

Mom always braided my hair in one simple style. I called it my "North, east and west." She made three braids, one braid pointing straight up in front on the top of my head and the other two braids hung down on opposite sides. My hair was short, about three inches in length. I always dreamt of having long, flowing, black shiny hair, just like the cartoon character, Rapunzel. One day, I saw Dad in the bathroom shaving. I asked him to mix up something that could make my hair grow long. He did, but it ended up smelling like rotten eggs.

When Mom saw what he was doing, she said, "Emeline, don't put that concoction on your head that your father made for you. You're going to end up with no hair." That ended my dream. I decided to accept my hair length.

Dad had his own unique way of repairing things in our house. In the summer, it would get extremely hot in our house, especially upstairs in our bedroom which reached temperatures into the mid-90s. Our family couldn't afford central air conditioning because it was expensive. Dad knew he had the perfect solution to get air to circulate through the house and upstairs. He purchased a large industrial-size ceiling fan. It was literally the size of a turbine blade on a 747. Dad decided to install the fan in the wall right at the top of the stairs. Dad had me measure and draw out the dimensions on the wall. He cut out the opening in the wall for the fan to fit in and secured the perimeter edges with plaster. He mounted the controls on the wall next to the fan.

It was now time to see how well this thought-out project would get us air. Dad told me to turn on the switch. The motor let out a big rumble and just when the fan's blower kicked in, we heard a loud, *"Ka-woosh!"* The fan caused a terrible backdraft that nearly sucked up everything in its path. I quickly turned off the switch. Dad realized the fan should had been mounted on the ceiling. Dad ended up removing the fan from the wall, plastering the edge and mounting it the correct way in top of the ceiling. Finally, we had air.

AUNTIE ELLA, DON'T STOP THE MUSIC

My parents did their grocery shopping on Thursday nights. They shopped at Farmer Jack's, which was the most popular supermarket franchise amongst the black people in my neighborhood. We weren't allowed to go out of the house when our parents were away and we knew the consequences if we did, so we stayed inside the house. We occupied our time by listening to the radio and making up dance moves and routines. Besides, there was mom's lookout person, her sister Aunt Ella who lived across the street, three houses over from us. We knew not to get into any kinds of mischief, or she would get the news back to our parents.

One day, Am and I wanted to have some fun. We waited for our parents to leave. Am would tell me to go stand by the front living room window and let her know when they left. I'd peek through the beige paisley curtains and watch for my parents to get in the car and drive off. The minute I saw the car's rear red taillights turn right onto Collingwood Street that was the cue that the coast was clear.

"Ammmmm, they gone!" I yelled out. We changed into our white ankle socks and got our dance party started. We rearranged the living room into our own private dance studio. We pushed the plastic covered cream couch with the wooden feet back up against the wall and the center table over to the side. I rolled up the floor mat to have more dance space.

Mom kept her records inside the cabinet of the brown high five stereo in the living room. Every week Am and I learned a new dance step and would make up routines. We took turns sliding back and forth across the floor, breaking out with dances moves like the Elephant Walk, the Temptations Walk, the Jerk and the Twist. I sorted through the stack of 45's and found my favorite record to make our dance routine with - "25 Miles" by Edwin Starr. This would be our finale song for the evening. We'd listen for Edwin start singing the best part, *"I got to keep on walking"* and then he starts the count down. Am and I would be dancing on cloud nine.

We cranked the music up so loud, that we didn't realized that we were being monitored from across the street by Aunt Ella. Seemed like she had eyes and ears in the back of her head. My song was about to go into its final stretch. *"I got five more miles to go,"* all of a sudden, we heard, *Screeeeeech!* The song came to an abrupt stop.

We turned around and there was Auntie Ella, standing with her five-foot tall, solid, big-boned frame in the middle of the living floor *livid* with her hands on her hips. She pointed her left index finger in the air and yelled out.

"What's going on in here? Y'all know gotdamn well not to be playing that music so loud. I heard y'all clean cross the street. I'm gonna tell Gene."

That ended our dance party for that evening.

EMELINE, YOU'RE YOUNG, GIFTED AND BLACK

I developed a strong interest to join the Glee Club while attending Keidan Elementary. I loved to sing, so I thought if I was in the Glee Club, this would make me popular with some of my classmates. Ms. Faye Robinson was over the Glee Club. She was tall and pretty, with a chocolate brown complexion. Her long black hair ran past her shoulders. Ms. Robinson had her favorite picks as to who she wanted to be in the Glee Club. Judging from all the girls who she selected were pretty and quite popular in the school. My childhood friend whom my mother used to babysit, Anita Baker, and I decided to audition for the Glee Club.

My first singing experience prior to auditioning was in my church choir at the Antietam Baptist Church on 24th & Hancock. My second was whenever Am was practicing for her upcoming piano recital, she would have me sing her recital pieces, "Born Free" and "Give Me a Clean Heart." Anita went first while I anxiously waited by the stage to go next. After she took center stage, she announced that she would be singing, "What the World Needs Now." Anita opened her mouth and out came this melodious voice from heaven that drew everyone's attention. Immediately after hearing her voice, Ms. Robinson made an announcement.

"I'm sorry boys and girls, no more auditions. I think we have found our final Glee Club member."

My feelings were shattered. Unfortunately, for me her audition sealed my fate of ever becoming a member of Keidan's Glee Club. I was just minutes away from fulfilling my dream; my voice wasn't heard. However, I was happy and very proud that Anita made it. She deserved it. Anita was gifted, talented and a beautiful person with a "one in a million" voice. Anita grew up and became a famous Grammy award-winning R&B recording artist.

I was embarrassed about not having a chance to even audition. I thought all hope had ended for me because I was not selected for the Glee Club but, little did I know sitting in the audience was the Glee Club's vocal music teacher, Ms. Vardy. She was a petite framed, elderly Caucasian lady. She approached me and asked me to come to her room. I followed her not knowing what was about to happen. Ms. Vardy sat down at a beige, wood-colored upright piano and told me to stand next to it. She began to play softly a song that was unfamiliar to me.

"Emeline, are you familiar with the song, 'To Be Young, Gifted and Black?' by the legendary Nina Simone?" she smiled and asked.

"No," I replied.

"I'd like to teach it to you and have you sing it for me."

She played the melody and sang the lyrics. After she finished, it was my turn. I took a deep breath and in my soprano voice, I belted out the song and she listened attentively.

"Oh my, Emeline, you have a unique, lovely voice. Just because you didn't get a chance to audition for the glee club shouldn't discourage you from singing and auditioning," Ms. Vardy said. "I'm sure there are other places and opportunities for you to use your God-given talent. Emeline, is there someplace else you could sing and use your gift?" I thought about the one place where I could sing: my church choir. I never had to audition there.

The following Sunday, I went to my church with a new refreshed outlook on singing. During Sunday morning worship service, my pastor, Rev. War, asked me to come up to the front of the church and sing a solo before the congregation. He also asked Evelyn to accompany me on piano. We both decided on "Give Me a Clean Heart." Evelyn sat down at the piano and played a beautiful introduction. I stood in front of the congregation and silently whispered a prayer that God would use me as a vessel. I wasn't nervous although this was my very first solo debut.

I was petite in stature, but when I opened my mouth, projected my voice and started singing with all my heart and soul, *"Give me a clean heart, so I may serve thee, Lord fix my heart so that I can be used by thee......Give me a clean heart and I'll follow thee,"* I felt the presence of the Holy Spirit. The spirit was high in the church. The congregation started shouting, crying and praising God. I knew then that God had blessed me and given me another talent besides drawing.

From that day, my journey as a gospel singer flourished. I must give props to Anita for going first at the audition, to Ms. Vardy for her words of encouragement and direction, and to Ms. Faye Robinson for letting me see that rejection can serve as a springboard to launch you beyond your dreams.

I learned that the windstorms of life didn't come to break me, but to redirect me to a new path to discover and appreciate my God-given talents, and to build me up to be stronger.

I GOT MUSIC IN ME

Both of my parents were musicians so it was destined for me to have music in me. Their talents and dedication influenced my desire to learn instrumental music. Mama learned how to play the piano at a very early age and later became the musician for her church, Good Hope in Camden, Arkansas. After moving to Detroit, my parents joined Antietam Baptist Church. Antietam was a storefront church filled with loving church members. Mama continued using her gift and became the musician for Antietam.

I was only 11 years old when I decided to take that walk up to the front of the church and sit down in one of those wooden chairs they always put out when the pastor asked who wants to give their life to Jesus. I accepted Jesus as my personal savior and wanted to be baptized. Pastor War always told my parents, "Emeline is a special child. She's a little light bulb. So if the stuff is in you, baby, you can't do nothing but shine."

On Sunday mornings, Mama would play the piano while directing the choir. The congregation would all clap and rejoice in worship service. Choir rehearsal was held on Tuesday nights and some of the choir members like Sis. Daisy Early and Bro. Faust would come over and practice at our house. We had an upright, brown Wurlitzer piano in our living room next to the dining room. They all gathered around the piano to sing. Bro. Faust had a beautiful, baritone voice. He would always place his finger in his ear to stay on key whenever he sang. Sis. Early sang soprano. Mama would play and sing along in her soprano voice. Hearing how those beautiful harmonies came from their voices while Mama played one of my favorite hymns, "Lift Him Up", on the piano, it was like we were at a private gospel concert. Am and I stayed in the back room listening to them rehearse.

I learned how to play the clarinet at Keidan. My band teacher, Mr. House, looked at my fingers and suggested that I play the clarinet. Mr. House was the shyest person I ever met. Each year, our band had to perform in the Annual Christmas Concert. At the end of the program, it was time for him to come up on stage, give remarks and thank the students, staff and parents. Mr. House would always stand to the side of the stage, behind the curtain and whisper: "Thank you all for coming and good night". I thought this was so funny because he'd do this same gesture every year.

LOOK, LISTEN AND LEARN

Daddy, Mama, Errol David (Bobbie), Emeline, Eugenia (Kizzy), Evelyn (Am), Earnest Jr.

When dad was called into the ministry to preach, he wanted Am, the oldest, to take lessons and learn to play gospel music. Unfortunately, I wasn't given lessons. I self-trained and learned piano from being observant at my sister's private piano lessons. One day while driving down Waverly Street, Dad noticed a man watering his grass. He stopped to get acquainted and met Professor Minor, a talented versatile musician and later owner of Minor Brothers School of Gospel & Classical Music. During their conversation, Dad asked if he could give his daughter piano lessons. Professor Minor agreed and scheduled lessons for Am on Saturday's at his home. I wasn't jealous or envious that I didn't get lessons. In fact, I would benefit just by being in that environment. I also was happy for my sister. It pleased me that Dad allowed me to go with her so she wouldn't walk home alone. I would enjoy the camaraderie. I felt like the devotional song we sang at church, *"I'm Glad to be in the Service."*

Professor Minor lived on Waverly Street which was a twenty-minute walk from our house. He introduced us to his beautiful wife and their two little daughters, Kelly and Kimberly. We headed downstairs to his basement. It was set up as a music studio. At the front of the room perched against the wall was an upright standard piano. Framed music accolades of Professor Minor hung on the wall. I sat quietly at the back of the room on one of the white plastic folding chairs, while his little black Cocker Spaniel constantly barked at me for attention.

For that next entire half hour, I focused my attention on everything Professor Minor taught Am to do on the piano. I listened, visualized and absorbed. He showed her fundamentals of music theory, gospel, classical, scales and selected a gospel and classical song for her spring recital. After lessons, Am would always treat me to the store and buy my favorite candy: a box of lemon heads. At home, Am would practice on the piano and get pointers from Mama. She was a gospel musician, too. Since I loved to sing, Am often had me to come, learn and sing the songs she practiced for her upcoming recital. My favorites were, "*Exodus Born Free, It's Wonderful and Give Me a Clean Heart.*"

Whenever Am wasn't at the piano, I practiced what I'd observed at Professor Minor's. It got to the point where I taught myself how to play the piano. It wasn't too long before Am was qualified to be a church musician. At the request of Dad's friend, Pastor Joseph Ware, who needed a musician for the choir, he asked if Am could come play for the Sunday morning services at Northwestern Community. Am's first paying job! In the meantime, Dad was called to Mt. Calvary to pastor. The church had a piano and a C3 Hammond organ, but no musician. Dad saw my interest and paid for me a few organ lessons. So, I volunteered and played both instruments, directed and organized a mass choir for Mt Calvary.

MISCHIEVOUS "PK"

By our father being a preacher, my siblings and I were labeled as PK's (preacher's kids). I admit to sometimes being a little mischievous, and a little sneaky while attending junior high school at Winterhalter. On one occasion, Am and I were leaving Professors Minor's headed home. Mama trusted us to always return home the same route. "Don't go venturing elsewhere", she said. I wanted to go visit Bruce, the bowlegged boy in my classroom. He told me he'd lived in the second house on Tuxedo, a couple streets over from Waverly and Sturtevant. I had the biggest crush on him! He reminded me of my favorite karate character, Bruce Lee. After telling Am, she immediately said, "Emeline, you betta not go over Bruce's house. Mama told us to stay on Sturtevant Street!" But, being hardheaded, I didn't listen. I told Am, "You go ahead. I'll run up and catch you later."

It wasn't shortly before I got one foot on the step of Bruce's front porch when Mama pulled up in that gold Cadillac Seville. Busted! When I saw the look on her face, I hauled ass and jumped into the car. Mom didn't say one word the entire ride back home. I was sweating bullets. Mama made me pick the biggest branch out of our backyard and told me to meet her in the basement. I knew I was in big trouble.

"Emeline, take off every stitch of clothes you didn't bring with you when you came into this world."

I can testify when we came back upstairs, I couldn't sit down for weeks. That was my first and last whipping I ever got from my Mama. Oh yeah! My big crush on bowlegged Bruce? Over!

I BET YOU CAN'T BLOW THAT SAX, LENNY GIRL

I picked up my woodwind instrumental talent from my Dad. He played the tenor saxophone and would often hold jam sessions with his friends over at the house. Bobby Barnes, John Garland, and Melvin Anderson practiced their saxophones with my Dad in our basement. Sometimes, they'd be down there for hours going over scales and playing jazz standards like *Satin Doll*, and *Song for My Father*.

Every time they got ready to practice, Am and I would sneak up to the front living room and put our ears up to the vent in the floor and listen to Dad and his friends play. Those sweet sounds coming from the basement penetrated my soul. I found another new love.

I was 15 years old when I learned to play the tenor saxophone. It all started from a bet that Daddy made with me. Daddy was sitting on the living room couch, practicing on his tenor saxophone. I walked in the room and was mesmerized by his playing. When Dad showed me his shiny brass saxophone and said, "I bet you can't play this, Lenny Girl," I said to myself, "Oh my, it's on Daddy!"

I picked up the saxophone, put on the strap around my neck, placed my mouth on the mouthpiece and with all my might and strength, I blew as hard as I could. I stood there waiting to hear those same sweet sounds that resonated from basement, coming from the bell of the horn as I blew. Surprise! It didn't happen.

Only the excruciating sounds of *"Screech! Bonk!"* expelled from the saxophone. Dad burst out laughing.

"Lenny Girl, if you ever want to duplicate those sounds you heard coming from the basement, you first need to let me give you some lessons, learn how to breathe properly, learn your horn, and practice, practice, practice your scales."

I took Dad's advice and it helped me to become a better professional saxophonist today.

DADDY-DAUGHTER MINISTRY

Dad was called into the ministry when he was at Antietam Baptist Church. Our family, friends and the entire church was there to hear Dad's first trial sermon. After Dad had been up before the congregation for about 30 minutes, it was time to bring his sermon to an end. At the close of his sermon, Dad's preaching style and his tone changed. After each sentence, he started taking in long gasps of air. Hearing that sound scared both me and Am. We didn't know what was happening to Daddy. We later asked him what was that he was doing.

"*Whooping* is a typical style of preaching used by most of the African American preachers in churches within the Baptist and Pentecostal denominations." It wasn't too long after that when Dad started to get invitations to preach at other churches and run revivals. I was still leading songs in the church choir and getting engagements to go out and perform solos at different churches. I was happy when Dad called upon me to sing after he preached. We were a team. My ministry was gospel singing, and Dad's was preaching God's Word. I felt honored to be a part of ministry with my father by rendering my gift of thanks by singing back to God, a gospel songstress delivering songs of comfort and enlightenment to God's people. I also sang in a gospel group, "Rev. Earnest Fowler and the Witnesses." Rev. Fowler was my father's close friend who met him when he served as the interim pastor at Morning View Baptist Church. Rev. Fowler was the church organist. He came from a gifted family of musicians, with some connected to the Motown Gospel label. I always admired Rev. Fowler's gifted style of playing on Sunday mornings at church. Rev. Fowler could make an organ rise up and walk! How elated I was when this talented musician asked me to join his gospel group, which consisted of Rev. Earnest Fowler, Rev. R. Foster and me. Rev. Fowler's nephews were the group's percussionist and guitarist. The group performed concerts at churches throughout the City of Detroit and in other states. I continued to use my God given ministry gift of singing with my Dad.

Rev. Earnest Fowler & The Witnesses

FEMALE TRUMPET PLAYER INSPIRED ME

On Saturday mornings after we finished our chores, I sat in the back room and watched my favorite dance shows like *American Bandstand* and *Soul Train*. The shows would feature a variety of artists like Diana Ross and the Supremes, The Jackson Five, Patti LaBelle, The Temptations, Prince, Chaka Khan, Tina Turner; Earth, Wind and Fire and many more. The one group that caught my attention was Sly and the Family Stone. They were singing two of my favorite songs, *Everybody is a Star* and *Dance to the Music*. What captivated me was Sly's band member, Cynthia. She was a tall, black female wearing a huge afro and playing the trumpet. This was quite out of the ordinary in that time for a female. Seeing her play inspired me to want to play the saxophone even more.

FEASTING WITH THE KINGS

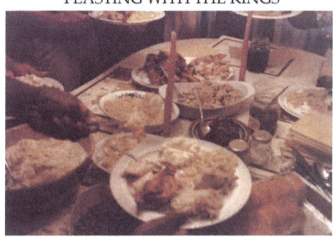

After I graduated from Cass Technical High School, my father was called to pastor Mt. Calvary Baptist Church located on St. Aubin and Frederick in Detroit. I cried for days when I found out our family would be leaving Morning View Baptist Church. I didn't want to go because I was having fun participating in BTU showing my art and leading solos in the choir.

Every third week in September, Dad hosted Mt. Calvary's Annual Fall Revival. The sanctuary would be packed with Mt. Calvary members, along with visitors and several of Dad's pastor and minister friends. Dad would invite one of his out-of-town evangelist friends like Pastor Hayes, Grandpa Randall from Arkansas, or Pastor Turbough from California to run the revival. It was a festive, yet spiritual, soul-saving event that we all enjoyed. Am and I could hardly wait for Friday to come because that was the last day for revival and enjoying Mama's homemade cooking. After the service, all the ministers would come over to dine and have fellowship at the home of Pastor King and his family. This turned out to be a yearly affair that everybody looked forward to.

Mama would start preparing her meals early Friday morning for that evening's occasion. Cooking on the stove would be large, shiny, silver pots filled with turnip greens, mustard greens and black-eyed peas. Mom made all the desserts the day before: coconut, caramel and German Chocolate cake. And oh Lord, please don't forget her sweet potato pies! The potato salad was chilled in the refrigerator; the tender beef was roasting in the oven along with the macaroni and cheese. The chicken was well seasoned, battered and frying in Mama's favorite black cast iron skillet. The cornbread was sliced and the sweet tea was made. I helped set the table and set out extra serving trays. All the adults would eat in the dining room while the King children would either eat in the kitchen or in the back-room den.

I was so amazed at how much food and desserts Mom prepared. It was plenty for everybody to enjoy and take some home for later. Feasting with the Kings was worth the weekend wait.

SEVEN HISTORICAL EVENTS THAT TOUCHED ME

Seven historical events took place during my childhood. I remember watching them on our 21-inch screen black and white RCA television. Those moments will always be remembered:

1. The 1967 Detroit Riot
2. The assassination of President John F. Kennedy on November 22, 1963
3. The assassination of civil rights leader Dr. Martin Luther King, Jr. on April 4, 1968 at the Lorraine Motel in Memphis, Tennessee
4. Less than two months later, on June 5, 1968, Senator Bobbie Kennedy was shot and killed in the Ambassador Hotel.
5. It was an exciting day for me as a teenager, sitting in my backroom den with my family watching television for the arrival of the famous British group, the Beatles from Liverpool, England. In 1964, four young men stepped off the plane in New York City to thousands of screaming, infatuated teens for their first American

debut. It was worth the wait to hear them perform their number one hit, *I Want to Hold Your Hand.*

6. What a defining moment in space technology on July 20, 1969 when Commander Neil Armstrong and lunar module pilot Buzz Aldrin became the first men to land on the moon. I heard those famous words, "That's one small step for man, one giant leap for mankind." It was total excitement just witnessing something of this nature that was over a billion miles away from me.

7. The Lunar Roving Vehicle, which was called the "Lunar Moon Buggy," a four-wheeled rover vehicle was used on three of the missions to the moon. Seeing the image of this strange mechanical object, the Lunar Moon Buggy, traveling roughly up and down on the Moon's surface on television took me back to my childhood experience of driving Al's go kart. What a close resemblance! I wondered who designed that. This only developed a stronger love and appreciation for anything with four wheels.

1967 DETROIT RIOT

We lived on the west side of Detroit at the time. Although the 1967 Riot started in the area of 12th Street and Virginia Park, there were several adjoining neighborhoods that were impacted. Am and I sat on our front porch, listening to the fire engine sirens rushing to put out fires from burning buildings, store front businesses and people's homes. Some of which were destroyed by people throwing Molotov cocktails. You could smell and see dark smoke fill the air.

We were in walking distance to Dexter Avenue, which was one of the major streets close to where the riots were taking place. The news of these uncontrollable riots reached Washington D. C., where President Johnson had issued a state of emergency with federal troops being deployed to Detroit. The National Guard was dressed in Army apparel and carrying rifles. They could be seen shooting off tear gas in the air, trying to control the crowds. A military tank drove down 12th Street. Mayor Jerome Cavanagh asked Governor George Romney for assistance. Curfews were in effect, and anyone found on the streets would be arrested and placed in jail.

Every news station reported and interviewed the injured victims, and the death toll was constantly rising. The neighborhoods which were once adorned with elegant homes and established businesses were now burned down to the ground. Supermarkets, convenient stores, jewelry stores, etc. were broken into by looters, who could be seen running and stealing merchandise right off the shelves. Uncontrollable arson, shootings and murder; Detroit was in total chaos.

AMERICA MOURNS
JOHN, BOBBY AND MARTIN

It was a sad day for America with the assassinations of President John F. Kennedy and his brother, Senator Bobbie Kennedy. I was in the back room watching our black and white television. I saw on television when Senator Bobbie Kennedy got assassinated and seconds later, Jack Ruby walked up to the man who was taken into custody for killing Senator Kennedy, and he shot him point blank.

I remember the day Dr. Martin Luther King was shot on the balcony at the Lorraine Motel in Memphis, Tennessee. My grandmother Leonia was up here visiting from Camden, Arkansas. I remembered seeing her sitting in the living room on the green paisley plastic-covered couch, head buried in her hands murmuring, "Oh Lord, have mercy. They done killed Dr. King."

THE BEATLES

I watched a lot of musical performances on my favorite television show, *American Bandstand*. On February 7, 1964, I was one of those screaming teenagers watching The Beatles step off the airplane in New York City and wave to the crowd. Paul, John, Ringo and George were the first British group. The Beatles aired their first debut arriving in the United States to perform at the Coliseum in Washington D. C.

BTU (BAPTIST TRAINING UNION) LAUNCHES TALENT

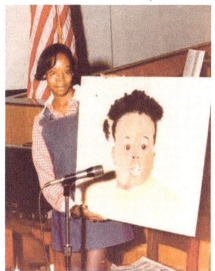

Portrait Sketch (cousin) Jackie Williams

In 1976, Dad was called to Morning View Baptist Church to serve as their interim pastor until the church found a newly elected pastor. The former pastor, T.J. Prince, left Morning View and moved to Texas to pastor another church. My mother would often take us there to hear Daddy preach at Morning View. Later, we moved our membership from Antietam to Morning View. I had a wonderful time there, especially their BTU (Baptist Training Union). It was the platform that launched my drawing career and exposed many other gifts. Every Sunday at 6 p.m., my mother took my sisters, brothers and me to Morning View's Bible Training Union.

We would pile in the back seat of our parents' 1979 yellow Ford Maverick for an evening of fun and learning. Morning View sat on the corner of 5646 Lawton and Grand River. Rev. Marion Myers, Sr. was the pastor. Our family attended BTU faithfully, learning about the books of the Bible, doing Bible drills, and reading Scriptures.

If you had a talent or gift, you could showcase it there. Deacon Ted Givens was our BTU instructor. Mr. Givens was wise, friendly and full of knowledge. He'd always greeted you with a smile. He was a professional photographer. He would take pictures of every special occasion that occurred in my life, framed the picture in a liquid tinted colored, plastic resin using various sized geometric, fruit shaped images and present them to me. During our Bible drills, Mr. Givens would say in a loud, boisterous voice, "Draw Swords!" We raised our Bibles in the air, and at the sound of his command, we'd race to find the Scriptures and read them. Everybody in the congregation would race to see who would be the first person to open their Bibles, find the Scripture, stand up and read. I was always in competition with the Dubois brothers, Sequoia and Ramey. They were smart, young men with high IQ's who later became prominent lawyers. I was the winner the majority of the time.

After the Bible drills, it was time for my favorite part of the evening: the BTU Talent Showcase. I looked forward to giving my presentation before the audience and showing my latest artwork. Math and Science weren't my favorite subjects in school, but I was exceptionally good at drawing. Most people started out trying to draw stick figures. I was more interested in drawing the muscular and skeletal structures of the body. I could illustrate just about anything I saw. It didn't matter whether it was a car, boat, airplane, still life, architecture, fashion, person, place or thing. I kept my first drawing that I drew in kindergarten of a turkey with multicolored feathers. I was proud of it. I used every color in the 64 pack of Crayola Crayons.

My father worked at the Design Center. He noticed that I liked to make an impact by drawing my subject's life size. Dad surprised me one day by bringing home 30x40 sized white illustration boards for me to draw pictures on. My mom had subscriptions to both *Ebony* and *Jet* magazines. I drew life-sized portraits of famous black celebrities who graced their front covers. This made quite an impression. I used assorted colored pencils, pastel chalk and magic markers for my art supplies. Sketching my family members and futuristic cars were easy. My drawings would always win first prize in the talent showcase.

Later, I saw how standing before the congregation and talking about my artwork would benefit me in my career. Attending Baptist Training Union enhanced my public speaking skills, strengthened my confidence, and enabled me to make presentations before audiences of any size.

Pencil Sketch (Child Actor) Rodney Allen Rippy

Acrylics Painting – Future Mobile Transport/Mobile Fuel Station

CHAPTER TWO
SHE WAS EXPOSED TO IT

MY FIRST MENTORING LESSONS AT THE STUDIO OF MR. OSCAR GRAVES

My parents played a major role in shaping my art career. Had they not exposed me to art at an early age, my life would have gone in a different direction. My father worked for Ford Rouge for three years. Faced with continuous layoffs where he worked four months and was off for six to seven months of the year. With this dilemma, in search of a permanent job to sustain his wife and young family, he decided to quit and look for better opportunities. Dad also enrolled in the Wolverine School of Trades, where he learned the skill of Metal Casting. He worked twelve years at both places for Pressure and Plaster Cast developing experimental parts for both automotive and aviation metal casting from the plaster mold.

Saturday mornings was Daddy/Daughter time. It was at the "pressure cast" foundry where my father met Mr. Oscar Graves, a famous black sculptor from Detroit. They established a camaraderie that lasted for years. It was at the Oscar Graves Studio on Grand River where Dad assisted Mr. Graves by helping make plaster molds, bronze plaques, etc. for Mr. Graves' commissioned art sculptures. Oscar Graves' Studio is where I was first exposed to black art and was mentored by Mr. Graves. I saw him create some of the most magnificent works of art in his studio. I was inspired the very first time I met him. He stood six feet tall, a thin-framed man with a smooth, caramel-skinned complexion. Mr. Graves kept his salt and pepper goatee well-trimmed, which made him look like a prestigious French painter. He always wore a white smock with a black beret shifted to the side of his head. I thought it was comical when he spoke with his cigar hanging out of the side of his mouth. It constantly bobbed up and down.

Mr. Graves must have favored jazz music because each time I walked into his studio, I heard smooth jazz playing softly in the background. Famous jazz vocalists and musicians: Ella Fitzgerald, Sarah Vaughan, John Coltrane, Miles Davis, Dizzy Gillespie, and other greats would fill the room with a calming atmosphere as Mr. Graves worked diligently on his sculptures. He was a graduate of the Cranbrook Art Academy, a prestigious art institute located in Birmingham, Michigan. Some would consider him a modern-day Michelangelo. He was inspired by Roman classic sculpture and was a protégé of famous Michigan sculptor, Marshall Maynard Fredericks. The Spirit of Detroit, a famous and iconic statue located in front of the Detroit City County Building, is one of the works of art by Mr. Graves. However, he was never given the credit for it; favor was directed toward Marshall Fredericks. One can see Mr. Graves's masterpieces represented in the renovation of the interior of the luxurious Fox Theater on Woodward Street. Inside the theater, above the stage at the top of the ceiling, are decorative plaster relief sculpture pieces created by him surrounding the moldings. Located at 7333 12th Street near West Grand Boulevard is a bronze replica bust of civil rights leader Dr. Martin Luther King, Jr. that Mr. Graves sculpted.

I was able to watch Mr. Graves use his talent to develop the most beautiful sculpture pieces. I was fascinated to watch him take pieces of green clay, roll them up in a little ball, shape it, and then apply it to a sculpture armature he made. I was like a kid left alone in a factory filled with free, unlimited candy.

I enjoyed the fresh smell of clay that filled the entire studio. Hanging on the walls and displayed on the countertops were a variety of Mr. Graves' tools, Afrocentric sculpture plaster molds, and 8X10 black & white head shots of people he had been commissioned to sculpt. He had a variety of African pieces, such as side reliefs of African women dressed in headwraps, carrying their child on their backs. There were two pieces that were my favorites: One was the flowing water fountain that sat on the floor in the foyer of the studio. It had three bronze fallen horse sculptures surrounding the top of the fountain. Another was a life size bronze bust of the late President John F. Kennedy. Mr. Graves gave it to my father, and I cherish that in my home today.

I would listen and take in all the knowledge and wisdom that came out of Mr. Graves' mouth. Our conversations included his travels to Europe: visiting Rome, Italy, to see the Trevi Fountain and tossing three coins in it with a wish to one day return; seeing the whole city of Paris from the vantage point of the Eiffel Tower; visiting the Leaning Tower of Pisa, Mona Lisa's smile, Michelangelo's David, Notre Dame, the Colosseum, the Parthenon, the Sistine Chapel, and several other wonders of the world. I never imagined that one day through my work with my future employer, Ford, I would visit and work in these countries on Foreign Service Assignments and experience the same wonders Mr. Graves shared with me.

DADDY, WHAT'S BEHIND THE BLUE DOOR?

Another favorite pastime that my father and I shared was him taking me to his company events. He once took me to his company's Christmas party. It was held in the Ford Motor Company Design Center's showroom. I was excited not only because it was the first time I visited my father's workplace but it sparked a dream of mine to one day work with him at the same company and in the same building. That trip was the catalyst in helping me choose a career in the auto industry. We drove to the Design Center's parking lot. I could tell from the outside appearance of the building that whatever took place behind the brownish, smoky privacy glass would be exciting and spectacular. We entered the building where we met a Caucasian security guard who was seated behind a desk. He said, "Hi Ernie, how you doing? You're here for the Christmas party?

Dad politely said, "Hello, Frank. Yes, we are."

Then he proudly told him, "I'd like to introduce you to my daughter, Emeline."

After the friendly introduction, both my Dad and I proceeded down the hall to the showroom. I noticed how beautiful the long corridor was. The white tile floors were polished, and the walls were painted white. We were only a few feet from the entrance when my eyes caught the blue door. It stood out against the white walls. I was curious as to what was behind the door, so I headed closer. As I leaned forward, I caught a sniff of a familiar scent. It reminded me of the smell of clay every time I went to visit Mr. Oscar Graves's studio. I quickly turned around to my Dad and asked him, "Dad, what's behind this door? It smells like clay in there." That's when my father explained to me the total breakdown of what goes on in there.

He informed me, "This is just one of our design studios, and it's called the International Studio. That's where cars are designed. Behind this door is where you have talented men known as *transportation designers*. They sit behind cubicles and sketch two-dimensional concept cars and trucks on paper based on guidelines from upper management, engineering and marketing. If their two-dimensional concept drawings are approved and selected by management, they are turned into full production, manufactured driving vehicles and made available for the public to buy and drive. Emeline, every vehicle that you see on the road today had to start in a design center, and it first was created in the mind of a transportation designer who had an idea and turned it into reality."

In an enthusiastic tone, I asked my Dad, "What's a transportation designer?"

That's when he said, "It's a person who can design all types of transportation vehicles, such as passenger cars, sports cars, sport utility vehicles (SUV), commercial vehicles, aircrafts, boats, trains, etc. Every vehicle that you see on the road had to start with a transportation designer".

I asked my Dad, "Do you work in there?" He told me that he works in the fabrication shop on the other side of the design studio.

"Once the concept is sketched out two-dimensionally—both interior and exterior—it is developed into a three-dimensional, full-size clay model. After this transformation, it moves over to my area to be fabricated, where we make a mold of the car in fiberglass. The fiberglass model is painted and all interior components like the seats, doors, instrument panel, console, graphics, mechanical armatures, etc. are further developed in the trim, wood, metal, shop, and graphics departments. At this point, the car has the appearance of a real car, made out of fiberglass and not sheet metal. The next process is manufacturing the car into sheet metal, marketing the product, and the final stage into the showrooms, where this concept designed by the transportation designer is now a profitable vehicle available for the buying public."

It was so interesting how my father explained to me the entire process from start to finish of how automobiles are designed. I was so proud to know that it all started here at the Design Center. I gained greater respect for the men who thought of ideas for a concept that would be drawn and later created into the cars that we drive.

After Dad gave me the overall description of how cars were designed and made at the Design Center, it raised my level of anticipation and desire to be a part of it. I wanted to go inside to see, but we couldn't. We had to have access, so we proceeded to the showroom. As we entered the showroom that was decorated with holiday decorations, Christmas music filled the air. The record made by Burl Ives, "Have a Holly, Jolly Christmas" was playing over the speaker, putting everybody in the holiday spirit. The jolly, old Santa Claus was dressed in his red and white suit, handing out Christmas gifts, and joking about which employees had been naughty or nice. The room was filled with hundreds of Design Center employees and their families. You could count the number of black people on both hands. For entertainment that evening, the black ventriloquist, Willie Tyler, and his companion, Lester, took center stage, causing the audience to laugh at their comical jokes and anecdotes. Dad would always introduce me with pride to his coworkers as they shared about their job specialty at the Design Center. From that day forward, my passion intensified for wanting to design cars. After we ate and socialized, it was time to leave. We made our way back down that same hallway with the blue door. Just as we were about to exit the building, I stopped, turned around, and looked down the hall to where that blue door would get a view of its future employee. I made a promise that one day I would return as a transportation designer, come to work with my father, and make major contributions in the automotive industry.

CASS TECHNICAL HIGH SCHOOL:
MAMA KNOWS BEST
MY INSPIRING ART TEACHERS

My parents choose only the best schools for me to attend that would develop my art skills and talents. I went with my mom to the parent-teacher conference at Winterhalter Junior High School. I decided to bring my portfolio of drawings that included portrait drawings of my family, famous musicians, celebrities, and futuristic cars to show my counselor. My teacher was impressed after seeing my work. She stated, "Emeline, you have talent. You should consider a career in art and go to an accredited school here in Detroit. I would suggest Cass Technical High School. They have an excellent Art Program that would benefit your talent development, plus all of the instructors are experts in their fields of study."

The teacher said, "I did some research about what the school offered. Their art programs are the best and they have a variety of classes: commercial arts, graphic design, illustration, figure drawing, sculpture, painting, printmaking, fashion design, drafting…the list goes on and on. Emeline would be amongst a group of talented and diverse students by attending Cass. The school is rated number one amongst high schools in the country". When she mentioned Cass Technical High School, Mom's reply was "Yes". She said "I've heard the school has an excellent reputation and yes, I've made my decision. Cass Tech is the school Emeline will attend. She will obtain a solid education, enhance her talents and abilities even more in such a good environment.

Mom was quite pleased from what she heard about Cass and all it had to offer me; however, her choice didn't sit well with me because I had spoken earlier with my girlfriends: Barbara, Sharon, Anita, Cassandra and Julia about what high school they were going to attend. Graduation was a week away, and I still was undecided.

My friends already decided on several of the neighborhood schools. They told me Central, Northwestern, Mumford, Denby, or Cooley — any school except Cass Tech.

I asked them, "Why you all don't want to go there?"

One friend commented, "That's the school for nerds. Why you think they call it, 'The Pickle Factory.' Their school colors are green and white." Another friend said her Mama told her she can make her own choice about where she wants to go.

After talking with my friends, I made my mind up that I wasn't going to Cass Tech. My only dilemma was how I was going to tell my mother of my decision that I didn't want to go to a school known for nerds. I wanted to be with my friends.

When I shared my concerns, Mama told me, "You are not going to school to socialize and follow after your friends. You are there to learn, period." My counselor told my mother that she made a wise choice and offered to write a letter of recommendation on my behalf. She knew the head of the Art Department, Mr. Irving Berg. Mama gave me that stern look and told me, "Emeline, you're going to Cass Tech. You have zero options."

Mama's next task was getting me enrolled as soon as possible. Registration and orientation were scheduled for 6:00 that evening, and before I could get the words out to tell Mama why I preferred not to go there, she was pulling in the parking lot at Cass Tech telling me to get out of the car and make haste. We headed straight to the auditorium, where we met the head of the Art Department: Mr. Irving Berg, a tall, friendly Caucasian man who walked with a limp. One of his legs was shorter than the other. I was still upset and began contemplating what other tactics I could use to get out of enrolling in Cass Tech. When Mr. Berg asked me to fill out the application form, I wrote my last name as my first and my first name as my last, then checked the box "male" for my gender. I handed the form back to Mr. Berg. He read it and looked at me with a confused expression on his face. My mother noticed his reaction and asked to see what I had written. She then turned and glanced back at me and gave that look. From her reaction, out of fear and humiliation, it caused me to suddenly change my mind to develop love, appreciation, and gratification for selecting Cass Tech.

Throughout my eight semesters at Cass, I excelled in my art classes. I still kept in touch with my old friends and made new ones. It was fun being around a diverse group of talented students. We were all smart and learned from each other.

One particular friend, Babette Taylor, was in the same sculpture class with me. Babette Taylor was a talented black girl who loved playing hockey. In those days that sport was more favored by Caucasian men. I admired how she made beautiful relief sculptures of her favorite hockey player, Mr. Gordie Howe.

My major was Commercial Arts. I took courses in painting, life drawing, graphics, drafting, and sculpture. Some of my favorite influential teachers were Dr. Cledie Taylor, who taught design composition, and Mr. Irving Berg, who taught sculpture. Mr. Berg was amazed at my unique skills in making armatures, creating clay sculptures, and making plaster molds. I never mentioned to Mr. Berg about my former training I received learning this craft from my mentors, Mr. Oscar Graves and my father.

WINNING MY FIRST POSTER CONTEST: BICENTENNIAL NEW YORK STOCK EXCHANGE – IT'S AMERICAN, JOB EQUALITY

Mr. Noyer, my Graphic Arts teacher, gave the class an assignment to design a bicentennial poster promoting the American economic system. This contest was sponsored by the New York Stock Exchange. Each contestant was to submit a poster and select their own theme. I chose "It's American, Job Equality." My poster illustrated equal pay for men and women in America. I designed my poster to have six white individual stars mounted on a blue 18x24 poster board. Each star contained a symbol, from one of the six governmental departments: Corporate, Transportation, Law Enforcement, Medical, Judiciary, and Military. I used red Helvetica font with three-inch cut-out letters for the title: *It's American, Job Equality*. Just to be more creative, I replaced the letter 'O' in the word 'Job' to look like the combined graphic of the male and female gender symbols.

Three weeks later, Mr. Noyer informed five of the art students: Alexander Wilson, Mark Reed, Paul Lusch, Patrice Rowlett, and me that we were to be guests for a luncheon at the Hotel Pontchartrain in downtown Detroit that day. We all piled in the backseat of Mr. Noyer's white Volkswagen Beetle. It was funny; we looked like a can of sardines, bobbing up and down every time he hit a pothole in the street. When we finally arrived at the Hotel Pontchartrain restaurant, we headed toward the elevator. That's when Mr. Noyer asked me to press the button that read, *Top of the Flame*. When the elevator doors opened, the room's decor was like a five-star restaurant, and at the front were five brass easels with our posters.

We all sat down at the table for lunch. The waiters were dressed in white tops and black bottom uniforms and served us our meals. A plate in front of me appeared to be an over-decorated small piece of steak covered with green leaves and flowers. I leaned over and asked Mr. Noyer, "What is it?"

He told me, "It's called Filet Mignon, a thick tender boneless slice of steak. It's a French term for 'dainty'" Well, it didn't resemble anything my mom would have prepared. Her steaks were big and always covered in succulent brown gravy and onions. I asked if it would be all right if they brought me a cheeseburger. The waiter said, "No problem, madame."

After we ate, it was time for presentations and announcing the winners of the poster contest. School board members from the Detroit Public School District, the business sector, New York Stock Exchange, and William C. Rodney & Co., a Detroit-based securities firm, presented the five contestants with a trophy and a beige burlap sack that contained twenty-five bicentennial silver dollars. A photographer from the *Detroit News* was there to take our photos with our posters.

My mind wandered off to thinking I'll have to take the Iron Pimp home. That's the term black people in the hood called the Dexter bus. How was I going to make it home safe? When I thought about having to ride carrying a beige sack filled with money in my neighborhood, I thought about how that would draw attention to the inquisitive thief.

After the event was over, Mr. Noyer took us back to school. From there I took the bus home and prayed a long prayer for God to please protect me. I arrived home safely and showed my family what I had won. They were proud of me. Winning the New York Stock Exchange Bicentennial poster contest was the first time I was featured in the newspaper, and by choosing a career in the art field, it wouldn't be my last time.

PERSEVERANCE REWARDED ME WITH
A PERFECT ATTENDANCE AWARD

I graduated from Cass Technical High School on January 21, 1976. It was one of the coldest winter semesters, and for the record, my Class of 1976 would be the last winter graduating class. Graduation was held at the Adlai Stevenson Building on Grand River. Everyone was there, including my parents and siblings Evelyn, Earnestine, Eugenia, Earnest Jr., and Errol David. Mr. Ted Givens, my Baptist Training Union (BTU) instructor, and his wife came. Following the ceremony, we walked across the stage, received our diplomas shook hands with the faculty, and returned back to our seats. Our principal, Mr. Donald Carmen, approached the podium to make his final announcement. He addressed the audience, "Ladies and gentlemen, Class of 1976, you have one student among you who hasn't missed school in her entire four years. This graduate has shown consistency, perseverance, and determination to maintain perfect attendance, especially when the elements in Detroit can be challenging and distracting. No matter how she felt, somehow she managed to get up every morning and make it to school on time." I sat in my seat listening to him but didn't have a clue as to whom he was referring. I tried blocking out the sarcastic comments my classmates were saying, "I wonder what fool is that? They must have lived, ate, and slept at Cass Tech to never miss a day. Can you imagine when we have our 10th year class reunion? Classmates will probably say, 'I don't remember you,' and that person will have to remind them, 'I'm the one who won the perfect attendance award.' Then, the other person would say, 'Oh that was you? Now what's your name again?'"

At that moment, I was hoping I wasn't that person the principal was talking about. To my surprise, he called out my name. "Emeline King, congratulations! Out of the 600 graduating students, you are the recipient of the Cass Technical High School Perfect Attendance Award. Please come down and receive your award." I got up from my seat feeling somewhat embarrassed after hearing those remarks from a few students. I made my way down to the stage and the surprised looks on my classmates' faces were Kodak moments. The audience gave me a standing ovation. I could see how happy and proud my family was. My parents instilled in me how important it is to go to school, be on time, stay focused, and get a valuable education. There's no time to miss school, and lateness wasn't an option in the King family.

WAYNE STATE UNIVERSITY

After I graduated from Cass Technical High school, I was still pursuing a career in the arts and getting closer to my dream. My parents made the decision for me to go to

Wayne State University, which was located on Cass Avenue in the cultural center. I would always ride past the campus on my way to Cass Technical High School.

Wayne State was surrounded by a variety of museums: the Detroit Institute of Arts (DIA), the Historical Automotive Museum, The Children's Museum, and The International Institute. There was also the Center for Creative Studies, a highly accredited art school I would be attending later in the summer. I majored in Industrial Design at Wayne State and would be applying for my bachelor's degree in Fine Arts. My classes included Painting, Anatomy Drawing, Printmaking, Product Design, and Art History.

My special interest was in art history. I was fascinated with the ancient Egyptian civilization, their artifacts, and the pyramids. I found it captivating how these magnificent structures were built in ancient times without using modern machinery. I could always relate to the Renaissance era paintings and sculptures. The artists depicted biblical stories and symbolism that I was familiar with from studying the Bible and learning about these stories in Sunday School. My Art History professor would show slides of these masterpieces. I fell in love with the paintings of some of my favorite Renaissance painters: Michelangelo and Rembrandt. Their interpretations and passion created emotional works of art, leaving me feeling like I was right there experiencing a historic event.

During one of several lectures my professor asked, "Who can describe this painting?" I would always be the only who volunteered the answer. My responses finally caused him one day to slowly turn around, look over his glasses, scan the room, and seek out the individual who was well versed in these religious paintings. Impressed with my knowledge, he called upon me to give a special presentation of my choice before the class. I received an A+ for my final grade. I promised myself that one day I would visit these famous works of art.

Throughout my college years, I developed good study habits and applied them to my lecture classes. I set a standard for myself to learn all my subjects thoroughly. I preferred recording the lectures instead of taking notes. My attention would be focused one hundred percent on what my college professor was presenting. I noticed how the majority of the class would be involved in taking notes, thereby missing out on hearing what the teacher was saying. How could they focus on the professor if they're doing several things at once: listening, remembering, and writing down what they think they heard before it's time to write something new?

I resolved this problem by bringing my tape recorder to class and recording everything discussed. I think my professor may have been offended every time I came to class and set up my ritual. I always sat in the middle seat in the front row and set up my tape recorder on my desk. It had a built-in microphone that I positioned directly in front of the teacher to capture his every word. After I finished all my classes for that day, I'd go home where I would study for hours in my room. It was unlike being in the lecture hall, where I couldn't always stop the teacher and ask him to repeat everything he said. I could replay the tape as many times as I wanted, summarize what I had heard, and then write it down. I had complete understanding of the lectures. I'd also listen for pertinent information about what material the professor said would be on the next exam. My good study habits and my ability to retain information enabled me to get 100% on just about every assignment. Things didn't play out quite the same at home.

Earnest, Jr, Mama, Emeline, Bobbie, Daddy and Earnestine

I recalled only two whoppings from my Dad. The first was when I was twelve years old. One day, Dad told Am it was her turn to wash the dishes, a chore she hated to do. Am was as stubborn as a mule and refused to do the dishes. To top it off, she wouldn't cry while she was getting whooped by Dad. Although I tried to inform Am that if she cried and dropped those big crocodile tears, she'd lessen the number of strikes Dad would give her. Being the compassionate 'lil sister, here comes Emeline to the rescue. I jumped in front of Am and told my father, "I'll take Am's whooping for her. She gonna do the dishes!"

The second incident happened was when I was twenty-one years old! That's what I get for being a smart mouth and disobedient. Yes, I was still living at home, eating Mama's good cooking, enjoying free room and board, but grown and didn't want to follow their rules. My boyfriend Herbert wanted to take me out to celebrate New Year's Eve which fell on a Saturday. This would be the first time ever for me to go out on New Year's Eve which meant missing our family tradition. We always prayed the New Year in together as a family. Each year, we would gather in my parents' bedroom around their queen-sized bed on our knees. On the floor with heads bowed, we listened over the loud gunshots ringing outside the bedroom window while Dad prayed from 11:50 p.m. until midnight. After which, my siblings, parents and I wished each other "Happy New Year!" and then turned in for bed.

I really wanted to go out and celebrate. So, I sort of asked and smartly told my Dad, "I'm sorry, but I'm going." His first comment was "Emeline...it's 10:30 at night. You don't need to be out in those streets this late. People be shooting, drinking and acting like fools. Bullets don't carry names. You need to be at home. We... got church tomorrow." Well, from his remarks and tone I sensed his answer was definitely 'NO'; however, I'm grown and I decided to go anyway.

It was well over into the New Year, roughly around 1:00 Sunday morning when I told my boyfriend, "Herbert, I enjoyed my time out with you, but I need to get home." I turned the key and slowly opened the front door. I made my way over to the first step into the living room and headed straight toward the hallway, upstairs to my bedroom. Assuming everybody would be sound asleep, but to my surprise, Dad was up! He was seated at the table in the dining room reading his Bible and preparing his sermon. I tried to tip toe slowly and sneak past him without getting noticed. All of a sudden in his slow, soft pastoral tone, Dad said, "Didn't I tell you not to go out?" He closed his Bible. The next thing I knew, he got up and took off his belt. That's when I sarcastically asked, "Daddy, you're studying! I know you're not fixing to whip me?" He raised the belt in the air and came down swinging toward my back side, but missed as I dove for cover toward the green, paisley design, plastic covered sofa chair. It turned more comical because the chair received the majority of strikes from his belt than my back side. Noticing he was out of breath from those few swings by chasing me with the belt with me dodging him from side to side, we looked like two NFL players going in for a tackle. I constantly told him, "Dad, you're going to wear yourself out. Now you know you have to preach today?" My concerns didn't help. He kept on wackin' and missing.

Embarrassed, he finally gave up. I went to bed and tried to get in a couple hours of sleep.

Later that morning at breakfast, Dad asked me would I like to go with him to Bethel Baptist East Church where the pastor, Dr. Carl D. Hughes, invited him to preach and Dad wanted me to sing after the sermon. I told him, "Yes, I would love to." His sermon title was "Drop Your Nets" based on Jesus' parable when he met some fishermen by the seashore who had been toiling all night trying to find fish. Jesus commanded them where to drop their nets to find fish. Parable of the story: Following Jesus made them "Fishers of Men". My mother taught me always pick the appropriate song to fit the occasion or sermon. Not too pleased about what took place New Year's Day between me and Dad, I sung an old Negro spiritual, "Nobody Knows the Trouble I've Seen" instead of "I Want to Be a Follower of Christ." One of the older nurses, Sister Jessie McDowell also known as "Big Mac," who often served Dad after he preached walked over to me and asked, "Emeline, why you sing sumtin like that? Child that der song don't have a darn thang to do with fishen!" Jokingly, I told her, "You would have sung it too if you got a 'hit and miss whooping' from your father at twenty-one years old!" I smiled and looked over at my Dad who was nearby. We all couldn't help but to break out laughing.

MY FIRST TRANSPORTATION DESIGN MENTOR: MR. SAM MAYERS

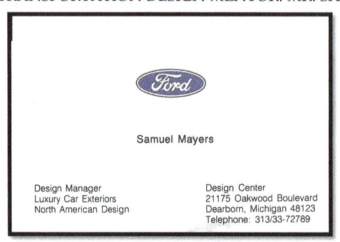

Meeting my mentor, Sam Mayers, for the first time had a profound impact on my design career. It was on a Saturday morning, and I was in the kitchen eating breakfast with my parents. Mama had made her delicious biscuits, served with rice, scrambled eggs, and bacon. I heard the doorbell ring and excused myself from the table to see who was there. Standing on our front porch, behind the white screen door, was a medium built, dark-brown African American man who had the biggest smile on his face. He seemed to be cheerful.

I asked him, "Sir, may I help you?" He told me his name was Sam Mayers and that he worked at the Design Center with my dad, who invited him over to talk to his daughter.

I told him "Oh, really? I'm his daughter, Emeline. Wait right here, I'll go tell him." I returned to the kitchen to let my Dad know. I wondered if Sam had something to do with designing cars, since he mentioned working in the Design Center. Dad went to the door and greeted Sam. Dad introduced Sam to me and told me, "Lenny Girl, since you love to draw cars and are interested in becoming a car designer, I invited Sam over to talk to you about his career and job duties at Ford. Sam is a talented car designer, and he would be able to give you good advice and direction."

I was excited about meeting Sam. I learned he was a product of the Detroit Public School System and that he had attended Eastern High School. Sam studied design at the Center for Creative Studies. He loved cars. He had been employed at Ford Design Center for seventeen years and had several acclaimed accomplishments. Just to name a few, he was lead designer of the Probe 1979 Mustang Project, which won "Car of the Year Award" and also the 1989 Lincoln Town Car. Sam had a unique style. His designs were timeless.

Sam told me how Ford had a talented group of black male designers, clay modelers, and engineers that have contributed to the auto industry. Even more historic was his coworker, Mr. McKinley Thompson, Jr., the first black male car designer. Both McKinley and Sam were the only designers to be promoted into middle management. Sam had a cousin, Nehemiah Amaker, who was a Transportation Designer. There was only one black in each of the shop departments at Ford. My father worked in the fabrication shop. Frank Woods represented the Wood Shop. Tom Jones worked in the trim shop. There was one black male named Julius in the metal shop. Ray was in engineering. With the exception of the paint shop, which had two black males: Al Poole and David Ramsey, there were two blacks who worked on special events: Benny Bailey and Diane Fox. Diane was a beautiful, elegant lady—I'd call her the Halle Berry and Lena Horne of the Design Center. Art Berry worked in administration. There were five clay modelers: Calvin Morrison, Charles Leak, Charles Purnell, Jasper Garrison and George Rogers. There were two other African American men who worked in the studio who were in charge of the clay ovens: Andy Walker and Melvin Edwards. Andy worked at Ford since he was 16 years old and looked good for being age seventy plus. He had the most beautiful smile with a warm, friendly, kind-natured personality. Andy was a veteran. Each year in honor of Veterans Day, he stood at the front entrance to the Design Center and handed out little red poppy flower pendants to everyone at the Ford Design Center, but please don't let that smile or his attitude fool you! Charles Purnell, one of the modelers, shared a story with me about Andy.

One time Andy went to the modeler's back area of the studio to take a nap on his lunch break. Upon awakening, Andy noticed his shirt was missing from where he had placed it on the bench next to him. When he found it, he noticed clay stains. I don't know who it was, but someone must have mistaken it for a rag. Andy was heated! He came out in the middle of the studio, stood up on a chair bare-chested and yelled out, "Who's the M----F--- that took and messed with my shirt?!"

There was Melvin Edwards who must have had an important position at Ford. I recalled one day when Melvin took me out for lunch. When he and I returned, I noticed that he parked in his own named parking space. Charles Purnell informed me that Melvin used to be the personal chauffeur for one of the executive Ford patriarchs. Each of these men and women were not only talented in their careers, but they were also professionals outside of Ford: a golfer, military bomb specialist, author, classic car collector and restorer, sculptor, licensed pilot who owned his own plane, photographer, musician, Motown graphic artist, skeet shooter, pastor, deacon, minister, Little League coach, and an attorney. As I sat there listening to Sam, I was looking forward to the day when I would meet these hidden jewels. I was appreciative that Sam exposed me to a unique, talented group.

At that moment, Dad interrupted our conversation and asked, "Sam, are you hungry? Would you care for some breakfast?"

Sam replied, "Yeah, man, I never turn down food." I noticed Sam could eat, and once he tasted Mama's biscuits, his conversation about designing cars would go on and on and on. He had my utmost respect and attention. I asked Sam to critique some of my car drawings I had been working on. I showed him a rendering of a Lincoln Continental.

He acknowledged that I had talent and suggested I come over to his house on Ferguson off of Seven Mile. He would help me to further develop my drawing and rendering skills and show me the role of a car designer. He mentioned how he had trained several aspiring black male car designers in his basement studio and that I would have an opportunity to meet them.

I spent many evenings with Sam and Dennis Moses, another aspiring talented designer who once designed toy cars for Mattel and later became a Ford Transportation Designer, in Sam's basement watching him do demos using a pencil, vellum, magic markers, and pastel chalk. Sam created some of the most beautiful, eye-catching, and timeless concept car renderings. Sam told me the importance of making sure I drew the car proportions correctly. He would call me "Weezy." He gave me that nickname because I reminded him of the character "Weezy" on the television sitcom, *The Jeffersons*. Sam mentioned, "You should first get the drawing right, then the rendering, and all those pretty fancy drawings comes second."

CENTER FOR CREATIVE STUDIES:
RON HILL, TRANSPORTATION INSTRUCTOR

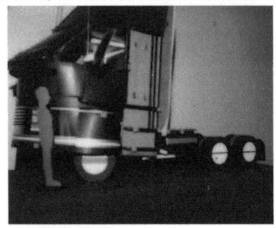

I was already a full-time student majoring in Industrial Design at Wayne State University when my mentor, Sam Mayer, suggested I should get more training directly from a designer working in the auto industry. He told me to enroll in the Center for Creative Studies, located on John R and Ferry Street. They offered a course in Transportation Design, and it was held every Saturday from eight in the morning until noon for eight weeks. My parents paid my tuition.

My instructor was Ron Smith, a professional transportation designer who worked for General Motors (GM). I heard he was a prolific, talented designer who had his own private design studio in the basement at GM Tech Center. One of my favorite class projects was to design a futuristic sixteen-wheel tractor trailer. I went through the entire design process by developing two-dimensional concept sketches, selecting a theme, and making a three-dimensional model out of construction cardboard paper.

Being a perfectionist, I had a habit of staying up all night, adding the last-minute details on the model, and rehearsing my presentation speech in front of my family. We would all assemble in the living room where I would stand before them and give my presentation. After I finished, everyone would give me a critique, which always helped. The critiques helped me get out all the kinks before I made my final presentation in class. My final design project was a fifth scale model of a futuristic tractor trailer designed for the year 2000. I built it out of colored construction paper and cardboard.

The color scheme was a charcoal grey exterior with a pink and light grey interior trim. The exterior represented a smooth, cocoon-shaped body with aerodynamic integrated side view mirrors and enclosed wheel openings with a futuristic flush exterior cab spoiler designed to enhance the vehicle air flow and eliminate wind resistance. On the day of my final after my presentation, my instructor, Ron, told me and my mother that I was a creative designer ahead of my time and that I could become a great transportation designer. Although it was a short summer class of eight weeks, what I learned from my instructor got me closer to pursuing a career in designing cars and mastering my craft.

FORD BLACK DESIGNERS AND ENGINEERS MAKE HISTORY AT MT. CALVARY'S YOUTH CAREER DAY

A historic event took place the second Sunday in June 1980, at my church, Mt. Calvary Baptist, located at St. Aubin and Frederick. My father was the pastor. I was chairperson for our Annual Youth Career Day. This affair gave youth an opportunity to meet and interact with representatives from diverse occupations within the industry.

This year, I wanted to make it personal and different. After having a conversation with Sam, I thought it befitting to invite a select group of black men working at Ford to share about their careers. I wrote a personal letter to Mr. McKinley Thompson, Jr., the first black car designer at Ford, asking him if he would come and enlighten the youth as our guest speaker. The accomplishments that he achieved would be inspiring to them. After learning about the blacks at Ford and their specialties, I wanted to expose this hidden culture to our youth.

I selected a theme: "Each One Mentor One, Each One Expose One." Mr. Thompson talked about his life as a car designer for Ford and the steps he took to accomplish his dream. There were a lot of obstacles he faced, and he shared how he overcame them. His encouraging words to our youth were that they should never give up and always pursue your passion. I had also invited all the Ford Design Center's black designers, clay modelers, engineers, and fabrication shop people. A diverse group of people were well represented for Mt. Calvary's youth.

Ford's talent enlightened the youth. It was a diverse representation of careers, so that if they were to all band together, they could incorporate their own automotive company. The advice that each one gave on their specialty was priceless. Every youth pledged that day to be committed to strive for success. It inspired me personally to become whatever in life I chose. My only limitations are the ones where I don't apply myself. I knew that I was surrounded by greatness that day, and it was bound to rub off on me.

I was happy to introduce this unique, talented Ford group to our youth just as my Dad had introduced Sam to me. This exposure was something the youth never would have known existed in the auto industry without Sam sharing this information with me. Now when these young people are riding in their family cars or see an exciting car on the street, they'll know that a part of their black culture played a significant role in it.

TED FINNEY, TRANSPORTATION DESIGN INSTRUCTOR AND FUTURE FORD MANAGER

Sam informed me that Wayne State offered evening classes in Transportation Design on Tuesdays and Thursdays from 7 p.m. to 10 p.m. Ford Motor Company had partnered this program through Wayne State. The students could obtain hands-on training from an experienced transportation designer currently working in the auto industry. They learn techniques on how to design cars and develop a portfolio to show potential employers upon graduation. Ted Finney, who was Caucasian, was assigned to teach. He worked at the Ford Design Center with Sam and my father. I was the only female in the class along with seven other males. The class was structured like an exterior design studio. Ted Finney would act as our design manager, and he was responsible for telling the class and the transportation designer the type of car we would be designing. We drew several concept sketches and chose a theme in which we developed our idea and made a presentation about our work before the class. Mr. Finney would critique our drawings and often give demonstrations.

Our final assignment was a portfolio of our best concepts. This would be our showpiece to landing a job in the auto industry. The renderings reflected the skills and talent of what we were capable of doing and would hopefully make one a potential candidate for hire. I wanted to make a great impression with my portfolio. I chose a format of 30 x 40 for all my drawings to be, instead of the standard 18 x 24 size.

A week before graduation, Mr. Finney recommended I reduce my format size and redo my entire portfolio. This request would require a lot of work and me staying up late each night to finish. I needed to have a portfolio in order to graduate. So, I decided to redo the assignment with a few special alterations. I redrew all my 30 x 40 drawings onto an 18 x 24 format. I placed them in a flip chart arrangement and mounted the stack on a 30 x 40 illustration board. This arrangement was more impressive and made it easier to view while describing my concepts during my job interviews. It looked professional. My Dad made me a 30 x 40 brown vinyl portfolio case with handles in which to carry my work.

I STOOD UP FOR WHAT I DESERVED

There was an incident that proved to me to always stand up for what you believe, deserve, and know is right. After the class had given their portfolio presentations, it was time for final grade markings. I received my grades in the mail. I was shocked. Mr. Finney gave me a B for my transportation design class. In my opinion, this marking did not reflect the quality or quantity of work I did over the course of six months, in addition to his last-minute request for me to redo my entire portfolio. I deserved an A, and I wrote him a rebuttal letter explaining several reasons why.

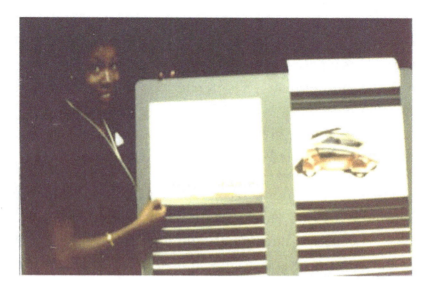

After some thought, Mr. Finney told me, "Out of all my years in teaching, I've never had a student question a grade choice or ask to change a grade. He told me, "All right, Emeline, I'll give you an A."

I replied, "No, Mr. Finney, I don't want you to 'give' me an A. I 'deserve' an A." After my comment, he changed my grade from a B to an A plus. I'm glad I stood up for what I deserved.

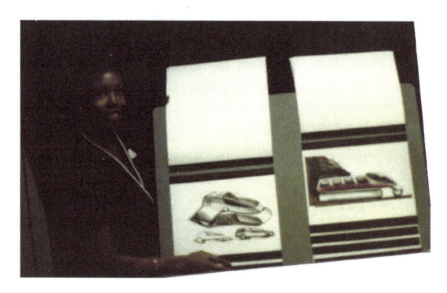

CHAPTER THREE
SHE DREAMED IT

MY FIRST JOB INTERVIEW AT GM

After I graduated from Wayne State on May 7, 1981, I was anxious to find a job in the automotive industry. I was equipped with my portfolio in hand, but before scheduling an interview with Ford, my dream employer, I wanted to do a test interview with one of the other big three automotive companies: General Motors at the Tech Center on Mound Road in Warren, Michigan. I remember having to borrow my Uncle Jack's car to drive to GM.

When I got to the lobby and informed the secretary that I was there for a job interview, she asked me to please take a seat in the lobby and someone from Human Resources (HR) would be out to assist me. I did as she asked and waited in the lobby. The place was immaculately designed with modern white office furniture. Finally, a tall Caucasian male wearing a black suit appeared from HR. He appeared to have a cold and distant attitude about him. He introduced himself and asked me to follow him to the office.

I thought I was on my way to be interviewed; however, he asked me for my portfolio and told me to wait in the office. He said he would be back and let me know what they said. He walked over into another adjacent room with my portfolio. He didn't return until about 45 minutes later.

He told me, "Thanks for coming, I'm sorry we aren't hiring right now." I thought it was strange that I wasn't invited in for the interview. Maybe that's how they interview potential employees. To this day, I left that place with the gut feeling that they may have photographed my concept drawings and used them for some of their own future products.

FIRST JOB INTERVIEW AT FORD: DID THESE DESIGNS COME OUT OF YOUR HEAD?

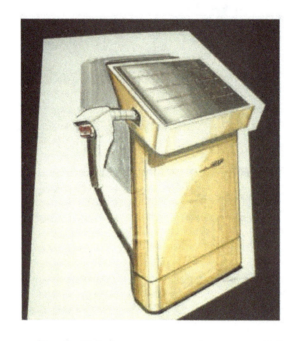

My first job interview at Ford didn't turn out the way I had planned, either. My creativity was questioned. I had just graduated from Wayne State University with a Bachelor of Fine Arts Degree in Industrial Design. I had an excellent portfolio that included my best design pieces, futuristic cars, my sketch book, and concept drawings of products. I knew my portfolio was on a top professional level, so it shouldn't have been a question that I had the talent, skills, and qualifications to design cars for Ford Motor Company.

My father came with me to the interview at the Design Center in the HR office. The office was small and my portfolio was a 30 x 40 format that practically took up the whole desk. I presented my work and explained each concept. That's when the HR representative looked down at my drawings and asked me, "Did all of this come out of your head?"

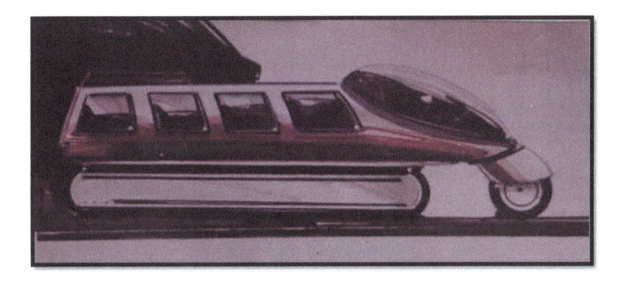

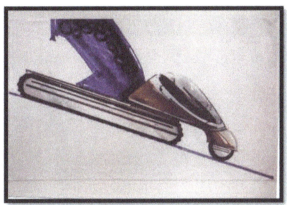

I quickly glanced over to my father who had a look on his face that wasn't too pleasing after hearing HR make the comment about my intelligence.

I told him "Yes, I created and designed everything that you are looking at." I even had a sketchbook that I kept with me showing what I imagined Ford cars and trucks would look like in the near future. He quickly flipped through the pages and told me how bad the economy was and they're just not hiring at this moment. "Emeline, when the economy picks up, we'll give you a call." Dad wasn't happy and neither was I about how the interview went. After leaving the Design Center, we headed to the car to go home. I was trying to be strong and silently hold back my tears. I was disappointed, but not destroyed. I asked my Dad about getting me an interview with Mr. Jack Telnack, Global Vice President of Design for Ford Motor Company.

My Dad said, "Lenny Girl, I'll see what I can do. Don't you worry."

I PROMISE I'LL BE BACK FOR MY INTERVIEW, MR. PRESIDENT

Two weeks later my Dad managed to schedule an interview with Mr. Jack Telnack. He was the Design Center's President. One thing I knew about my father was that he was persistent and unafraid to approach or speak to anybody, no matter what their position was. It could be the President of the United States or the average Joe on the street. Dad would always tell me, "Emeline, it doesn't hurt to ask. What do you have to lose? They breathe the same air you breathe".

I had my interview in Mr. Telnack's office, which was on Mahogany Row, in the Design Center. This is where all the design executives' offices were located. He reviewed my work and commented honestly on how creative my designs were and that I had a professional looking portfolio. He told me he wished he could hire me right then. Unfortunately, because of the economy, Ford is just not hiring.

So I told him, "You know what Mr. Telnack, I've been informed that the economy might be down right now, but it's not going to be down forever. So, I plan on going back to school, continuing my education, and after that, I would like to get hired as a Transportation Designer to work here at the Design Center."

At that moment, my Dad politely asked Mr. Jack Telnack, "Sir, what college did you attend to get your training in Transportation Design?"

Jack Telnack told my Dad, "Ernie, I went to Art Center College of Design in Pasadena, California. It is the top school of design in the country. Some of the top designers and design executives got their training in how to become a Transportation Designer by going to Art Center. What makes this school so unique is that the instructors are all professionals from all over the world who have worked as top CEOs in their industries." Mr. Telnack turned to my father and said, "Ernie, you should look into enrolling Emeline there. That would be an excellent choice for her to get an in-depth training, thorough knowledge about Transportation Design and the role of the designer. She'll experience how automotive companies are ran through its many departments and experience the total design process. Art Center instructors are the best in the design world. With her talents, skills and background education plus what she'll obtain at Art Center, Emeline will be a triple threat as a transportation designer".

I thanked him, and right before leaving his office, I turned to Mr. Telnack, shook his hand, looked him straight in his eyes, and said, "Mr. Telnack, after I graduate from Art Center, I'm coming back here to Detroit, and I want to be interviewed by you. I want to design cars for Ford Motor Company.

He told me, "Emeline, that will be great. No problem. When you graduate from Art Center, you'll be able to run this company."

MOST LIKELY SHE WON'T BE ACCEPTED TO ART CENTER

I was disappointed that I didn't get hired at Ford. This short delay would only be a minor pit stop for me. Once I completed my education at the prestigious Art Center, I would be even more equipped with the tools to get me back to my final destination: Ford Motor Company Design Center.

My father began the process of getting me enrolled in Art Center and my mentor, Sam, thought this was an excellent choice. It was on a Monday when my Dad called the admissions counselor at Art Center, a private college, and asked about their enrollment policy. She told him I would have to first submit my portfolio before I'd be accepted. Their standard format size is 18 x 24. Once the school board reviews the portfolio, depending on the applicant's level of talent, the board will determine whether or not they are accepted into the school's two-year program. My father explained to her that my portfolio size is 30 x 40 but it contains 18 x 24 drawings. She replied, "Well most likely she won't be accepted." Her remark didn't please my father at all.

Dad asked her, "How can you say she most likely won't be admitted when you haven't seen her work? I'll tell you what. I will fly Emeline, me and her 30 x 40 portfolio down to California for the board to review her talented work. I just need you to schedule a date for me and we will go from there."

She told my Dad, "I can book you an appointment, Mr. King, for this Thursday." Dad said, "That's fine." She must have forgotten that we lived in Detroit. Later that evening Dad made arrangements to book us a flight to California, but because of the short notice the tickets were pricey. I overheard Dad telling my mom what the counselor said, which made him even more determined to get me to California and enroll me in Art Center. Dad had minister friends in just about every state, so when he talked with his close friend, Rev. E. C. Bowdry, who lived in Los Angeles, California, and told him he was coming there with his daughter and her portfolio to Art Center for an interview, he also asked if E. C. Bowdry would be able to take him to the school located in Pasadena.

Rev. E. C. Bowdry told him, "Yeah Doc, I know exactly where that school is. It's waaaaaay up in those hills. I heard a lot of rich kids go to that private school."

Dad told Rev. E. C. Bowdry, "Man, I'm not worried about her not getting in because she has two things in her favor. Lenny Girl got the Lord on her side and she sho nuff got talent."

Rev. E. C. Bowdry picked us up from the airport in his white 1980 Cadillac Coupe de Ville. It was a beautiful, sunny day in Los Angeles, California, and the temperature was in the high 90s. This was my first trip to California. Looking out my window I noticed the green palm trees lining the streets in formation as we rode pass. I can see why people would call California, "God's Country." The scenery is breathtaking. Rev. E. C. Bowdry placed our luggage in the trunk, along with my 30 x 40 portfolio, and we headed straight to Pasadena. He took the 405 freeway heading north. I noticed ahead in a far distance a brownish haze that covered the city skyline. I asked Rev E. C. Bowdry, "What is it? "

He told me, "It's smog, a combination of smoke and fog. This air pollutant comes from the automobiles, heavy traffic, diesel- run vehicles, and industrial plants."

I noticed the traffic started to back up and Rev. E. C. Bowdry told us two things you can't get away from here in California are traffic jams and smog. Once traffic started moving, and we were getting closer to Pasadena, the scenic route turned into narrow winding roads, hills, and mountains. After driving for an hour, we finally reached 1700 Lida Street. I could see a black steel bridge at the very top of the hill, suspended in the air between two mountains. Rev. E. C. Bowdry pointed his finger up to the top and called out, "Emeline, there's your Art Center."

We parked the car and headed to the school. We met the head of the Transportation Department, Mr. Teter, a Caucasian petite man. He carried a cane and walked with a limp. Mr. Teter was a former Transportation Designer who worked for Ford at the Design Center in Detroit and after retiring, he was called to head up the Transportation Department at Art Center. Mr. Teter introduced us to the portfolio committee who would be reviewing my work: Mr. Joe Farrer and the admissions counselor.

I handed my portfolio to Mr. Teter. He noticed the size and said, "Wow, that's almost as big as you, Emeline."

I told him, "Yes, that's why we flew out here...because I was told the standard format size is 18 x 24.

Mr. Teter told my father, "Feel free to walk over to our student cafeteria and have lunch while the board reviews the portfolio. It should take about an hour." We made our way to get a bite to eat.

Rev. E. C. Bowdry, looking around, told my Dad, "Doc, this is some place."

Dad said, "Yes it is, now let's bless the food." Dad said a prayer on my behalf that God will provide and that favor be placed upon me to get accepted to Art Center. An hour had passed and it was time to find out my fate.

Mr. Teter informed me that the portfolio committee was highly impressed with my outstanding leverage and quality of work and unanimously voted to have me enroll in the school's Transportation Design program. They informed me that because of my experience, they would give me advance standing which would allow me to finish the program in 18 months instead of two years.

Mr. Teter assured me of three things. "Emeline, it's going to take hard work, dedication, and all of your time to complete and finish this program. My dear, you'll have no life outside of Art Center. But once you graduate, the doors of opportunity are limitless."

On the ride back to the airport, I remembered what Mr. Teter told me. I knew this journey wasn't going to be easy, but I was willing to give 110 percent. As we were leaving Art Center, I turned around and noticed the beautiful Art Center structure fading off in the distance. I whispered one of my favorite bible verses, Philippians 4:13 "I Can Do All Things through Christ Who Strengthens Me." When we made it back to Detroit, Dad started making arrangements with relatives about who I would be staying with in California.

MEET MY COUSIN, "MAC"

Art Center didn't provide dormitories for their students. I was very fortunate that my father had relatives and minister friends living in Los Angeles, California. I heard Dad talking on the phone with his cousin, Matthew (Mac) King who was in his late sixties, asking if it would be okay for me to stay with him while I attended Art Center. Dad mentioned he would send some money for Mac to find me a reliable car to get around. Mac stayed in Inglewood, California, which was almost 30 miles outside of Pasadena. The ride to Art Center would take at least two hours, depending on traffic. Mac told my father it would be a pleasure for me to stay with him. My family, friends, and relatives gave me a big send-off party. They told me they loved me and that I will always have their support. My parents reminded me to study hard, fulfill my dream, and most of all keep God first, pray, and trust Him always.

When I arrived at LAX airport, cousin Mac was at the gate waiting for me. What a character he was! This happy little man, standing only five feet tall, was wearing a pair of beige khaki pants, a bright red short-sleeved polo shirt, and a beige cap. He greeted me with a captivating smile and a country accent, "Hello, Emma. Welcome to CA-LEE-FORN-KNEE-AH." Seeing him for the first time, I would describe Mac as a carbon copy of Fred Sanford, who was played by actor Redd Foxx on the television sitcom *Sanford and Son*. Mac walked, talked, and portrayed that same sarcastic, outspoken, flirtatious, and charismatic charm of Fred G. Sanford.

Mac's demeanor would heighten each time he was in the presence of a female. He'd start off by saying, "Well, hello, my daaarling, and how are you doing today? You're so pretty." For some strange reason every female we passed in the airport on our way to the baggage claim was smitten by his comments. Mac was so full of energy, I could hardly keep up with him.

It was still early in the morning when we left the airport. Mac took the scenic route down Manchester Blvd. Mac mentioned to me, "Emma, I'm taking you to my own big, fancy, expensive restaurant to buy you some breakfast. I'm thinking that cousin Mac owned a restaurant, to my surprise, we pulled in front of "Big Boy." To me, it was your typical family restaurant, nothing more than that. Back in Detroit, we have plenty of Big Boy restaurants, but I wasn't about to bust Mac's ego.

We went inside, and a young waitress came over to seat us and take our order. That's when Mac started his flirtation again. Looking up at the waitress, he flashed that million-dollar smile and said, "Darling, you looking mighty beautiful today. Heaven must have fallen because beauty is written all over you."

She smiled and said, "Thank you Sir, you're so sweet." Mac told me, "Now Emma, you go ahead and order whatever you want. I'm paying."

After we finished our breakfast, it was time to go to Mac's house. We drove around for about forty-five minutes and came to a neighborhood adorned with beautiful pastel-colored houses. He parked the car in front of a yellow stucco bungalow house. Mac rang the doorbell and a lady came to the door. She was dressed in a blue and white track suit and had her hands folded. She looked upset and appeared to be in her late 20s.

Mac walked in and said, "Betty, this is Emma, my 'lil cousin from Detroit. She's going to that big college, Art Center in Pasadena. She's gonna get a good education. Emma, meet Betty." Clearing his throat, he spoke in a soft, low voice, "We gonna need a place to stay for a couple of weeks. Come on in Emma, make yourself at home." I looked at Betty, and she was just as surprised as I was. I politely spoke and followed right behind cousin Mac.

Later that week, we went to a used car dealership to look for transportation to get me back and forth to school. Dad sent Mac $1,500.00 to purchase a car. He was able to find me a used 1979 white Chevy Chevette. He spoke with the salesperson and asked to check out the mechanics. After Mac did a test drive and saw that it had a couple of miles on it, he was satisfied and said, "Emma, I think this will work." It turned out to be a good running car.

WILL THE REAL LOOK-A-LIKE PLEASE STEP FORWARD?
AUNT ESTHER MEET MAC

School would be starting in two weeks. Mac decided to take me to Walt Disney World. We knew that once school started, I wouldn't have time to do anything but concentrate completely on my studies. We stood in line to get on one of the amusement rides. I was behind this tall, middle-aged lady and she happened to turn around. I noticed she was the actress Esther Anderson Ross. She played "Aunt Esther" on the *Sanford and Son* television show, which was one of my favorites. What a coincidence!! I was so excited, I grabbed my camera and was just about to snap her picture when she immediately held her hand up in front of my camera and said, "Hold it, young lady. You're supposed to ASK a person for their permission before you take a picture of them." I apologized, and told her, "Ma'am, I didn't mean to be disrespectful. I guess I overreacted seeing a real movie star. This is my first-time visiting California." But, before I could retract and ask her permission, Mac stepped in between me and the lady and said, "Excuse me, Daaarling, you should be glad anybody would want to take your picture." It wasn't long before the people standing behind us started laughing and whispering, "This must be a taping for an upcoming episode on *Sanford and Son*. Little did they know that it wasn't. Although this lady was the actress, Esther Anderson Ross, who played Aunt

Esther, she looked puzzled and surprised, thinking Mac was the real actor, Redd Foxx, and her agent was playing a joke on her. However, Mac assured her that he wasn't.

She told him, "Well, you sho nuf had me fooled."

EMMA, IT'S TIME TO MOVE

I had to get up at 5:00 a.m. every morning and leave the house by 5:30 a.m. so I would be on time for school. My schedule was very intense. I was in school from 8:00 a.m. to 10:00 p.m., which meant I normally wouldn't get home 'til late. One particular morning, Mac and I headed downstairs to the kitchen to get breakfast. We noticed on the kitchen counter the top portion of a wedding cake had a large kitchen knife stuck in the middle and the groom's figurine head was broken off. Mac looked at me and surprisingly said, "BETTY," he paused. "Emma, that's not a good sign. We got to find another place to stay. Don't worry, we can move in with Tina."

I asked, "Who is Tina, Mac?"

He said, "That's my first wife."

Mac told me that Betty was very jealous because he would always wait up for me to get home from school every night. I thought it was strange she felt that way. Cousin Mac was only looking out for my safety. Art center was some distance, and some nights I wouldn't get home till 11:00 or midnight.

On our way to Tina's house, Mac pointed out a small building that had a giant brown donut on top of its roof. He told me they show this famous landmark on a lot of television commercials.

"Yes, I remembered seeing it." We turned on South Ash Street and pulled in the driveway to Tina's house. It was a white stucco ranch with a two-car garage and living quarters above it. We met Tina coming out the side door of the house. She was an older lady and close to Mac's age. They've been divorced going on five years, but they still remained cordial. Tina was the mother of Mac's two sons: Robert and Jerry. Tina was a Christian lady, but she was stern. In a kind, high-pitched and authoritative tone, she asked, "Matthew, ah, what's going on? What brings you here, Mister? The last time I saw you, you ran to Vegas to elope with that young thang Betty."

Matthew stood there as quiet as a church mouse and later said, "Tina, this is my 'lil cousin, Emma, from Detroit. She's going to college in Pasadena, at the Art Center. So, if you don't mind, we will need a place to stay." Tina started laughing and told Mac, "That's fine, I have no problem having Emma staying with me. Nice to meet you, Emma. Mac, you're welcome too, but you're going to be walking on eggshells, Mister." From that day on Tina and I had a good relationship. She treated me like a daughter. Mac and Tina were always looking out for me. Tina would often prepare dinner for me and show me around L.A.

For the first couple days of school, I had to follow Mac in my car going to Art Center until I became familiar with the route. By the time I got out of school, Mac would be in the parking lot talking and flirting with most of the students. I had no time for outside activities while attending Art Center, except for going to church. My father had contacted another one of his minister friends, Rev. Dudley, who pastored the Mt. Calvary Baptist Church in Los Angeles. My church was also called Mt. Calvary. Dad asked Pastor Dudley if I could be under his watch while I was there attending college. Dad shared with him that I had a beautiful voice and was a gifted gospel singer who would love to sing in the choir. Dad called me "the Jill of all trades" because I had many talents and interests.

I looked forward to singing in the choir on Sunday mornings. The church organist's name was Frankie. She was a talented musician who accompanied me whenever I was asked by Pastor Dudley to come sing a solo. Pastor Dudley loved for me to sing "Only What You Do for Christ Will Last" and "He Decided to Die." Frankie could make an organ talk. After I finished singing, the spirit would be high in the church, with the congregation shouting and praising God.

I needed my weekly Sunday church rejuvenation in order to keep my sanity. The workload at school was tremendously stressful. Quite often I'd find myself having to stay up late to pull all-nighters to complete projects that had to be perfect. There was no time for error. Art Center ran like Corporate America. Some students were so burned out, they'd pop pills just to keep up. I heard one student fell asleep at the wheel and crashed the car at the foot of a mountain. Thank God, no one was badly hurt. Aside from that one incident, I dealt with the strangest thing that occurred every Friday. My car always stalled at the foot of the mountain, near Art Center, and I had to wait for some student to come along and give me a boost.

ART CENTER COLLEGE OF DESIGN

I had been in school about two months before Mr. Teter, the head of the transportation design department, informed me that GM was sending HR representatives to see my progress. How strange that after going to GM for a job interview, HR didn't want to interview me with my portfolio, but now all of a sudden, they have an interest? It seemed like every other week I was approached by students who asked, "You still here?"

Although I had received advance standing, Art Center tuition was expensive. Unfortunately, I wasn't given a scholarship or any grants. I did not come from a wealthy family like the majority of the students who attended Art Center. By the grace of God, my parents worked to pay for my education. Art supplies costed a fortune. Dad did numerous hours of overtime working at Ford. He would jokingly say he would be the one who turned the lights off at Ford. Mom took on extra jobs teaching at Keidan Elementary. Never once did they miss or was late on my tuition payment. My family believed in tithing and that God would supply their every need and He did!

Mr. Teter told me that in attending Art Center, there was no time for outside activities. It was going to take hard work, dedication, commitment, assignments, and talent to succeed here. The workload was going to be heavy, and by the time you realize that in the first two weeks of school, you are already behind. He told me to get used to burning the midnight oil, numerous hours of staying up late to finish.

I took several courses: one in particular made Mr. Teter's statement true in my first semester. Joe Farrer was on the Art Center's portfolio committee who reviewed my artwork prior to me being accepted into Art Center. He headed the industrial design department and was rumored by his students as the perfectionist who showed students no mercy if they neglected to follow his class demonstrations. It was the week of finals when I presented Joe my last two class projects: a handcrafted, painted fiberglass vase and a set of clay model tools. The clay modeling tools were to be used by transportation design students who took the course *Introduction to 3D Design*.

For our senior project, we would be designing and using our personalized tools to create fifth scale clay models. Our final grade depended highly on the craftsmanship of our clay tools. I had been in school since 8:00 that morning, working on my design projects: a set of clay modeling tools and an oval-shaped vase. I was tired and hadn't taken time out to eat, but I managed to push through. Joe had given an intense demonstration on how to make clay tools. I made sure I followed his instructions on how to use the right texture of sandpaper and what order to apply it in. Plus, you had to allow each coat of paint to dry before applying another layer. I mixed the color mauve and painted it evenly onto the vase. I noticed the clock said 10:00 p.m., and I still had to put three coats of clear shellac on the clay tool handles and let them dry.

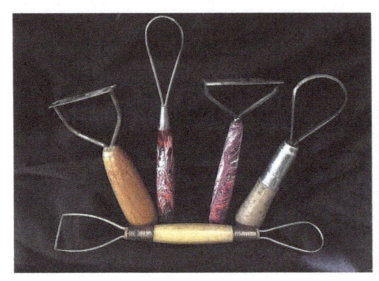
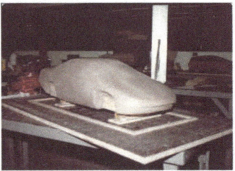

It was around 11:30 p.m. when one of my classmates — Mona, a biracial female who had the prettiest freckled face and was a talented environmental designer — stopped by the paint shop. She was a term ahead of me. She once did an internship designing the interior of a private jet for a sheikh in Saudi Arabia. I was frantically trying to finish when she told me, "Emeline, why don't you take a break and come over to my house. I stay close by." I can help you finish your clay tools." I followed her home, which was ten minutes away from Art Center. Mona had a beautiful house. She introduced me to her husband, a friendly Caucasian man. Mona shared with me that before meeting her husband for the first time, he came over to her house and cleaned her bathroom. After that gesture, she had to marry a man who was kind enough to do that for her. Mona made me a turkey sandwich and offered me an energy drink along with some no-doze pills. I passed on the pills and enjoyed the sandwich. Mona noticed I seemed a little discouraged. She gave me some encouraging words that lifted my spirit.

She said, "I don't care how early you start your projects in the beginning of the semester, you always end up burning the midnight oil the night before finals. You got to hang in there. Emeline, if you don't know it by now, you are making history. You will be the first black female to graduate from Art Center in Transportation Design and when you go back to Detroit you'll probably be a first for Ford. Art Center's graduates always turn out to be successful in life.

It was getting late and I glanced down at my watch. It was going on 4:00 a.m. in the morning. I knew it would be a long drive home from Pasadena to Inglewood—at least an hour and 45 minutes. Hopefully, I would be able to catch thirty minutes of sleep and make it be back to school by 8:00 a.m. for my class presentation with Joe. I asked Mona for some coat hangers so I could hang my clay tools. I placed them in front of my car's interior air vents and turned the air switch control on high. I rolled down all the windows so by the time I got home, my clay tools and vase would be completely dry. I drove 25 miles per hour because I didn't want the vase or clay tools to fall or touch each other. It was funny seeing my car's interior overcrowded with fixtures hanging everywhere. I made it home just in time to lay down and rest my eyelids. This was only for a minute after which I was awakened to the sound of my alarm. I set it to go off at 5 a.m. I hurried to the bathroom to get ready for school. I managed to get to school at 7:45 a.m. I had 15 minutes to get to class. We placed all our projects on a table at the front of the class. We were on pins and needles watching Joe scan over the top of his wireframe reading glasses as he held the vase up to the light and carefully inspected and critiqued the entire surface.

Unfortunately, there was one male student who must not have remembered Joe's instructions on how to properly make a flawless vase. In the beginning of the school semester, Joe warned each student if he or she didn't follow his instructions, he would automatically fail you. Joe happened to spot a hairline scratch on the surface of that one student's vase. The student neglected to let each layer of paint dry before applying another one, resulting in an orange peeled texture settling on the surface. All of this could have been avoided had the surface been prepped in the beginning. Joe showed a demonstration on how to achieve a smooth surface using various textures of sandpaper: hard, medium, and fine. Applying them in order to the fiberglass vase, next Joe mixed and applied the first coat of paint. Then, he let it dry between each layer before applying another coat of paint. Rushing the process resulted in a poor quality surface. What lies underneath will come thru the outer surface.

When my classmate saw the outcome of his project, he was so frightened that he begged, pleaded, and cried like a baby; however, his emotions didn't affect Joe's decision to fail him. After seeing the outcome for my classmate, I started to get nervous. I was next in line to go before Joe. He looked at my work and carefully inspected the surfaces and without saying one word, Joe turned to me and smiled. I took that gesture as an indication that I had passed his class. All I could think to say was "Thank you, Jesus!"

I left school that day exhausted. I had a frightening incident happen to me while I was driving home from school on the freeway. I had stayed up all night. I was tired and my eyes started to burn. I could barely see the road ahead. I suddenly swerved to the right side, and my car headed toward the side railing. I was so scared. When I realized that I wasn't hurt and my car was not damaged, I started thanking God again.

CHAPTER FOUR
SHE LEARNED IT

YOU'RE ALWAYS ON THE PHONE. ARE YOU A BOOKIE?

My father stayed in touch with me every day. He would call me during his lunch break on his company phone promptly at 11:31 a.m. Art Center had installed a phone for the students to use. It was located on the wall in the hallway outside the cafeteria. During my lunch break, which was thirty minutes, I would go stand by the phone at 11:30 a.m. and wait anxiously for Dad to call. We talked no more than two to three minutes each day about how I was doing in school and how everyone sends their love. He would tell me he went to the bank and deposited some money in his account for my school's tuition and for me to continue to do my best. The next day, I was on my way to the cafeteria when a white male student approached me and said inquisitively, "I've been noticing you are on that phone everyday around 11:30 a.m., you must be a bookie?" I replied, "No," I'm not a bookie."

The following day when I walked over to that same area, the phone had been removed from the wall. When I got home that evening, I called my Dad to let him know what had happened. That prank didn't stop me and Dad from keeping in contact with each other every day. I wrote letters home, and Tina told me I could use her house phone anytime I wanted to.

"EMELINE, YOU'RE MAKING THE BIGGEST MISTAKE"

The week before graduation most of the major car companies would be sending representatives to Art Center to review our senior portfolios and look for potential candidates to be hired. I had completed all my classes and a portfolio that represented my best automotive and design projects. My dream of becoming a car designer was fast approaching. I still had my sights on heading back to Detroit and fulfilling my promise of being interviewed by Jack Telnack, head of the Design Center at Ford.

It was a Friday afternoon when I was walking across the Art Center's atrium with Mr. Teter, who walked slowly with a cane because of health challenges. We were having a friendly conversation about how being an alumnus of Art Center has opened many doors of opportunity to all its graduates. He informed me that Ford Motor Company would be sending a Human Resources representative out to California to interview me and review my portfolio.

I told him "That is a kindhearted gesture for them to do. Unfortunately, I won't be here. I'm heading back to Detroit. I promised Mr. Jack Telnack that when I graduated, I wanted him to interview me."

That's when Mr. Teter looked at me strangely and said, "Emeline, you're making a big mistake by not being here for the interview. They are making a special trip out here on your behalf." By then, Mr. Teter seemed upset and hurriedly thrusting his cane at the ground, left me standing there. I literally had to run to catch up with him. I felt total numbness. I didn't know whether to start crying or what. When I got home, I stopped by the mailbox. There was a letter and a package from my Mother. She sent me a grey pinstriped two-piece suit to wear for my job interviews.

I broke down and cried. That night, I called my father and told him what Mr. Teter had said about my decision not to interview. I reminded my Dad of the promise I made to Jack Telnack that I didn't want to break. I asked my father if he would book a flight home for me and make an appointment for me to meet with Jack Telnack. He told me he would and for me to concentrate on graduating.

When Mama found out about my plans, she was hurt and just knew I had blown my chances of ever getting hired at Ford. Although she was upset, Dad assured her everything was going to work out in my favor. God had the final say.

MY PROMISE: I'll BE BACK FOR MY INTERVIEW, MR. PRESIDENT

Dad was able to get me my interview with Jack. On the morning of my interview, we rode into work together. While in the car, Dad was giving me my pep talk. He told me not to be afraid because God was on my side today.

"Lenny girl, you have all this training under your belt and your talent to prove that you are more than qualified. Look Mr. Telnack straight in the eye and speak with confidence."

When we arrived at the Design Center, I made my way toward Mahogany Row. I spoke to the receptionist and informed her I was there to interview with Jack Telnack. Surprisingly, my Dad walked right in with me.

The receptionist spoke, "Hi, Mr. King, how are you doing?"

He said, "I'm doing great, and yourself?"

She said, "Fine" then told us to please have a seat. She would let Jack know we had arrived. She shortly returned and said, "Mr. Telnack will now see you in his office." I didn't know Daddy was in on the interview too. I'm sure this was going to be a historic interview.

Both he and I were dressed professionally. I wore the two-piece gray pinstripe suit mama brought me, and Dad wore his black three-piece suit. Jack's office was immaculate with modern black and silver decor. He had a couple of fifth scale models of Ford cars displayed on his desks and inside a glass curio. There were trophies and several awards on the wall and a framed car sketch that he had drawn. Jack invited me and Dad to have a seat on his big, brown leather couch. I sat in the middle; Jack was to my right and Dad was on my left side.

I handed Jack my portfolio. That's when Mr. Telnack asked me, "Emeline, were you aware that Ford sent representatives out to Art Center to specifically interview you for a job position here? For some reason, they couldn't find you, Emeline."

I told Mr. Telnack "Yes, because I was on the plane heading back to Detroit. Don't you remember the promise I made to you, Jack? The promise was after I graduated from Art Center, I wanted to be interviewed personally by you. You agreed, so I'm here now." Jack laughed and said, "I do recall." I left that day confident that I would be hearing from Ford real soon. That next day I flew back to Art Center to prepare for finals and graduation.

MY ART CENTER EXPERIENCE: THE ORANGE DOT EXPERIENCE

Every time I saw the color orange in the shape of a small dot, which was Art Center's school logo, it reminded me of my experiences at Art Center. Art Center taught me six important things that I have maintained throughout my career as a car designer.

1. The importance of being disciplined
2. To seek knowledge by learning from the best
3. Maintain strong determination
4. Strive for perfection
5. Seek mentors as bridges to opportunities
6. Learn the quality of craftsmanship

First, I learned the importance of being disciplined, staying focused and avoiding distractions. Mr. Teter, who headed the transportation design department told me on my first visit to the school, "Emeline, you won't have any time for outside activities. Art Center has a strict curriculum for any student who gets accepted in this school to live, sleep, and breathe Art Center."

Second, I discovered that Art Center faculty and instructors are the best and are top professionals in their field. They will equip you with the tools you need to enhance your talent and abilities. What you obtain from them will allow you to become successful in your career. It's your responsibility to digest, retain, and apply everything you learn here.

Third, I learned to maintain strong determination, even if it means burning the midnight oil, staying up late to complete an assignment that your instructor gave you three weeks to complete and then decide they want it submitted early. You will do everything in your power to complete it in time. No excuses for incomplete or late assignments.

Fourth, each student must strive for perfection. If you can make it through Art Center, you can make it anywhere. Art Center has set high standards—never come short of them. Fifth, mentors are "Your Bridges to Opportunities." Depending on their construction, choose wisely. Sixth, the craftsmanship of your tools will determine the quality and outcome of your model's surface.

I found this lesson to be true when one of my assignments was to make and design my own clay tools to help build my fifth scale 3D clay model for my final senior project. In our shop class, our instructor, Joe Farrer, demonstrated how to use the various shop machines—band saw, vise, and lathe machine—to make our first semester clay tools.

In order to achieve a professional-looking surface model that's representative of my selected concept sketch, I had to design and make the tools right from the start. Using only a hammer, file, and a vise, I took strips of thin metal rods, then bent and shaped them into three different designs: an oval for carving the clay, one horizontal blade with two smooth sides, and another horizontal blade with two jagged edges. This process wasn't easy because I had to go through a couple of metal pieces before getting the shape perfect. I had to be careful using the band saw machine to carve three handles out of a small block of wood, which then had to be shaped, sanded, and painted with two coats of shellac.

Once my tools were completed, the next step involved taking my 2D design concept theme sketch and using the clay tools to transfer a 2D design into a 3D clay model. Provided that the clay surface underneath is smooth with no imperfections, Dinoc, which is a thin painted sheet of material representing sheet metal, is used to cover the clay surface. The final step involved detailing the clay model using tape to outline door cuts, window shapes, grille openings, lights etc. and then add on the wheels and tires, which had to be designed, carved and painted. All of these steps couldn't have been successful if the clay tools were made poorly in the beginning.

ART CENTER CLASSROOMS

Art Center wanted their students to get a feel of what's it's like to work in the auto industry after they graduate. For this reason, classrooms are running like a real automotive design studio. Studio agenda meetings are often held every morning to discuss and give the designers their assignment. Everyone from the studio who participates in the program is present. Based on upper management, engineering and marketing objectives for the program, everyone is informed about what type of vehicle is to be designed: sedan, sport, truck, or van, etc. Engineering specifications, the target market audience, benchmark and competitive vehicles are all considered. Each transportation designer now will have an opportunity to participate in designing a vehicle for mass production. The optimum goal for every designer is to have your theme sketch selected by management and be appointed to follow that concept vehicle from start to finish production. There are several sketch reviews until a theme is selected, then it is transferred from 2D sketch to engineered dimensions to 3D clay model development. This same design process would apply in a classroom. The only difference is it would be before your teacher and classmates.

I always did exceptionally well when it came time to make presentations before my instructors and classmates. I would explain my designs with supportive logical sketches that met the objectives. I was never nervous because I did a lot of public speaking at my church, in front of my family and other social events. I carefully selected the best pieces of work to support the program. When it came time to have my work critiqued in class, I learned not to be offended or carry my feelings on my sleeve because Art Center instructors had no time for that. If your work presentation was excellent, you would be commended. If it was a piece of crap, they would tell you. An excellent presentation, logically configured designs, and your model's craftsmanship all determined your final grade.

ART CENTER CLASSMATE GARTH NEWBERRY

While attending Art Center, I was the only African American female in the school, and I was in the transportation design department. There was a classmate I became friends with—a black male named Garth Newberry. He was from Akron, Ohio and was one semester ahead of me. Garth was a talented designer; he was supportive in encouraging me while attending Art Center.

Dad flew momma out to be with me for graduation. I introduced her to Garth. It was so funny . . . my mother went bonkers over Garth. I don't know exactly what nationality Garth was, but mom wasn't too shy in saying, "Emeline, he is handsome." Garth was just my friend, that's all. I had no time to even think of starting up a relationship. Many years after we graduated from Art Center, Garth came and visited me in Detroit. He surprised me for my 50th birthday celebration. My birthday was in December and it was a blizzard, but I was happy he came all the way from California to see me.

ART CENTER GRADUATION

Graduation finally came on September 16, 1983. Both my parents flew out to California to be with me. It seemed like my eighteen months of advance standing at Art Center went so fast. The sun was shining and it was a beautiful day, with the temperature in the high 90's. After the ceremony, we headed to the school's reception at a place called the Hill and that's exactly what it was. Praying that my little white Chevy Chevette would make it up this steep mountain, I floored it. When we reached the top, the building called the Hill stood over the city of Pasadena. It was a beautiful vantage point, seeing the city all lit up. I joined in the festivities with my classmates and school faculty. We danced, ate, and talked about our plans after Art Center. We had a wonderful time. I will always remember my Art Center experiences. I was under a lot of pressure, but I made it. I was the first African American female to graduate from that school and in that curriculum. If I survived Art Center, I could handle anything. I'm grateful to God for blessing me with parents who supported me both spiritually, financially, and emotionally. My new chapter was beginning, and I was determined to make my parents proud. I still remember Jack Telnack's words "If you make it through Art Center, you could run Ford."

CHAPTER FIVE
SHE APPLIED IT

MY FIRST MAGAZINE DEBUT REVEALED MY FUTURE EMPLOYER

The first time I was featured in a magazine was the February 1984 issue of *Smithsonian*, Volume 14, Number 11, page 78. The article was entitled, "Where tomorrow's cars are being shaped." The article was about the students who were studying transportation design and its well-structured program at Art Center College of Design in Pasadena, California.

These talented designers will design the cars of today and the future, it read. What made this article astonishing and meaningful was a full-size color photograph of me on page 78, seated with my arms crossed in front of my future concept drawings. I was twenty-seven years old, but looked like I was fifteen and hadn't slept or eaten for days. I remembered when they shot the photo I was in the midst of finals. I was totally exhausted from staying up late completing my assignments. The caption read: *Emeline King here displaying her concept sketches for a van, is now a designer for Ford in Detroit.*

I was overwhelmed with joy. Although I had only been at the Art Center for about a year and three months and was scheduled to graduate in September, the article stated that Ford had already hired me. The article mentioned in the caption, "Emeline King, a Ford designer, pictured with her concept van." What a surprise employment confirmation because I hadn't graduated and the caption mentioned I was already employed by Ford!

This article solidified that my dream of being a car designer and working for Ford with my Dad was meant to be. I called my parents who were in Detroit, Michigan, to tell them I was featured in the *Smithsonian*. It was hilarious because before I could hang up the phone, they were out buying every *Smithsonian* on the newsstands, in bookstores, and calling every relative and friend to go and purchase the magazine.

ART CENTER COMMENCEMENT SPEAKER
GRADUATING CLASS OF 1990

After I graduated from Art Center in September 1983, I started working for Ford on October 24, 1983. Fast forward ten years: At the request of Art Center, they asked me to be their commencement speaker for the graduation class of 1993. In the past, it was noted that Art Center would only invite CEOs from the top Fortune 500 companies to be the commencement speaker. I felt honored that I was chosen because I wasn't nowhere near an executive level, or in the vicinity of a Fortune 500 listing. However, I was the first black female to ever graduate in Transportation Design at Art Center and the first black female car designer for Ford. Ford's Public Relations department offered to write my speech. I was well skilled in public speaking, so I decided to write my own. I gave a copy of my speech to both Fords' PR and Mr. Jack Telnack. They were impressed.

Mama, Emeline, Tom Brown with daughter and Rosa Farrer

Ford flew me and my mom to California and paid for our stay in an expensive hotel. On the day of the graduation, I must have given a dynamic speech by the reaction of the audience. They gave me a standing ovation that lasted for several minutes. Joe, his wife Rosa, and all of my instructors and Art Center faculty were there. I was informed that Mr. Teter had passed away. Tom Brown, the president of Art Center, congratulated me on a job well done. He informed me that Art Center was a private college and expensive. He hoped I was given financial aid when I attended.

I said, "No sir, it was my loving, devoted parents who sacrificed financially to pay for my education.

That's when Mr. Brown directly told me, "Emeline, had I been the president during the time you were a student at Art Center, you would have been given a full ride scholarship.

JOE FARRER, SORRY I FORGOT TO TURN IN MY CHIP

On the first day of class, Joe gave each student a numbered silver circular metal chip. My chip was number 33. Joe stressed not to lose it if you wanted to graduate, you had to turn in your chip. Even though I was frightened of Joe and his critiques, he turned out to be one of my favorite instructors at Art Center. A year had passed since I graduated from Art Center and started working at Ford. I was in the international studio sitting in my cubicle sketching some car proposals. The phone rang. It was my former Art Center instructor, Mr. Joe Farrer. I was surprised. Nervous, I started to shake and nearly dropped the phone. All I could do is wonder why Joe would be calling me? I thought for a moment. It could only be one thing. I forgot to turn in my chip before I graduated. I remembered my first day of class, Joe handed out to every student a one-and-a-half-inch silver metal rounded coin with a number indented in the middle. I was given the number C33. Joe told the class not to lose this coin if you wanted to graduate. You have to turn it in. No excuses. Joe forewarned us that he would hunt you down and revoke your diploma. But, before I could explain to Joe on the phone my reason for not returning it, he assured me that he wasn't calling about my chip, but to inform me that he and his wife, Rosa, were in town on company business. He wanted to invite me and my mom out for dinner. We went to a restaurant in Dearborn on Michigan Avenue. I brought the chip to give to Joe. He burst out laughing and told me, "Emeline, keep the chip. It will always remind you of me and the story behind it." We enjoyed the evening talking about my job at Ford and how proud Joe was of me.

Emeline, Mama, Rosa and Joe Farrer (Art Center)

YOU'RE HIRED, EMELINE KING

On Thursday, October 20, 1983, at 2:00 p.m. I was sitting in the back room watching television, when the phone rang. A male voice said, "Hello, this is Mr. Powell from the Salaried Personnel department at Ford Design Center in Dearborn, Michigan. May I please speak to Emeline King?"

I answered, "This is she. How may I help you?"

He replied, "Ford Motor Company would like to hire you for a salaried position as a transportation designer. We are offering you a base salary of $1,950.00 per month, plus cost of living which is currently $1,284.40 giving you an annual income of $28,000. Do you accept this offer?"

I immediately said, "Yes."

Design Center
Ford Motor Company

21175 Oakwood Boulevard
P.O. Box 2110
Dearborn, Michigan 48123

October 21, 1983

Ms. Emeline King
10023 Quincy
Detroit, Michigan 48204

Dear Emeline:

This is to confirm our telephone conversation of October 20, 1983, regarding a salaried position here at Ford Motor Company's Design Center. Your base salary will be $1,950.00 per month, plus the quarterly cost-of-living which is currently $1,284.40. These two figures combined will result in an annual income of better than $28,000.

In addition, this offer includes the following benefits: Savings and Stock Investment Plan, Retirement Plan, Company-paid Life, Disability and Medical Insurance; liberal paid sick leave and vacation allowance, "A" and "B" Plan car discounts with eligibility as defined in the various benefit plans.

This offer is contingent upon normal reference inquiries and satisfactory completion of a medical examination administered to all employes at time of hire.

We are pleased that you have accepted our offer as I believe the Design Center is a challenging and exciting place to work.

We will look forward to seeing you at 8:30 a.m. on Monday, October 24. Please call me on 322-3637 if you have any questions.

Sincerely,

T. A. Powell
Salaried Personnel

He told me to please report to work on Monday, October 24, 1983, at 8:00 a.m. I should first stop by the personnel office to get my badge and photo taken. "You are assigned to the International Studio where Mr. Walt Golwitzer is your manager. Also, you should be getting a letter of acceptance in the mail."

After I got off the phone, I ran to the kitchen where Mama was washing some greens in the sink. I told her, "Mama that was Mr. Powell on the phone. Ford hired me, I got a job, Mama." She grabbed me by the hands, and we started jumping up and down, praising and thanking God. The joy on my Mama's face I will always remember.

On Friday October 21, 1983, I received my letter confirming the telephone conversation with Mr. Powell. It outlined the breakdown of my annual income: base salary of $1,950.00 per month, plus the quarterly cost-of-living of $1,284.40. The two figures combined resulted in my annual income of $28,000. There was also a list of benefits Ford offered: Savings and Stock Investment Plan, Retirement Plan, Company-Paid Life, Disability and Medical Insurance, liberal paid sick leave and vacation allowance, and "A" and "B" Plan car discounts.

FIRST DAY AT WORK: THE INTERNATIONAL STUDIO
I MADE IT BEHIND THE BLUE DOOR!

My alarm went off at 6:00 a.m. Today would be a special day, a long time coming for me. I wore a black two-piece suit with a white shirt. I met Mom and Dad downstairs in the kitchen. We had prayer at the dinner table. Dad thanked God for blessing me with a job at Ford. Mama made us a light breakfast. After we finished eating, Mama kissed Daddy and me.

It was time for us to head to work. My dream was finally fulfilled. This ride into work today with Dad was special. We both were now Ford employees. We entered the Design Center and headed toward that long familiar corridor. What a coincidence! It's exactly how I envisioned my first day at work with my father. I was assigned to work in the International Studio. It was located behind that curious "blue door," which first caught my attention during my initial visit to the Design Center with my father. Walt Golwitzer was my manager. I don't know who was more excited for me working at Ford: my father or some of his black coworkers. My manager took me around the studio and introduced me to all the employees in International. I met designers, engineers, and clay modelers. I was the only female in the studio. The photographer from Ford's newsletter, *The Highlighter*, came and took a photograph of me seated at my cubicle. Sam came around still sporting that big friendly smile and greeted me by saying, "Welcome aboard, Weez." Thank God I had mentors like Sam and other black designers, modelers, and engineers, who were there to guide, encourage, and help me along the way at Ford.

ONE GOLDEN OPPORTUNITY
MEET THE MAN I DESIGNED CARS FOR: WILLIAM CLAY FORD, JR.

It was at one of our studio staff meetings when my manager announced that William Clay Ford Jr., CEO of Ford Motor Company, would visit the Design Center at 11:00 a.m. that day for a quick walk through of the International Design Studio. He asked that we have the studio cleaned and all studio models set out for display. After hearing this announcement, I hoped there would be a chance for me to see or at least meet the top man for whom I had been employed to design cars. Growing up in the Motor City, I was fortunate to have lived a few miles from where Henry Ford, the grandfather to William Clay Ford Jr., who built his first Ford Model T at the Piquette Avenue plant back on October 1, 1908 and established the second American production facility at 91 Manchester Avenue in Highland Park.

It was around eleven o'clock when the blue door at the far opposite end of the studio opened and in walked an entourage of Caucasian male executives: the president of the Design Center, Mr. William Clay Ford Jr., our studio design executive, a representative from Ford Public Relations department and a small group from marketing. It wasn't too long before the subtle sound of talking and laughter from the group filled the studio. They made a quick stop through the studio, viewed a few of the full-size fiberglass program models and a couple of in-progress clay models. They then proceeded down toward my area. That day, I wore a blue pinstriped two-piece business suit. I stood at my desk sketching new concept designs for the Sierra G two-seater sports car program. I heard the sound of footsteps getting closer to my desk. I assumed they would have to pass by my cubicle, which was next to the blue exit door, in order to get out of the studio. This was a once in a lifetime opportunity for me to see my employer, William Clay Ford Jr. I took three steps out of my cubicle and there he was, Mr. Ford! With an elevator speech ready, I introduced myself. "Hello Mr. Ford, my name is Emeline King. I'm a car designer and I love designing cars for Ford Motor Company." I extended my hand to him and politely said, "What a pleasure to meet you, Mr. Ford." The studio got quiet. You could hear a pin drop or better still something my mother would say, "You could hear a rat piss on cotton." Mr. Ford smiled at me, shook my hand and kindly said, "Nice to meet you too, Emeline. Keep up the good work designing Ford products!" Next to fulfilling my childhood dream to work at the Design Center designing cars for Ford with my father, meeting Mr. Ford was tops, inspiring, sentimental and historic for me. I'm glad I got a chance today in those few seconds to meet the highest ranked echelon person at Ford, the company where I design cars.

UNIQUE BLACK DESIGNERS MEET DR. CHARLES H. WRIGHT

I recall one afternoon when some of my black coworkers—Sam, Calvin Morrison, Charles Purnell, Jasper Garrison—and I went to have lunch at a restaurant located on the Grand Boulevard in Detroit. Parked up the street, we noticed a white trailer with a sign that read *Dr. Charles H. Wright Museum*. Curious, we took time to stop in. Inside the trailer, we met the owner, Dr. Charles H. Wright, who was an African American physician who in his spare time traveled all over the world collecting African American artifacts for his museum. He gave us a tour. We were amazed to see some of these cultural, historical exhibits. We each introduced ourselves and told him we worked for Ford Motor Company designing and making cars. We let him know that we were a unique group. Some were Transportation Designers, Modelers, Trim, Wood, Fabrication Specialists, and Engineers. Sam let Dr. Wright know that I was the new kid on the block and the first black female car designer ever employed at Ford. We shared with him our accomplishments and how few people really know that there is special group of talented men and a lady at Ford who are making an impact and contributions in the auto industry. Dr. Charles was astonished with what we shared with him; he thought we were unique, rare, and interesting. He asked if we didn't mind contributing some of our "personal artwork" to be displayed in his museum. We agreed and were proud to be a part of Dr. Wright's historical collection. It was an honor to have met such a brilliant man like Dr. Charles H. Wright. Today, what was once a little trailer of collectible African American artifacts has now become a multimillion-dollar enterprise: the Charles H. Wright Museum of African American History, located at 315 East Warren Avenue in Detroit.

EBONY MAGAZINE: MY MENTOR SAM MAYERS

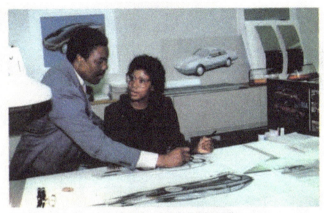

Emeline King, a first-year designer at Ford, gets some surefire tips from 17-year veteran Sam Mayers. Mayers has a management role as design specialist. Ms. King is the newest of the designers.

Next to meeting Dr. Wright, another highlight for me was when Ebony magazine asked to do an article on the few blacks in the auto industry who were playing a major role in designing the cars. What great exposure it was for us. Ford had the largest representation of black designers, engineers, clay modelers, fabrication workers, etcetera in the auto industry.

We were featured in *Ebony* magazine in the January 1984, Volume 39, No. 3, article entitled, "Black Auto Designers, Talented Few Help Shape the Future Ford" on page 84. After 28 years, only nine Blacks worked as artists in demanding creative fields. Featured in that issue of Ebony at that time were nine transportation designers. Four of the designers were from Ford: McKinley Thompson; the first male African American car designer, and myself, the first female African American car designer. What a coincidence that the article, issued in January 1984, has the same two last numbers as the article that features me on page 84 with my mentor Sam Mayers and his cousin, Nehemiah Amaker, who worked as a designer for Ford, too. Chrysler's designers were Ed Wilburn, Marietta Kearney, and Fred Edwards. General Motors was represented by Arthur Pryde and Ken Hill. I was honored to be a part of *Ebony*'s article because of its exposure to the world and especially to little girls and boys who might have never been privy to know about this field or how a unique group of talented African Americans had a major role in designing cars for the auto industry. We can be role models to all young people, knowing that every time they see a car on the road and ride in it, they can say "If they made it, so can we!"

LEARNING TO DRIVE MY FIRST MANUAL SHIFT
FRANK WOODS: STOP STRIPPING MY GEARS!

I met Frank Woods my first day at work in the International Studio. Frank was the only African American male who worked in the wood shop at Design Center. It was a coincidence his last name was Woods. I nicknamed Frank "Belly." For obvious reasons: he loved drinking beer. Frank was like a big brother to me. Frank designed a beautiful, monogramed business card holder for me that he personally created out of mahogany wood. Inscribed with gold letters was my Ford work service date 10/24/1983 on it. He gave it to me on my first day of work. Frank was a professional skeet shooter and an expert hunter. He drove a red Mercury Capri. It was fully loaded. A five-speed manual with a V8 engine, Frank had it decorated with a special rear aero spoiler and lower front fascia kit. I loved Frank's car so much that I went and purchased one as my first car, a red Mercury Capri. I couldn't afford all the bells and whistles that Frank's Car had, so I settled for the base model. I didn't know how to drive a stick so my Dad drove it home and it was parked in the driveway until I learned how to drive it. I went to Frank and asked him to teach me on his car. I purchased my first car, a red 1979 Mercury Capri, two-door hatchback, 4-speed manual shift V6, and I couldn't even drive it home that day.

It was on a Saturday morning when Frank picked me up from my house. I could hear his eight-cylinder engine roar several blocks away. We headed to Belle Isle. Frank found an open parking lot for me to practice. He showed me how to use the clutch and switch gears. He told me, "You have to listen to the sound of the engine. It will help you know when to change gears. Whatever you do, take it easy, come off the clutch slowly. Please, please don't strip my gears. Eventually, you'll start to feel the rhythm, that's when you know you've learned how to drive a shift. You won't be bucking and jerking."

After his demonstration and drilling, it was time for me to get behind the wheel. I was excited. I placed one foot on the pedal and the other one on the clutch, and my right hand on the gear shift. I was left-handed, so it felt a little awkward. Frank told me to ease up off the clutch, and when you're ready, shift the gear and go for it. When I tried putting everything together, the car started bucking up and down, the engine let out a loud grinding sound, and I was starting to see black smoke coming from the hood of the car and all four tires. That's when Frank told me "Stop! Put it in park."

"What happened?" I asked.

He said, "You were about to strip all my gears. Emeline, I'm taking you back home. You can practice and strip your own car's gears." I was disappointed my lessons with Frank ended so soon. I later found out he had no intention of teaching me how to drive after almost destroying his car.

CHAUFFEURING DADDY TO CHURCH

Another week passed before I finally got enough nerve to drive my car around the block several times. I still couldn't get that smooth pattern that Frank was talking about because I kept bucking and grinding. Later that evening, my Dad had to go preach for a revival. The church was located on Grand River and Evergreen. It was ten miles from my house. Dad asked if I wanted to chauffeur him to church. I immediately told him, "Yes." That's when my mischievous 'lil sister, Kizzy (Eugenia), and Bobbie (Errol David), who were playing outside overheard Daddy and asked if they could come. They hopped into the backseat, being typical ten-year-olds. Every now and then, I noticed in my rearview mirror that they were mimicking me with their hands and moving their bodies back and forth every time I switched gears. We bucked the whole ten miles to the church. People passed me in their cars giving the thumbs down signal. I'm sweating bullets and frustrated. Dad was on the passenger side, sweating and looking nervous. He took out his handkerchief, wipes his face and looked up toward the sky and jokingly cried out "Oh Lawd, please get me and my chillins to church in one piece, so I can preach your word."

That's when Kizzy and Bobbie yelled out, "AAAAA....Men." I did manage to get us there safely. The ride home was good because I finally got the feel of the shift, managed to drive and change gears without bucking.

DADDY TO MY RESCUE
SOMETHING'S FALLING AND IT'S NOT RAIN

I'd often walk over to Dad's department if I needed some work to be done or when following up on a model. On a personal note, I'd go if I needed some encouragement from my Dad, especially when I was being mistreated on my job. If I had forgotten my lunch, I knew Dad would have some great snacks stashed away in his desk cart for me to eat. Dad was always there at my rescue. I recall when I was assigned to work in the mid-size luxury studio working on the 1989 Thunderbird Super Coupe. I had to make a presentation, and I decided to leave my cubicle and walk across the studio. I wanted to double check and make sure everything was in order for my presentation before management. The sketches were lined up properly on the display boards. The full-size clay model was all dinoced, giving the appearance of a real car. I always dressed professionally. Sometimes, I loved to coordinate the same color scheme as my project. I wore a cream-colored two-piece suit and beige heels. As I walked across the studio, I could hear a faint whisper coming from behind me. It was my manager, Ted Finney, my former Transportation Design teacher at Wayne State.

He came up to me and whispered in my ear "Something's falling, Emeline." I looked down at my feet and the slip under my dress had fallen down to my ankles. Embarrassed, I grabbed my slip and immediately ran back to my cubicle. All I could think about was calling Dad to see if he had a piece of string to tie it up and could he bring it over right now. I had a presentation before management in the next 15 minutes. While I was waiting in my cubicle, Dad comes in wearing his white uniform. I nearly busted out laughing. It took all I had not to laugh because what Dad was holding in his hand was a ten-foot, heavy duty rope. When I told him what had happened and that I needed a piece of string, we started laughing. I just ended up stepping out of the slip and placing it in my purse.

PROUD FATHER STUDIO VISITS

I looked forward to every time my Dad stopped by my studio cubicle to visit. I could hear him from afar walking thru the studio in a slow but hurried pace: *swish, swish, swish*. Dressed in his work clothes, a pair of white plastic coveralls, he looked like the "Man from Glad" from the Glad Wrap commercial. I listened as my coworkers in the studio say to Dad as he passed by: "Hey, Ernie, how you doing?" You could see the expression of a proud father coming to see his daughter.

Prior to being hired in at the Ford Design Center in Dearborn, Michigan as an Exploratory Fabrication Plaster Specialist, my father worked at the Ford Rouge Foundry for three years. Faced with the working conditions in the foundry, the low pay wages, and being an hourly instead of salaried employee, my Dad made a wise choice to quit and look for better opportunities. He met a man who made deliveries to the Foundry who informed him that the Design Center, another division of Ford, had an opening in the fabrication shops and that the job was a salaried position. The Design Center was the crème de la crème in the automotive industry. Dad knew that working at the Design Center as a salaried worker would place him in a better and higher pay bracket than staying at the Foundry as an hourly worker.

He had the skills and qualifications from his previous experience working in the Foundry with plastic and plaster casting. Moreover, he had several examples of pieces of artwork he made at the studio with famous sculptor, Oscar Graves. Dad knew his portfolio of work would demonstrate his skills and be a tremendous asset to the Ford Motor Company. A salaried position was a top priority that he wanted. My Dad called Human Resources for an interview and brought his portfolio of samples of his work from the foundry and Mr. Oscars Graves's studio. After viewing his work, Mr. Lee from the personnel department asked my Dad if he would accept his offer for an hourly position in the plaster shop at Ford. In a confident tone, my Dad told him he wasn't there for the hourly position but would accept work in the fabrication department in the salaried position. He was hired as a salary employee working as an exploratory fabrication specialist in the plaster department.

Dad took his job serious and was a faithful worker. Dad often would joke and say, "I had to turn the lights out at Ford. Quite often management needed a job done for a review the next day. It might require making a cast off of the clay models or finishing up a part. Sometimes it would be right before Dad was to get off work when his supervisor would ask if he could stay and get it done. Dad never complained or turned it down. That overtime pay came in handy for two special reasons: my parents were able to put all the King children through college. Secondly, a phenomenal accomplishment, after we all graduated from college, Daddy promised mommy he'd buy her a house after the kids finished college. But, that changed with Daddy's carpentry experience. He decided to build her a house from the ground up. It was a two-and-a-half-acre ranch style home in the prominent area of West Bloomfield Hills, Michigan.

Daddy commissioned me to design the entire house structure, and my cousin's dad's nephew, Robert Randall Jr., was the architect. Dad hired his friend Willie Talley to be the constructor. The house was enormous. The house sat on two acres. There were three bathrooms, full kitchen, living room, dining room, a foyer, three guest bedrooms, and my parents had a master bedroom with full bath Jacuzzi, heated floors, a walk-in closet and a balcony. The family room was adjacent to a full walk out patio deck, the basement was the entire length of the house with a walk-in lower pathway, a kitchen, family room, and a full-length basement area for dining. There was a two-car garage, a full circular driveway, and a beautifully decorated landscape. We would tell Dad: "Don't be surprised if commercial planes mistake your circular driveway as a landing strip."

It was so well lit up at night. I asked Dad how much his house was worth. He told me one million dollars. He said when he had finished building his house, the only money they had to pay was five hundred dollars.

Dad was filled with wisdom and knowledge and was never afraid to speak up to anybody. He let his supervisor know that he worked for Ford and was a loyal employee, but being a minister and pastor was his calling and service to God came first. So, if he needed to attend a funeral or a wedding, he would. His coworkers respected Dad so much that they asked Dad to perform some of their weddings and eulogize some of their loved ones. My father set a milestone in that department up to the day he retired from Ford, which was in 2003. With 32 years of service, he had been the first and only African American male ever to be hired to work in that department.

Dad's favorite pastime at work was talking on the phone. He could call out-of-state friends and relatives. The studio had only one phone that was shared by all his coworkers, so there was a time limit. Dad used that phone so much that when he retired, Ford's Fabrication Department presented him with the studio's rotary phone. They painted it gold.

THE DESIGNER PERKS: COMPANY VEHICLE'S OVERNIGHT EVALUATION

One of the perks of being a Transportation Designer at Ford included overnight evaluation of Ford's competitive company cars. I've driven several cars, but three of my favorite vehicles were the 2002 Audi TT two-seater convertible, the Chrysler Sebring Convertible, and a Ferrari Testerossa 408. I was still living on Quincy Street in the hood and having expensive cars in my neighborhood was an open invitation for certain folks who had no respect for other people property. For safety reasons, at night I'd have my parents sandwich their cars one in front and behind of the Ford vehicles I brought home to test drive. I enjoyed seeing the looks on the faces of the boys and girls in my neighborhood every time I brought home a competitive car to evaluate. I'd park in front of my house on 10023 Quincy Street, and before I could get out of the car, I would be surrounded by little bright eyes, curious stares, and inquisitive minds from the neighborhood.

Each one would anxiously ask me, "WOW! Miss King, what kind of car is that? Is that your car? Ohhh . . . man, that's a cool car! I bet it cost a whole lot of money. Can it go real fast?"

I felt proud I was able to explain to the youth the type of car I was driving and that Ford had assigned me to do an overnight drive to evaluate the interior components. I informed them I was a transportation designer and I designed cars for Ford. One little boy, who had two of his front teeth missing, was occupied with his toy truck. He suddenly stopped, looked up, pointed his finger toward me, and said, "You draw cars? You a girl. "

I told him, "Yes, I was a little girl when I started liking and drawing cars. Now I design cars for Ford." I shared my story how my Dad got me first interested in cars when I was around their ages. I stressed to them the importance of getting good grades, staying in school, respecting their teachers, mastering their craft, and choosing something that they really love to do. "If you love cars, like I do, you can have a career in the auto industry, too."

You never know when someone might be driving around in a car you designed. Some of these kids were probably never privy to such information, let alone get this close to a vehicle and meet a car designer. I hope I sparked an interest in them to one day follow this same path or do something else they loved.

WHO WOULD BELIEVE IT, EMELINE DRIVING A FERRARI?

On another occasion, a coworker and I had a special opportunity together. The coworker was Dennis Moses, a black male transportation designer who was hired after me and was one of Sam's protégé students. Prior to coming to Ford, Dennis used to work for Mattel Toys designing miniature size cars. Dennis also was a professional photographer. One morning during our staff meeting, Dennis and I were assigned to test drive one of the company cars, a 1986 Ferrari Testarossa 408. We rode around in the city. Dennis stopped by his house and got his camera. I suggested to Moses that we should take photos of ourselves inside the vehicle. I knew this was a once in a lifetime moment. Two African American transportation designers: a male and female, sitting behind the wheel of a red Ferrari. A rare opportunity indeed.

CAREER DAY PRESENTER

Emeline with Ms. Zaats, Keidan Kindergarten Teacher

I was always getting letters and requests from the various elementary, middle, and high schools to come and talk to the students about my job as a car designer for Ford on their career day. The students would be delighted when I would give a demonstration on how to draw a car. I told them how important it was to stay focused, study, and never give up on achieving their dream. May 17, 1993, was a special event for me when I was the career day speaker during Career Week at my former elementary school: Henry B. Keidan. I was surprised to see hanging on the walls throughout the school 18 x 24 magazine articles of my accomplishments at Ford. My mother was there, and she was so proud. Mom worked as a paraprofessional at the school.

SAM MAYERS AND HIS PROTÉGÉ'S HOST
SATURDAY MORNING HIGH TRANSPORTATION CLASS

My mentor, Sam Mayers, along with me and another talented black designer, Dennis Moses hosted a Saturday morning class teaching young people about transportation design. It was held at The International Institute on John R and Kirby in the Detroit Cultural Center. The course was sponsored by Ford. I felt honored to be an instructor introducing transportation design to future up and coming designers.

TAKE YOUR DAUGHTER (BRING YOUR CHILD) TO WORK DAY

Mt. Calvary Youth, Emeline and Brianna Torrence (niece)   Errol Lonell King (nephew) and Emeline

The Ford PR Marketing department presented a special project to the Design Center. I was a part of the committee of women who worked at Design Center and first introduced the concept: "Take Your Daughter to Work Day." This affair was to take place on the third week in April 1992. Design Center employees would have a chance to bring their daughters to work and experience a day filled with experiencing their parents' careers within the auto industry. Some of the male employees in the Design Center heard about this event and were offended that it was only being offered to girls. They felt that boys should be included. So, in order to meet their request, the committee changed the name from "Take Your Daughter to Work Day" to "Bring Your Child to Work Day." It was such a success that it became an annual affair. Every department displayed their specialty with hands-on participation for an excited group of young people to see how cars were made and to experience their parents' daily activities.

"Bring Your Child to Work Day" grew from a local scale to a national one, and it still exists today. Also, my little sister Eugenia ("Kizzy") hadn't too long been hired in at Ford working as a mechanical engineer. She and I took our nieces, nephews, the neighborhood kids, plus a group of young girls and boys from our church, Mt. Calvary to this exciting and historical affair. They each had an opportunity to visit my studio, the Design Center, my father's fabrication/plaster department and my sister Eugenia's engineering department. The girls dabbled in clay and watched me do a car sketch demo. The group saw a fiberglass casting of a car door being made and learned about engineering mechanics of a car. The boys posed with me in a convertible Mustang and other Ford products. This milestone event was twofold for the King family. My father and his two daughters were two generations of Ford employees who worked and made design contributions in the auto industry. Secondly, the "Bring Your Child to Work Day" brought back fond memories of when my father first took me to the Ford Design Center.

PUBLIC RELATIONS SPEAKING ENGAGEMENTS REPRESENTING WOMEN IN DESIGN

I was always being asked to represent the company by giving speeches on women in design. On one occasion a group of women from each discipline at Ford—Design, Marketing and Engineering—was invited to New York to be on a panel to present women's roles and their impact in the auto industry. We stayed at the New York Royal Plaza Hotel. It was a beautiful hotel. This was the closest to high luxury that I ever experienced. I had to ask God for forgiveness because I "borrowed" from the bathroom the plaza's monogrammed white, plush cotton towel.

I was called upon numerous times to give speeches on design representing Ford before major organizations like the Industrial Designers Society of America (IDSA) and the University of Michigan.

CHAPTER SIX
SHE DESIGNED IT

MY FIRST FOREIGN ASSIGNMENT: TURIN, ITALY
BLACK FEMALE FORD DESIGNER LEAVES FOR EUROPE

I worked in the International Studio for approximately eleven months prior to my first foreign assignment. The majority of my time was spent developing concept sketches, renderings, and packaged full-size tape drawings of vehicles that were produced for the

United States and Europe. Today's studio staff meeting played a historic part in my life. Our staff meetings were held on Monday mornings and included all the designers, a master modeler, the senior engineer, a marketing representative and the studio manager.

My supervisor, Walt Gotwitzer, updated the studio on the status of each car program to which the studio was assigned. He reviewed the current projects and discussed each designer's next assignment. One of my coworkers, a designer named Darryl, was a graduate of the Center for Creative Studies and the son of a design manager who worked at Ford. Darryl was the "golden boy" who climbed the corporate ladder at Ford faster than one could blink. He had just returned from his Foreign Service Assignment in Koln Germany and at the Ghia Studio in Turin, Italy. Walt informed everybody that, Joe Siler, another designer, would be leaving in June for Italy and that I was scheduled to go in October. It took every inch of me to sit still and hold my composure after hearing that I would be assigned to the Ghia Studio for four months. I could hardly wait to tell my family when I got home. The furthest I had traveled was Little Rock, Arkansas for my family reunion.

The notion of me going to another country was something I never imagined. My mind reflected on previous conversations with my mentors Oscar Graves and Sam Mayers. Their experiences and European culture truly influenced their craft. Sam's first Foreign Service assignment was in Sydney, Australia. I had read about Europe in school, but actually going there to live was far out of my radar. Joe and I decided that we might need to brush up on our Italian. So after work, I stopped by the Barnes & Noble bookstore at Northland Mall to purchase audio tapes and books on learning how to speak Italian. I knew it would be beneficial if I learned the basics of Italian, like how to order my meals, ask for directions, and hold a casual conversation. This was a milestone for me because it would be the first time anybody in my family got an opportunity to travel out of the country. A black girl from the west side of Detroit on her way to live on the northern side of Italy! Thank you, Jesus! When I got off work, I drove as fast as I could in my red Capri. When I arrived home, my parents were seated in the living room watching the news. I ran up to them and shouted, "Mama! Daddy! You're not going to believe this! Ford is sending me to Turin, Italy to design cars! I'll be leaving in three months." I swear…my parents were so elated that they told every relative, friend and every person they came in contact with that their daughter, Emeline, was going to Italy to design cars for Ford.

BON VOYAGE
BLACK FEMALE DESIGNER HEADS TO EUROPE

My family planned a surprise Bon Voyage party for me. It was held at Morning View Baptist Church in their lower fellowship hall. All of my relatives and friends were there. Mama hired a reporter from the Michigan Chronicle[1] who took photographs of this historic and festive occasion. Everybody wished me well and gave me encouraging words.

Ford's personnel department handled my traveling, lodging and passport arrangements. I had to take a physical exam and get my shots which I passed with flying colors. I was scheduled to leave on September 23, 1984. My parents and my boyfriend, Herbert, went with me to Delta's International airport terminal. When it was time for me to board the plane my parents walked with me as far as they could go before I entered the cabin. I turned and told them I love you. The stewardess directed me to first class section. I watch the looks on the people faces who were in first class. I was the only black person in that section. The flight would take 10 hours. I fastened my seatbelt and looked out my window as the plane taxied onto the runway. While the engines was preparing for takeoff, I bowed my head and whispered a prayer that God would be with me and everyone on the plane and get us to our destination safe. I didn't know that this experience was the beginning of numerous first class trips, perks and foreign assignments for Ford. I enjoyed the ride and admired God's masterworks. After the plane landed, I gathered my small luggage that was in the overhead bin and exited the plane. I noticed two people standing in front stood waiting at the gate for me. One was a tall, blonde-haired male and a petite, Italian lady.

He spoke to me in Italian. "Benvenuto in Italia" and I replied "Grazia." He told me his name was Michael and introduced me to Petra, the secretary from the Ghia Studio. Michael was an American Italian car designer, fluent in Italian who worked for Ford at the Ghia Studio. We made our way to luggage claim to get the rest of my things. Michael decided to take the scenic route of Italy. Showing me some of the famous buildings and sculptures of the city. When we arrived to the housing complex Michael helped me get my luggage. Later that evening, Michael and the secretary took me to a beautiful Italian restaurant. The decor was fine, white linen on the tables and china. I was hungry and looked forward to my having my first Italian dinner. The waiter handed me the menu and I ordered what was most familiar to me on the menu; pollo (chicken), pasta and pomme frites (french fries). Michael suggested a nice bottle of wine. After dinner we left the restaurant and headed back to my complex. I'd be staying here for the duration of my foreign assignment. Michael told me to get a good night's rest and he'd pick me up in the morning around eight o'clock and take me to the Ghia Studio. Turin, Italy was five hours ahead of the time zone at home in Detroit. I called my parents that night to let them know I made it safe. They were so happy. We talked for hours. I thanked God and prayed that he continue to watch over me, my family, and that my stay here in Italy be a blessing.

FIRST DAY: GHIA SPA STUDIO

The Ghia Spa Studio was similar to Ford's Design Center Studio in Dearborn, Michigan with one exception. Instead of having individual, enclosed cubicles for the designers to work in, the Ghia designers sat openly in the studio at individual office desks. Mounted on the walls were full size tape drawings, sketches and renderings of concept cars. During my stay at Ghia, I was assigned to work on sketch proposals - full-sized tape renderings for a small, mid-size European car, and to make a final presentation to management at the end of my stint. I would also visit some of the International Auto Shows.

Michael took me around the studio and introduced me to all the designers. The majority of them spoke Italian and very little English. As we made our way around the studio, there was one special designer who stood out amongst all the male designers. Michael told me, "Emeline, this is Marilena, you two have something in common. You're both "female designers." You don't know how elated I was to meet another transportation designer who happened to be a female from another part of the world.

MARILENA CORVASCE, FORD OF EUROPE'S FEMALE DESIGNER

Marilena Corvasce was the first female Italian transportation designer working at Ford of Europe, Ghia. She was hired in at Ghia in 1968 before leaving Italdesign. Although I had never heard about Marilena, it still was an honor to meet another female who had successfully climbed the corporate ladder and broke the glass ceiling that had been dominated by males and was making an impact in the auto industry. We shared a common bond.

Marilena smiled and spoke in a soft, low voice, "Bongiorno Emeline." I replied "Bongiorno Marilena. Nice to meet you." Later that week, I got a phone call. When I answered the phone, a soft, female voice started to sing a familiar Stevie Wonder Motown song to me, "I just called to say I love you." What a pleasant surprise; it was Marilena. She called to invite me over to her place for dinner. She lived with her sister in a small apartment. We discussed our backgrounds, how we became interested in cars and how that passion lead to a career in the auto industry. We enjoyed a wonderful time we had that day and established a friendship. Despite our language limitations, we were able to communicate with me speaking some Italian and Marilena speaking some English.

Several years later, I came across an article in the Hemmings Motor News written by Daniel Strohl on June 25, 2018 about Marilena Corvasce. She made history as the first woman designer given the task to design both the interior and exterior of a car for Ford of Europe, the 1982 Ghia Brezza.

MOLTE LIRE (LOTS OF LIRE)

Ghia Coworkers: Marinlena Corvasce (center) and Emeline

The following day after work Michael drove me to the bank of Italia where I could exchange my traveler's checks. Ford provided my lodging, a daily per diem for food and for transportation, a two-door white manual Fiat. When we got to the bank the teller asked me, "Ciao, how much American dollars would you like to exchange? I told him, I wanted to exchange two hundred American dollars and handed him some of my traveler checks. He took the checks and walked to the back room to make the transaction. I noticed he was gone for a long time. When he finally returned, he counted out a stack of Italian lire which appeared to be five times the amount of traveler checks that I had given him. He looked at me, smiled and said, "Signorina King, it's a good day for you today. Currency is up for the American dollar, and down for the lire."

DRIVING AROUND EUROPE

We left the bank and went to Ford's Human Resources Department so I could get transportation. I ordered a white Fiat two-door coupe. I tried to get familiar with the driving route from where I lived to Ghia. It took a couple of weeks before I got the hang to get around in Italy. Back home in the States, the street signs were located on poles on the corner of each street. In Italy, they're placed high up on the sides of the buildings. The streets were made out of mixed cobbled stones. Some of the streets were so narrow that only one small vehicle at a time could pass through them. One time, I was leaving work driving on my way home. I was approaching a red light when an Italian lady jumped out of her car from behind me. She ran up to my car door and tapped on my window using both of her hands to express how upset see was. She said to me, "Guarda!!! GUARDA!!!!! vedi come guidi? Molto cattivo. "Look!!!! Look!!!! See how you drive? Very bad." I never had that happen to me before, so I told her, "Mi displace" which means "I'm sorry" and drove off.

IN ITALY DO AS THE ITALIANS DO: VINO

I never drank much wine back in the States before coming to Italy. As a matter of fact, hardly any. Every Italian restaurant I visited, they served wine, or "vino" as it's called, with all the meals. On one occasion, my mother was visiting me and I wanted to treat her to one of the Italian restaurants where I ate frequently. The decor inside was rich and elegant with white linen and fine china laid out on the tables. Italian sculptures and figurines surrounded the entrance. Renaissance paintings were displayed on the walls. The men and women were dressed in fine Italian apparel. Just hearing the sound of the Italian conversation filled the room and created a warm, friendly atmosphere. The hostess seated us and shortly after, a waiter came over to our table and took our order. I spoke in Italian to him, "mayi hanno due bicchieri di Chardonnay, una bottiglia da portare a casa la carne di vitello con pasta e un gelato al cioccolato, favore". This translated in English to "May I have two glasses of Chardonnay, a bottle to take home, the veal with pasta and for dessert chocolate ice cream, please?"

Mom blushed as she listened to me order our meals in Italian. In a high-pitched voice Mama, somewhat puzzled, asked "Emeline, baby, when did you start drinking wine?" I laughed and told her, "Mama, you've heard that old saying, when in Rome do as the

Romans do? Well, I'm here in Turin, Italy and it's full of art, fashion, and I migliori vini (good wine)!"

I took a strong liking to Italian cuisine: antipasto, veal, prosciutto lasagne, tagliatelle alla bolognese, and "Oh my!" those desserts tiramisu and gelato. Although pizza originated in Italy, it's made different from the fast-food pizzas I would order in the States. Italian pizza is made with a thin crust with marinara sauce and hardly any extra toppings - totally opposite from the thick crusted pizza I'd order from franchises like Little Caesar's, Domino's or Jays, the neighborhood pizza place and gas stations. The sky is the limit to what you can order on your pizza. They had every imaginable topping plus the kitchen sink…pepperoni, chicken, fish, pineapples, olives, Italian sausage, beef, barbecue, and a variety of cheeses.

Each morning before going to work, I would walk across the street to a small cafe on the corner and order an Italian breakfast: a flaky pastry croissant called a brioche and a cup of cappuccino. I loved to sit and listen to the Italians speak their language and would occasionally try to converse using a few words like "buongiorno e come stai oggi" for "Good morning" and "How are you today?" or "Ciao" for "hello" or goodbye".

THE PEEPING MERCHANT

Some evenings after I got off work, I'd come home, park my car in front of my complex and walk down to the piazza. Every city had a gathering place where people went to enjoy the scenic view of the city, shop, eat and have fun. You'd see all types of people, both local and tourists. They did a lot of walking in Italy. The piazza had several shops and even outdoor flea markets. Italian soft leather was popular. I remember going to a flea market and saw this beautiful brownish, full-grain Italian leather jacket that caught my attention. The material was as smooth as butter. I asked the short, stocky male merchant who was seated on a stool, "How much for the jacket? May I try it on?" He told me "Si, per favore, vieni" and directed me to go behind the curtain in his tent. As I began to pull off my jacket to try on the new one, I sensed someone was watching me from above. I knew my instinct was right when I looked up and staring down from the top of the curtain was the merchant grinning ear to ear, smiling like he had just gotten a free peep show. It startled me. I begin to make so much commotion in English! I was calling him everything but a child of God. He may not have understood what I was saying in English, but he knew I was upset about what he had just done. I looked in my

Italian dictionary and spoke to him in Italian. "Quanto per guests giacca gratis? "How much for this free jacket?" He said, "Liberal ora vai" which translated "Free please go." I ended up with a beautiful, expensive Italian leather jacket that day!

TERROR ON ROAD TO MONACO

I wanted to see as much of Italy as I could. Since we didn't have to work on the weekends, I used that time to tour other countries. One good thing about Europe is the countries are so close together that it only took a couple of hours to get from one to the other. My coworker Tony asked me if I would like to drive down to Monaco with him for the weekend. I told him "Yes" and looked forward to seeing Monaco.

It was a beautiful sunny day as we drove through Italy. Little did I know that this trip would turn out to be the most terrifying ride of my life! There were a lot of hills, mountains and narrow paths that we had to drive through. It was getting late in the evening and I noticed the fog was starting to thicken. Tony turned the headlights on and proceeded.

Tony told me how he had traveled all over Europe. Based on his conversation, Tony and his family were wealthy. As we're steadily climbing up this steep and narrow mountain, I glanced out the side of my window and it appeared like we were getting too close to the edge and would run off the road. Tony was driving quite fast and assured me we would be okay. To make matters even worst, he made mention that on this particular road, two years ago in 1982, Princess Grace of Monaco died after her car crashed and went over the cliff. Grace Kelly was a beautiful famous American actress who was married to Rainier III, Prince of Monaco. By this time, the fog was so thick that you couldn't see the road ahead. I was afraid we were riding on the edge. I pleaded for Tony to slow down, pull over and stop the car until the fog cleared up, but he wouldn't. Thank God, we made it there safe! My only regret was if we had to travel back that same road, I hope the weather would be sunny and nice.

Our excursion ended on a much happier note. We visited the city, toured the Prince of Monaco's palace, saw the Monte Carlo Casino, and had lunch by the Marina observing all of the expensive and exotic cars like Lamborghinis, Ferrari's, Jaguars, Bentley's and yachts. Later that evening we dined at Tony's favorite restaurant, Lauduree Carousel, in Monte Carlo.

MY COWORKER, MICHAEL

Michael was quite helpful to me during my stay in Italy. Michael spoke fluent Italian and English. The day he invited me over to his apartment, I was surprised to see that there was no elevator. When we walked into the foyer, Michael told me to keep walking until you get to the top stairs. I looked up and from where I was standing and it had to have been eight flights of steps! Michael said sorry for the inconvenience but there's no elevator; it's one of the main reasons he bought the place. Besides, climbing the stairs kept him in physical shape. Michael introduced me to his girlfriend and her daughter. Michael had the pleasure of being the translator for the evening. We sat down and enjoyed an Italian meal together. Michael told me he'd like for me to meet his father. You never would have thought this man was in his nineties by the way he acted and looked. When I visited his home, he took me mountain climbing and to a wine orchard to pick grapes and sample vino. We were several thousand feet in the air! He was a craftsman who showed me how to carve a vase out of wood using a lathe machine, which I kept as a memento.

MY WEEKEND EXCURSIONS

I had one month left before my foreign assignment was over and I would be returning to the States. What a surprise when I found out dad would be sending Mama to Italy to visit me for her birthday. I was so excited. I picked Mom up from the train station. I was so happy to see her! I really missed my family. I planned on to taking Mama to all the places she loved reading about in Sunday School, especially Rome, Italy where the

Apostle Peter, Jesus and his disciples traveled. I made sure this was a top priority on my list.

Prior to mom coming, I tried to take in as much of Europe's tourist attractions as I could. There was a lot to see in so little time! Luckily, European countries are remarkably close together – it reminded me of traveling from Detroit to Windsor, Canada. Just a short drive over the Ambassador Bridge or through the tunnel and you are in another country. One of my weekend travels to another country included a visit to Barcelona, Spain. I was surprised to see the world's tallest church, the Basilica de la Sagrada Familia was still under construction. Although it had its groundbreaking on March 19, 1882, the church building won't be completely finished until the year 2026. I toured Florence, Italy and tossed a coin into the Trevi Fountain with a special wish to return one day. I visited some museums and saw some famous Greek sculptures like David, Venus de Milo, Pieta and the Thinker. I also took a bus tour to Pisa, Italy. I wanted to see the Leaning Tower of Pisa and climb the hundred spiraling steps. I enjoyed the scenic view but didn't enjoy the bus ride.

Unfortunately, I had to apologize to this little Italian man who sat next to me. Terrified by the way the driver was riding the bus, weaving in and out of traffic and driving close to the edge of the mountain, after hearing of dangerous tour bus accidents, I was praying that this trip wouldn't end that way. The centrifugal force was causing the passengers to rock from side to side. In a panic, I grabbed the first thing closest to me, his hand, and nearly squeezed the life out of it. I don't know which appeared to be in the most pain, his facial expression or his throbbing hand. I was amazed to see these magnificent structures that have been in existence for years and still in some of their original format. I've read about theses art works, but to stand in the midst of them was breathtaking.

One weekend, I had the pleasure to take a train ride to Paris, France. I visited the Louvre Museum and saw several exhibits including the original famous painting of Mona Lisa by Italian Renaissance artist Leonard da Vinci. There was a long line of anticipated tourists who waited to view the exhibit. When the attendant opened the door for everyone to come in, there was a mad rush but somehow I managed to work my way up to the front of the exhibit. As I stood before this masterpiece, I was tickled and astonished to see all this excitement over a century oil portrait of a lady with the slightest gesture of a smile painted on a canvas no bigger than the size of an 11x14 piece of paper.

I took advantage of traveling on the Paris Metro to get around to visit several sites like the Jardins du Chateau de Versaillles (Gardens of Versailles) and the Palais Garnier (Opera House). I took a wonderful stroll down the Champs-Elysees which ended at the Arc de Triomphe where the Unknown Soldier was buried at the base of the arc in 1921. I enjoyed the beautiful panoramic view of the city atop of the magnificent Eiffel Tower and ended my excursion at the Cathèdrale Notre-Dame de Paris which turned out to be both physical, adventurous, frightful and unforgettable.

Prior to going inside to tour Notre Dame, I waited outside with a young Parisian man named Andre who spoke English and was taking photos of the exterior of the Cathèdrale. We struck up a friendly conversation and shared our interest in the Cathèdrale architecture and all of the wonderful Paris attractions we had visited. He had just finished the tour of Notre Dame and told me to go atop the Cathèdrale to view the city. He mentioned to be careful since there are plenty of steps to climb. The pathway was narrow and hot. I asked Andre if he would mind holding my backpack, which was filled with souvenirs, until I finished the tour. He said, "Oui profiter je vais attendre" (Yes, enjoy. I will wait for you.)

When it was time to enter Notre Dame, the tour guide informed everyone that after the tour of the interior to feel free to climb the steps and tour the outer perimeter which is decorated with sculptured gargoyles and a magnificent view of the city. Once inside the Cathèdrale, I admired its interior décor, the structured flying buttresses and the decorative religious themed stained-glass windows. After the tour, I took the challenge to climb the stairs along with two other daring male tourists and the guide. The closer we got to the top, the narrower and hotter it became. Finally, we reached the top balcony. It had to have been over 100 stairs! The view of the city was fabulous. I photographed the moment and had a close-up view of the decorated stone carved sculpture gargoyles. I managed to look over the ledge and down onto the ground. The people appeared like a little cluster of ants.

All of a sudden, it dawned on me that I didn't have my backpack! I remembered that I had given it to Andre, the Parisian man. What was I thinking? I could only pray that he would still be down there and hadn't left with my backpack filled with souvenirs and the most important thing, my ticket back to Italy! I would be up the creek without that! I made a mad dash down all those stairs.

When I got outside, there was Andre seated on the steps of the Cathèdrale waiting patiently with my backpack in his arms. All I could yell out was "Thank you, Jesus!" Surprised, he turned around and smiled, then asked "Amalina, how did you enjoy the view?" Frantic and out of breath, I managed to pull myself together and told him, "Andre, you really don't want to know. It was quite an eye opener." He asked if I had time to join him for lunch. I said yes and suggested somewhere close. My train wasn't scheduled to leave until later that evening. He shared with me that I looked frightened when I came out of the Cathèdrale and asked if something was wrong. Embarrassed, I told him that I couldn't find my bag. "I had forgotten that I had given it to you. I couldn't see you from where I was and I thought you might have walked off and left." He said "No, no. Amalina, I wanted to wait for you. You climbed many steps, femme formidable (superwoman)." We both laughed. We enjoyed our afternoon talking and eating our lunch near an outdoor café along the banks of the river Seine. I had a wonderful time in Paris. We wished each other safe travels. I returned back to work on Monday and shared my excursion with my coworker, Michael.

MAMA COMES TO ROME

During our stay in Italy, Michael was very hospitable with his Italian culinary. He invited me and my mother over for dinner. Mama passed on the vino, but I sure didn't. Petra, the secretary at Ghia was helpful in assisting me with booking my travel arrangements for my weekend excursions.

Since the train station was walking distance from my complex, I thought it would be nice for me and mom to take the train and enjoy the scenic route down to Rome and on to Venice. We toured The Colosseum which was a magnificent structure. Our tour guide told us the history behind the construction of The Colosseum.

It had held several events like Roman gladiator games, chariot races, and the most barbaric of all, public executions of the Christians. Even though The Colosseum was capable of holding thousands, the Romans had developed a unique way to evacuate the building in a few seconds. I was surprised to see numerous cats running throughout the complex. We had a chance to see Roman temples and the Parthenon. Next, we visited the Vatican City and toured St. Peter's Basilica.

We stood in awe as we walked through and looked up at the famous Sistine Chapel ceiling. Witnessing all of the works of Michelangelo Frescoes which depicted every religious and Biblical scene from the beginning of time reminded me of my art history classes at Wayne State. I told my mom "This had to be true dedication of an artist in its highest form. Being commissioned to do a masterpiece which took several years to complete, with a majority of the work being painted on a semi-curved ceiling while lying on his back suspended several hundred feet in the air, was breathtaking! After the tour, it was off to Venice. Leaving the Vatican City, we had to be careful because I almost had my camera snatched by some gypsies.

I noticed mom was getting tired and with the weather in Venice being damp, it brought on a few sniffles for her. I suggested she get some rest and I would come back for her in a couple of hours so we could pick up where we left off. We checked in at the hotel's front desk while the Italian bell boy, who was petite in size, offered to carry our luggage to the room. The rooms were small but cozy. I'm assuming he overheard my conversation with my mom because he told me he was about to go on his hour lunch break and invited me to come. He said he would like to show me some nearby famous sites. I told him "yes." What was I thinking? He showed me the location of Michelangelo's home, but he almost caught me off guard when tried to lean over for a kiss. I told him, "No, No, No". He smiled and said he was sorry then I told him, "It's time to take me back to the hotel. Do you understand? Capisce!"

I returned to hotel where mom was well rested, so we continued our tour of the city. Our first stop was the Piazza San Marco formally known as St. Mark's Square. We watched a man give a glass blowing demonstration and toured the interior of Saint Mark's Basilica which was decorated with beautiful glass-stained windows depicting religious themes. We sat and ate Italian pizza, watched the Venetians and the tourists take part in the different activities in the piazza. It was a beautiful day. We took a boat ride on the gondola, a flat-bottomed Venetian rowing boat, to the other side. We enjoyed our scenic tour along the river and was serenaded by the melodious gondola singer. One of my coworkers suggested that I must visit the Rialto Bridge also known as the "Bridge of Thieves."

This is a popular tourist attraction to purchase expensive fourteen karat gold and bargain with the merchants for a much lower price. European fourteen karat gold is a softer metal than the harder eighteen karat which is more popular in the States. I saw a beautiful fourteen karat gold bracelet which I bought Dad and got dirt cheap. We visited the Royal Chapel of the Cathèdrale of Saint John the Baptist in Turin, Piedmont which is located in the northern part of Italy. It housed the famous Shroud of Turin, the burial clothes that Jesus was wrapped in after he was crucified. After viewing the display, I headed toward the back of the building to purchase some souvenirs.

1 Colosseo
2 Foro Romano
3 Piazza S. Pietro - Veduta aerea
4 Foro Traiano e Monumento a V. Emanuele II

Hello Mt Calvary
We miss you and hope to see you soon. Our tours through Europe have been exciting.

Love,
Mom + Daughter
Imogene + Emeline

Mt. Calvary Bapt. Church
5301 St. Aubin
Detroit MI 48204
U.S.A.

I'M BLACK. IT WON'T RUB OFF

This had to have been the world's smallest souvenir shop I had ever seen. When I walked in, there was only enough room to hold a small wooden desk, a chair and standing room for three people. Seated behind the desk was this little, old Italian lady who was the exact image of mother Theresa. She was dressed in identical white apparel wearing that traditional white and blue trim head piece. I told her I wanted to purchase a souvenir of the shroud. All of the souvenirs where hanging on the wall behind her. She looked up at me, smiled, and immediately she took her hand and reached toward my face rubbing it gently. My only thought was that she had never seen a person with a dark or caramel skinned complexion and thought that by rubbing, it would come off. Mama and I often got a big kick from the reactions of star struck Italian teenagers and men who saw us on the streets of Italy. They'd approach us, point their fingers and shout "Bella! Bella!" which means beautiful in Italian.

"CIAO GHIA"

For my last day at Ghia, the studio threw a party for me. My mom came and joined in the celebration. Ghia Studio designers prepared light Italian refreshments. The table was decorated with an assortment of cheese, thin slices of prosciutto, pepperoni and a bottle of vino on table.

They gave me a bottle to take back home. I still haven't opened it. I will cherish the time spent with my friends at the Ghia Studio and the opportunity to share once in a lifetime European trip with my mother. Later that evening, Michael invited me and my mother over for dinner before going back to the States. To show my gratitude I brought a fine bottle of Italian vino for Michael.

ARRIVEDERCI ITALIA!

The next morning we were packed and ready to head back to the States. For our last night's stay in Italy, Ford arranged for limousine service from my apartment to a hotel, the Lord Baron. When we arrived at the Lord Baron, it had the appearance of a five-star hotel. The outside looked like an expensive chateau. White marble and Italian sculptured figurines adorned the steps. We checked in at the front desk. The front clerk gave me a box that contained a beautiful white and lavender orchid flower. She welcomed us and informed us that reservations for dinner had been made for the evening. The bell man took our luggage and escorted us to our room. When we got to the room, Mama and I changed into our new outfits I bought for us while we were in Italy on a shopping spree. We wore them to dinner. My dress was a beautiful grey wool material with a sash that went over the shoulder and mom wore a cream and beige two-piece ensemble along with her black Italian designer leather purse. We went to dinner and dined on filet mignon, pasta and wine.

When we returned back to our room, we were surprised to find our bed covers were turned down with a piece of chocolate candy on top of our pillows. My mother and I headed toward the bed. You would have thought we were two little excited girls waking up early on Christmas Day running downstairs seeing the many presents left for us underneath the Christmas tree. We grabbed each other's hands and jumped up and down on the beds. We had a ball.

 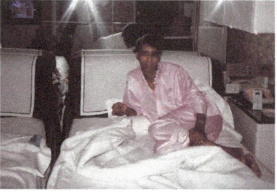

That morning, after breakfast, it was time to leave. We checked out of the room and headed down the stairs to get into the limousine outside and headed toward the airport. All of a sudden, the concierge ran down the stairs and was frantically calling, "Señorita, YOUR PASSPORTS!! Oh my gosh! The lady at the front desk forgot to return our passports.

HOME FLIGHT FIASCO

It was a two-fold blessing for me on December 16, 1984. First, my once in a lifetime wonderful Foreign Service Assignment in Turin, Italy had come to an end. Second, I celebrated my twenty-seventh birthday while in Europe. When Mama and I arrived at the airport, I was booked in first class, but mom was in coach. We boarded the plane. There were only two people seated in first class – a Caucasian man who sat across the aisle reading his New York Times, and me. The rest of the section was empty, so I asked the stewardess if it would be okay for my mom to sit in first class next to me since I noticed in coach where she sat, one of the passengers had a pet and this was going to be a problem for my mother since she has allergies. The stewardess acted arrogant like she didn't want to honor my request, so I got up and left first class and sat in coach with my mother.

It was quite unbearable and uncomfortable in coach. Women were pacing up and down the aisle holding their irritable infants while the unattended children sat in their seats continuously throwing a tantrum, yelling and kicking the back of our seats. The lady with the dog decided to take her pet out of the cage and play with it. I thought it was rude of the stewardess and the airline to allow such misbehavior from the passengers. After that flight experience, we were so glad to be home but I made a huge complaint to the airline on their inhospitable service.

CHAPTER SEVEN
SHE ACCOMPLISHED IT

LARGE CAR SPECIALTY INTERIOR STUDIO
THUNDERBIRD PROJECTS

After I returned from Italy, I was assigned to a large car specialty studio. My first studio assignment was to design the interior components for the 1989 Thunderbird, code named MN12. I designed the corporate airbag steering wheel, center console, gear selector (PRNDL), and gear shift. All components made production. It was fortunate after management reviewed my clay steering wheel design concept that it was selected to be the new "corporate" airbag steering wheel for all of Ford's upcoming car programs.

SKILLFUL MODELERS: EYES AND HANDS OF THE CREATIVE DESIGNER

Every designer should establish a good design relationship with the clay modeler(s) assigned to work on your design. It's important to understand exactly what you are designing based upon management's objectives. In the end, you want your finished 3D concept model to reflect management's vision and what they saw in the 2D sketch. The modelers are extensions of the designer's eyes, ears, hands, mouth and mind.

They are the catalysts who bring the design concept into existence. I remembered the advice that my mentor Sam Mayers shared with me as a young ambitious designer working with the modelers on my first interior design project for the Thunderbird program. It was essential to be prepared. Sam told me, "Wezzy, first start with a good two-dimensional sketch drawing and stay true to the objectives and theme selection which was reviewed and selected by management. Second, the designer should understand and be able to construct a mechanical drawing of the theme sketch. Third, transpose that theme sketch into a full-size tape drawing that meets the required engineered specifications. These early preparations make it legible and easy for the modelers to now transpose your design onto the clay model. It's important to know the design objectives and give clear, precise instructions to the modelers. Good communication between the designer and modeler creates a smooth transition for transposing the designers' 2D sketch concept into the finished 3D model. Two of my mentors, black clay modelers Charles Purnell and Calvin Morrison, were assigned to do the 3D modeling for my design project. By following my mentor Sam's guidelines, along with proper instructions and guidance, our teamwork turned out successful. We were able to interpret what management saw in my design concept to make full production. I could tell how proud Calvin and Charles were to be working with me on my design.

MY FIRST PRODUCTION CAR DESIGNS
THUNDERBIRD EXTERIOR: BASE, LX, SUPER COUPE

What a coincidence to find out my former instructor, Mr. Ted Finney, who taught me introduction to transportation design at Wayne State University, was my manager while I was assigned to the Large Car Specialty Exterior Studio. Ford developed several car series for the 1989 Thunderbird MN12 program. I made design contributions for the Thunderbird Base Model, Thunderbird LX (Luxury), and Thunderbird SC (Super Coupe), of which I designed the nomenclature graphics. 'Thunderbird SC' was located on the front and rear lower fascia.

1989 THUNDERBIRD WHEEL/WHEEL COVER PROGRAM
1993 FORD PROBE 14-INCH BASE MODEL WHEEL COVER DESIGN

After working in the Large Car Specialty Exterior Studio, I was given the task to design the entire the MN12 Wheel Program for the 1989 Thunderbird which included: 15-inch base luxury wheel cover and the 16-inch five spoke alloy wheel. Mark Kelly was my Studio Manager. The wheel program assignment served two milestone accomplishments for me. It was the first time a wheel cover design was patented. I received a phone call from Ford's legal department about documents pertaining to the designer of the 15-inch base wheel cover that needed my signature. Ford's legal department looked like a high-class Wall Street law firm. I signed the papers to verify that Emeline King was the designer of the 15-inch base wheel cover for the 1989 Thunderbird base series.

I received an outstanding performance rating for my design contribution to the 1989 MN12 Thunderbird wheel program. After my manager's approval on an excellent job of designing the MN12 wheel program, it caught the attention from another studio's design executive, Mimi Vandermolen, Design Executive for North American Small Cars. I was honored because Mimi was the highest-ranking female in design. She had succeeded the corporate ladder, a goal I hoped to one day reach as a female transportation designer for Ford just like Mimi. After Mimi spoke to my manager, it was her request that I be placed on loan to her studio to design the 1993 Ford Probe base wheel cover for Mimi's 1993 Probe program. Secondly, my designed 14-inch five-spoke base wheel cover made production. The wheel cover was used on all Ford Probe base models from 1993 -1997. After having a successful year in the Large Car Specialty Studio, manager Mark Kelly informed me about my next assignment - an 18-month Foreign Service Assignment at Ford's Dunton Design Center in Essex, England. This would be my second Foreign Service Assignment, yet another blessing for which God had favored me.

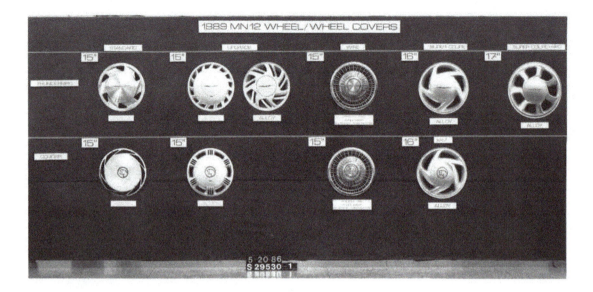

It was while I was in England that I happened to pass an outdoor newsstand. What immediately caught my attention was the three-quarter view of a red 1989 Thunderbird SC pictured on the front cover of Motor Trend magazine.

The magazine caption read: "'89 Thunderbird Super Coupe, Motor Trend's Car of the Year." Excited, I phoned my family in Detroit about the news. I also brought several copies to give to my friends in England. I realized God continually blessed me by letting my designs gain worldwide recognition. For generations, people can look back and see that a black girl from Detroit made design contributions to the auto industry.

SECOND FOREIGN ASSIGNMENT
FORD DUNTON DESIGN CENTER - ESSEX, ENGLAND

I was scheduled to leave for my second Foreign Service Assignment in England on September 1, 1987. I'd packed business suits, casual wear and other items needed for my trip. My mother suggested I wear my full-length blue fox fur coat. It was funny because I didn't think the weather got cold enough to wear a fur in England. The only times I had worn it previously was when the temperature dropped in Detroit while attending some fancy after five event or when I went to church. However, since Mama persisted, I wore it. My parents drove me to Detroit Metropolitan International Airport. We waited until it was time for me to board the plane. When the flight attendant called for passengers in first class. I kissed my parents and told them "I love you". I made my way down to the ramp then turned around and waved goodbye. My parents just stood there like two sad puppies who had lost their owner. I let them know not to worry, that I'd be okay. I said "God's with me and I'm going to do well designing over in Europe."

I appreciated all the sacrifices they made for me during my career. I couldn't be more blessed or asked for any other more loving and supportive people in the world than my parents. I boarded the plane and followed behind the flight attendant who showed me my seat which was in the first-class section. I sensed a few stares from the people who were in first class as I took my seat. I guess some wondered what my status was: an actress or a celebrity. The looks said they wondered what possible reason would a young, black female have to be dressed in a full length fur coat and hat while seated in first class.

When I arrived in London Heathrow Airport, I found it to be true what the song writer wrote in "A Foggy Day in London Town." I felt good about my second Foreign Service Assignment in the Ford Dunton Design Studio in Essex England. This design experience would help me to be more diverse, broaden my skills and heighten my career as a Transportation Designer. Europe's styling and packaging is totally different from the States. They tended to have a smaller size car market versus the States' larger size packaged vehicles. I planned on learning the European way of designing, travel the country on my free time, and make sure to take in all the culture of fashion, architecture and art during my stay in England.

CULTURE SHOCK

My coworker, Joe Siler, was at London Heathrow Airport to pick me up along with another designer who was English named Steve. He worked at the Dunton Design Studio. Joe had been on Foreign Assignment in England a couple months before me. We made our way to luggage claim and then headed outside. It was strange when we approached the curb where the cars were parked. Steve got into the small vehicle in front while Joe and I headed toward a large, greyish Ford Grenada sedan. Joe opened the right car door on the passenger side and asked me to get in. To my surprise, the steering wheel was located on the same side (passenger) and not the driver's left side. In Europe, people drove on the passenger side which was the total opposite from the States where I was accustomed to driving on the left (or driver's) side of the car. Besides hearing the different English dialects around me, driving on the passenger side was my first culture shock; however, I knew I had to get familiar with the driving if I planned on getting around in the city, back and forth to work.

Joe told me to follow Steve who led the way from the airport towards the city of Brentwood where I would be staying. We approached two circular intersections in the road called a roundabout, which were common throughout Europe at the time. To get to the other side of the road, we drove around the figure eight pattern. At first, driving the roundabout seemed awkward, but I managed to get comfortable the more I drove through the city. Thank God I learned how to drive a manual in back in the States! Had I not learned to drive a stick shift, this hour-long drive from London to Brentwood would have been a total fiasco. We arrived at Brentwood and parked in front of a brown and beige English Tudor Inn. Joe told me I would be staying there temporarily until my Foreign Service adviser found my permanent place. I got settled in, unpacked and called my family to let them know that I had made it safe.

Later that evening, Joe and Steve came by and took me into the city to see some of London's attractions and out to dinner. We drove through Piccadilly Circus, London Bridge, Tower Bridge, Wembly Stadium, Westminster Abbey, and Buckingham Palace. There was so much to see, but I knew I had plenty of time to come back and visit. Joe was quite familiar with London, so he filled me in and kept me abreast of things to do, where to go shopping, where to buy groceries, and other ways to make my stay enjoyable. "Driving in the city could be hectic", he said considering Joe lived in the next town and I stayed in Brentwood. "Feel free to take advantage of public transportation", he continued. England had a variety of mass transportation: trains, double decker buses, cabs and the UnderGround. The UnderGround is a public, rapid transit system. Learning to travel the London UnderGround was going to be a different experience compared to transit transportation in Detroit, which is slower and above the ground.

There were maps listed to help you get around the city. Just follow the color-coded, patterned map and it will get you to your destination. In Joe's opinion, some English foods tasted bland. That's why he'd often drive into the city, which was several miles from where he lived, to his favorite restaurant called Texas Long Horn. He claimed they served the best barbecue and the place reminded him of being back home in the States.

Joe was a talented designer and helpful during my stint. I had the opportunity to meet his parents when they came to visit him. Joe's dad was short in stature. He always carried a coin in his pocket which over the years he had rubbed all the surface off. After Joe and I finished our stint in England, a few years later, he and his fiancé invited me to sing at their wedding.

SETTLING IN

The following day Joe took me to Ford's Dunton Design Center in Essex, which was about a forty-minute ride from Brentwood. There, I met all the people who would be working with me. Everyone was warm, welcoming and looked forward to me coming aboard. I noticed that I was the only African American female in the building amongst the male designers; I really stood out. I also meet with my Foreign Service Advisor who assigned my housing which was located at 1 Jason Court. I would be moving there in two weeks. It was a comfortable one-bedroom furnished apartment. It was located right across the street from the Inn where I would stay during my Foreign Service Assignment. I opened a bank account at the Midland Bank. A designer could really save their money back in the States while on Foreign Service Assignment. Mainly, since the company took care of your housing, food (per diem) and transportation while on the Foreign Service Assignment.

I ordered a red Sierra G base model, two-door coupe as my company car. Although, it wasn't quite as powerful as the "granddaddy" Ford Grenada sedan that Joe ordered, it still had the horsepower to get up and go.

MEETING DERRICK MCCULLUM
EUROPEAN CAR DESIGNER

Before arriving in England, my mentor, Sam Mayers, gave me the telephone number to Mr. Derrick McCullum, a black male car designer who lived in England. Derrick used to work at the Ford Design Center in Dearborn, Michigan with Sam and a few of my other co-workers. He told me to make sure I contact Derrick who also was a protégé of Sam's. I never had a chance to meet Derrick because he left the Ford Design Center years before I hired in and went to work in Europe. I was able to contact him and later that week, Derrick invited me over to his home and prepared a wonderful home-cooked meal for me. I enjoyed a festive evening with Derrick and some of his friends. It was an honor to meet him and talk about our careers in the auto industry. Derrick told me how proud he was to have met the first black female transportation designer at Ford.

ADVENTUROUS JOE

One scary moment occurred when Joe, Rick, another designer from the States, and I decided to take a short excursion ride through the southern part of England. Joe always had a gung-ho nature about him so he decided to venture further from where he had planned on going. It started to snow heavily and effect the driving and road conditions, so I suggested that we turn around and go back home. But oh no, not Joe! He kept driving towards the border of Switzerland. We saw the border police who were armed with machine guns a few feet away. That's when Joe decided he would turn the car around and head back. We could have gotten in big trouble because our passports were only valid for the United Kingdom. We would have been cooked geese if we had gone a few more feet. Joe introduced me to Ron, another creative designer who worked at Ford's Dunton Design Center. His hobby included customized fifth scale toy model cars. Ron would disassemble every part on the model car, repaint it to look more realistic and assemble them back together.

Joe and I were always in competition on who had the largest collection of customized model cars. Personally, I had purchased over thirty of Ron's customized cars. When my foreign assignment was over and it was time to have my personal items shipped back to the States, I had the packers come and individually wrap my model car collection. Concerned about their safety, I wanted to have them insured; however, they assured me that my car collection would get to the States safe.

JOHN, WHAT A BLACK SURPRISE!

I was fortunate to meet another Dunton Design Center coworker, John Snooks, who lived not far from me. He was a car designer who befriended me and was supportive while I was there, eventually becoming my mentor. John worked at Ford for several years. Now John was your typical English man – a tall, slender, Caucasian, who spoke with a British cockney accent. One day, he invited me to his home, which was a couple miles from where I lived, to meet his family and have dinner. He introduced me to his beautiful daughter Cora and his lovely petite girlfriend, Anna, who happened to be black and British. Wow! At first, I was a little startled because I wasn't expecting his girlfriend to be black. I had never ran into or saw any black people in the area where I was staying. They were truly a happy couple in love. It wasn't long before John and his family took a liking to me and vice versa. I was their extended overseas family member. On several occasions, I'd visit and we sat around laughing and watching the "telly" which was their slang for television. They taught me about their British and English culture and I'd share with them the things we like to do in the States. They taught me to say phrases in an English dialect like "I'm going to the Loo, (I'm going to the bathroom)"; "Are you waiting for the Q? (Are you waiting in line?)"; or "Top of the morning to ya (Good Morning)" and addressing the police as "Bobby". It was so unusual seeing them walking the beat (which was the street), carrying sticks, not guns like back in the States. It seemed like everybody addressed you by saying "Hello, Love." or "Yes, love". It wasn't long before I had acquired an English accent and their eating habits. I got accustomed to eating mayonnaise on my french fries and ordering fish and chips. We'd often have beans and franks which was pork & beans and hot dogs. I even tried Shepherd's pie which didn't sit well with me at all. Drinking Earl Grey tea and scones throughout the day became a daily ritual. I really felt loved and at home with John and his family.

LOSING UNCLE LONELL

While I was in England, my uncle Lonell, my Dad's oldest brother passed away from a heart attack. I was at work and John was there with me when I got the news from my parents who called to inform me. Uncle Lonell lived in Cleveland, Ohio with his wife, my Aunt Tee, and four daughters, my cousins, Diane, Kimberly, Beverly and Debbie. Uncle Lonell loved to come visit us in Detroit. He'd always drove his cherished gold 'Deuce and a quarter.' When my oldest sister "Am" was little, Uncle Lonell would love to take her for rides in his car. She was his "'lil riding buddy." I fell in love with that car and tried my hands at sketching it. My dad would always take our family over to Cleveland to visit. We had a great time playing with our cousins.

I was sad that I couldn't go home to be with the family. Since it wasn't an immediate family member, Ford wasn't obligated to pay for me to fly home and attend the funeral. Mama told me it was okay if I didn't come home for the funeral. I'm sure the family understands and knows that you care. Uncle Lonell will be missed, for he was a strong pillar in our King Family. John was concerned about how I was handling the news about my uncle's passing, so he invited me after work to spend some time with him and his family.

TRAVELING WITH THE ROBINSONS AND STONEHENGE

During my stay in England, I met a wonderful couple, the Robinsons, who were from Michigan. Mr. Robinson was over on Foreign Service Assignment. He was an engineer and the former manager to my youngest sister, Kiddo (Eugenia). Mrs. Robinson worked for one of the universities. They were an adventurous couple. Mrs. Robinson planned all of our weekend excursions. We started off with the museums: British, Tate Modern, National Gallery, the Victoria and Albert Museum. We traveled to various cities like Birmingham, Canterbury, Nottingham, and Edinburgh. We toured the great castles: Bodiam, Windsor, Warwick and Leeds. The higher schools of learning like the University of Cambridge, Oxford, St. Andrews and the Imperial College London were next plus many other exciting places in England. We never needed a tour guide because she was well versed on the history of every artifact and every tourist site we visited. Mr. Robinson served as the designated driver. He was quiet and soft spoken, the total opposite of Mrs. Robinson whose personality was more extroverted. She was a long-winded talker. I practically had to clear my throat and jump in the conversation wherever I could. However, I loved traveling with the Robinson's who were caring and fun to be around. During my bereavement when Uncle Lonell passed, they called and offered condolences and insisted I spend the night at their home.

Out of the many trips we explored together, my most favorite was Stonehenge in Wiltshire, England which was a three-hour ride (127.4 miles). Mrs. Robinson kept us informed about what we would be doing for the day. Not leaving out any details, she talked from the time we got into the car until we reached Wiltshire. When we arrived, the scenery was mysterious, mystical and breathtaking. These ancient massive stones stood 13 feet high, seven feet wide and weighed 25 tons. We looked like ants standing in the midst of prehistoric monuments. I was amazed how the stones were arranged in a circular format without the assistance of modern technology to mechanically lift and space them. Capturing this "Kodak" moment, I took a beautiful photograph of the sun setting behind these stones.

SUB B COMPACT VEHICLE PROJECT
COPYING: THE HIGHEST FORM OF FLATTERY

John, my newest mentor, gave good advice and words of encouragement whenever I ran into a situation on the job. There was one particular incident with another male designer. I nicknamed him "Copy Cat." We were assigned to work on the Sub B project. The objectives were to design a small two-seater compact vehicle for the European market. This was going to be an exciting project and my opportunity to showcase my design talent. We presented our sketches of which one was selected as a theme by management. From there, we developed the theme sketch into a fifth scale 3D clay model.

Each theme were totally different in styling and design appearance. Management had specific design direction for each designer's theme. The next step was to transfer each fifth scale clay model design dimension onto the full-size split clay model. Each designer shared the same clay model armature. I'd worked on one side of the split model with my design theme along with a team of modelers and the other side was designated to Copy Cat's design. We both were strong competitive designers.

However, I became upset when I noticed "Copy Cat" started making design changes to his clay split model to look identical to mine. I wanted to blatantly let him know what he was doing and I wasn't too happy about it. The modelers and John noticed it, too. John called me over to his desk and told me, "Emeline, you shouldn't get upset; he's actually doing you a gigantic favor. I'm sure when management reviews both projects, they will ask him, "Where's the design theme management selected for you to represent on your side of the split model? Your side is identical to Emeline's theme." They will see he copied your design. I couldn't help but laugh. *Copying is the highest form of flattery.*

FAMILY AND A CLASSMATE VISIT ME IN ENGLAND

Both my parents and my 'lil sister Kiddo (Eugenia) had an opportunity to come visit me. This would be my father and sister's first time traveling to Europe and the second trip for my mother. When I picked them up from the London Heathrow Airport, not only were they shocked how the people in England drove on the passenger side of the car but surprised how familiar I was in traveling around the city. Mom made a statement, "Emeline, I don't see how when you were home in Detroit you'd get lost driving around block. You come over to England and know how to maneuver around town like you're a seasoned cab driver?" We toured the city and shopped at Harrods, the world-famous department store. Each floor was elegantly decorated with its own specialty department. We visited Buckingham Palace with the changing of the guards in their bright red, black and brass decorated uniforms plus Tower Bridge, Westminster Abbey, Tower of London and several other sites.

They met the Harrison's and got a chance to taste Daddy Harrison's special Jamaican jerk chicken dish. We went to church on Sunday with the Harrison's and I introduced them to the pastor who had been pastoring for many years. Both he and my father shared a lot in common.

The following month was a big surprise for me when my classmate, friend and coworker Robin Anderson visited me during my stay in England. Robin worked for Ford. A talented mechanical engineer, we'd been friends for years. Although her visit was short one of my friends, Delroy Harrison, volunteered and drove us around to see some wonderful tourist attractions.

BRIXTON, LONDON
MY MUSICAL BLESSING

One evening after work, I ventured out and drove down to the city of London. I turned on the radio to find a station that played music. In my searching, I came across a station that played gospel music. I loved gospel music and was awfully familiar with the song that was being played. "Going Up Yonder" performed by my favorite gospel idol, Tramaine Hawkins. We had something in common, both talented gospel singers from the United States. After the song ended, the DJ made an announcement that turned out to be my musical blessing. He spoke with a Jamaican accent. "Listen up, to all of me gospel lovers and singars out thar in radio lawn, if a ta want ta buy some gospel record come visit me at mer shop right down here in Brixton. We have everything you need." I listened for the address. Wow! Did I just hit the jackpot?

That next day at work I told John about what I heard on the radio and asked, "Where was Brixton? I wanted to go visit the gospel music store." He told me the best directions on how to get there and that I would find a lot of Jamaicans living in that part of town. He told me that "If you plan to go, please be careful in that neighborhood. There are some rough areas." I assured John that I would. Don't worry I'm from Detroit and I survived the hood. I grew up in neighborhoods that were way rougher than Brixton. I was able to find the store and John was right, it was a melting pot of black people everywhere on the street! Black merchants and their black owned businesses, etc… I fit right in! But, that didn't last too long. Once I opened my mouth and spoke to the clerk, he noticed my accent along with other people in the store and asked me, "Where are you from, my love? I told him I was from Detroit, Michigan. He smiled and said "Ah yes, Motown, The Jackson Five. Gospel music with those beautiful singars." I told him, "I design cars for Ford and I'm here on Foreign Service Assignment." Surprised he asked, "You design cars? A gurl? I told him, "Yes." He was excited to meet me and hear my story how I became a car designer. He asked, "So, what can I do for you, my love?" I told him I heard announced on the radio station that this place sells gospel records and music. I'm a gospel singer and wanted to purchase some items. He mentioned, "Since you love to sing you might be interested in performing with the Angelica Voice Choir, my love." Their manager is Simon Wallace. I'll give you his number. He informed me Simon promotes gospel artists from the States to perform in concerts in Brixton. I thanked him for the information and said I would be back to visit. That evening when I got home, I called Simon and we had a long conversation about my music background, the Angelica Voice Choir and some of the artists from the States he and I both knew. We arranged to meet later that week with the choir at their rehearsal. It turned out to be a warm, friendly fellowship. They asked me to sing a solo. Everyone was impressed with my singing, so much that Simon asked if I'd like to be a part of the Angelica Voice Choir. I ended up joining and gained some new friends.

SIMON WALLACE AND THE ANGELICA VOICE CHOIR

The Angelica Voice Choir had about thirty members and their own band, an excellent group of talented musicians. Simon selected the song "Dear Jesus, I Love You." performed by the Edwin Hawkins Singers featuring Tramaine. He said my range and delivery was similar to hers and asked me to sing the lead. It was an honor because Tramaine's my favorite gospel artist. The Choir entered a gospel singing competition which was televised on the BBC (British Broadcasting Communication). We came in first place. What I liked most about everybody in the choir was they were all saved Christians. I enjoyed their company, praising God, witnessing, and ministering through song to people everywhere.

We performed in several church venues around the city and even toured the Netherlands. I even had my debut performance on television with Angelica Voice Choir. One enjoyable trip was when we performed church concerts in Holland and Utrecht Amsterdam. We had our own tour bus. Simon made arrangements for each choir member to stay overnight in the people's homes.

The family I stayed with was very hospitable. I did experience some strange things that occurred in the people homes. While I slept someone came into my room that night and opened all the windows in the bedroom. I was freezing. My friends in the choir forewarned me this would happen. I also noticed when I went to use the bathroom, the walls were covered with calendars from the previous years. To top it off located in the bedroom stood a large white circular container in the middle of the room. I assumed it was a bathtub, so I used a small pan filled it up with water and climb inside to wash up. After our concert, it was time to head home. Everyone shared their experiences. One guy stayed with a family who was a dentist and was helpful to him when he developed a bad toothache and need an emergency tooth extraction. Another choir member got fitted for a pair of wooden Dutch shoes. I informed my friends I had a chance to take a bath in the strangest shaped tub. Everybody busted out laughing and told me, "Emily, we don't know what that contraption was used for, my love, but it wasn't for bathing!"

Lee Magid, Emeline and Tramaine Hawkins

When we got back to England, I met and took photos with some of the gospel artists from the States Simon had invited over to perform in concert. There was the Maestro, Thomas Whitfield, Fred Hammond, and Commission, the Hawkins Singers. My most cherished moment was when Simon had arranged for Tramaine to stop by our rehearsal one evening and meet the choir. We would be singing background for her upcoming concert performance the next night. This event would be an after-five affair. So now I know why mom insisted that I bring my fur. This would be the perfect occasion for me to wear it.

The "Maestro", Minister Thomas Whitfield   The Hawkins Singers

I got a chance to talk with Tramaine. I shared my career background, and how I've always admired her. She gave me some sound advice about singing and encouraged me to use my God-given gift to be an open vessel and let Him fill me up with his blessings. I also met her manager, Mr. Lee, an older Caucasian man who told me I should be an actress because I had that same sparkle in my eyes and drive which reminded him of the famous movie star Diahann Carroll, when she was a young up and coming actress.

MY SUNDAY MEALS WITH THE HARRISON FAMILY

I had the pleasure of meeting Delroy Harrison's family, one of the Angelica Voice Choir band members, who played the keyboard. The Harrisons were from Jamaica and lived in Brixton. This was another family that befriended me and adopted me into their

family. I'd often go worship at church on Sunday with the Harrison's. They would get so excited every time the pastor would always ask me to come up and sing a solo while Delroy accompanied me. After church, we'd return back to the Harrison's home to have tea, listen to gospel music and then sit down to enjoy Delroy's father, Mr. Harrison's special Caribbean dish, jerk chicken, plantains and yellow rice. I looked forward to my favorite home-cooked meal every Sunday. The chicken was so tender and well-seasoned - that the aroma of those spices penetrated throughout the house and neighborhood. Delroy, his sister Sharon, brother Paul and cousin Conrad would always tease me saying, "Oh, Emily, you know pops puts a lot of TLC (tender loving care) in that chicken. He prepared it especially in honor of his new, lovely daughter from America."

Delroy, Sharon, Paul, Delton and Conrad were devious and loved to play pranks on each other. This often occurred when we went into the city and ate at their favorite pizza spot: Pizza Hut. We ordered pizza and sat down to eat. After we finished, one by one they each would get up from the table and sneak out of the restaurant without paying.

EMELINE, BE CAREFUL WHAT YOU WISH FOR

One Saturday morning, I was in my apartment watching the 1988 Seoul Korea

Olympics on the telly (British English name for television). Being athletic, I enjoyed every track and field event. What caught my attention was seeing this six-feet, two inch, dark chocolate complexion, athletic built, British Jamaican male named Linford Christie setting up running block. Once the announcer said "Set," and the starter gun sounded, Christie took off full force sprinting like a seasoned thoroughbred leaving his opponents far behind. Christie leaned his head forward crossing the finish line setting a new world record and winning gold for England in the 100 meters races.

I could hardly take my eyes off of him. I murmured to myself, "What a phenomenal man! I sure would like to meet him some day." Well, be careful for what you wish for it might come true and to my surprise it did. It happened that his sister Angie sang in the Angelica Voice Choir and informed me that her brother, Linford Christie, would be coming home. He had just won bronze in the Olympics. So amazed I asked her "Do you think I could meet him? She told me, "Sure no problem." Although, I never revealed to her or him that my crush ignited after seeing him in motion on the telly.

THANK GOD I HAD MY FORD BUSINESS CARD BACKSTAGE PASS

I heard on the radio that Grammy award R&B artist Anita Baker would perform at London's Wembly Stadium. My parents babysat Anita when we were little. We both attended Henry B. Keidan Elementary. It had been years since we saw each other. Hopefully, I'd get chance to see my former classmate at the concert. I purchased two tickets and thought it would be good to invite Linford to go with me. I called Angie, his sister, and told her to please have him call me. I have two tickets to go see a classmate friend of mine, Anita Baker. I had barely hung up the phone before it was Linford calling me. "Hello. May I please speak to Ms. Emily? This is Linford Christie." Oh my God! I literately jumped out of my skin after hearing his sexy British accent call out my name. I tried to hold my composure. I caught my breath and answered, "Yes, this is she. Hello Linford. How are you? Are you available tomorrow night to go to the Anita Baker concert at Wembly with me?" He said, "Yes, I'd love to, my love" and thanked me for the invitation. He suggested we met near the main entrance at Wembly. He asked, "What color will you be wearing?" I told him I would be wearing a red dress. I bought the dress at one of my favorite stores in London: Next.

ANITA BAKER

We had a wonderful time at the concert and Anita was fabulous. After the concert I told Linford, "I'm gonna try to get us backstage and meet Anita." I got the attention of the guard and handed him my business card to give to Anita. I had written on the back it, "Enjoyed concert, Anita. Working in the UK 4 Ford, love to C U. P.S. I'm with a guest… Olympic Medalist Linford Christie. Emeline." It wasn't too long before the guard returned to where we were sitting and asked me and Linford to follow him backstage. There was a reporter from the London News and a small group of paparazzi who waited halfway down the hall. As we made our way pass them toward Anita's dressing room, someone noticed it was Linford and called out to congratulate him. They asked could they take a photo. We entered the reception area where we met Anita. She was dressed in all black looking cute and petite. The room was filled with people from her team including her backup singers, the Perry Sisters, and a few relatives. When Anita saw me she called out to me, "King! Emeline, what a surprise!"

We embraced and I introduced her to Linford and told her who he was. She was honored to have met Linford. We enjoyed the evening reminiscing and sharing our past experiences. I told Anita besides designing cars, I still was doing my gospel singing. She shared with me whenever she gets a sore throat and has to perform, she keeps her throat coated with a special tonic. It soothes her vocals like honey. Before we left, Anita handed me an envelope that had two complimentary tickets in it for tomorrow night's last performance. We took pictures and said we'd have to get together when we return back to the States.

Linford and I became good friends. On a few occasions, I would take the train down to Brixton and visit. Linford picked me up from the station in his white Mercedes Benz. He would jokingly say in his Jamaican accent, "Emily, don't cha be too surprised if you gonna see us on da cover of the tabloids." On one occasion, he prepared dinner for me and his beautiful girlfriend. He shared his stories about his adventures during the Olympics and gave me an autographed poster of his Olympic victory.

That next day I decided to contact my brother, Delroy. He was excited and looking forward to going to the concert and meeting Anita Baker his "BIGGEST" R&B artist. We took photos and from that day on Delroy continuously bragged every day to everybody about how he met and took pictures with his idol, Anita Baker.

ENGLAND'S STORM OF 1987

On October 15, 1987, the southern part of England suffered one of its worst storms ever since 1703. There was severe damage to homes, buildings, neighborhoods. Trees were uprooted from winds gusting up to 100 mph. It was reported that eighteen people were killed in the United Kingdom and four in France[2].

DETERMINATION AND DRIVE THROUGH THE STORM

I was scheduled to visit the Ford Cologne Design Studio in Cologne, Germany. One of my relatives Jean Markray who was stationed in the military. I spoke with her early that week to inform of my coming to Germany and I planned on visited her. My flight was scheduled to leave at seven that morning. London Heathrow Airport was about 34.95 miles from where I was stayed in Brentwood. It would take an hour to get there, so I left my apartment at 5:45am. I was about to walk out the door when the phone rang. It was my coworker John who called to tell me "Emeline, the weather's bad outside. You still planned on driving to the airport?" I told him, "Yes, I'd be alright. Thanks for your concern and I'll call you as soon as I get to Germany." Shortly after which the phone rang again. It was Delroy. He sounded worried and told me England has predicted a bad storm and I should cancel my trip. My mind was made up and I was determined to go. After being on the road for about fifteen minutes, I started to get worried. The sky steadily got darker. There weren't any cars on the freeway. I turned on my high beams to see the road while the wind started to pick up which caused my Sierra G sedan to rock from side to side. It rained, thundered and turned into a bad lightning storm. I saw the top of the trees bend over, sway back and forth like they were bowing and some were uprooted from the ground. Debris flew uncontrollably around in the air. What the hell was I thinking?! I wished I had listened to both John and Delroy and stayed my butt home. The only thought on my mind was to keep driving and pray that I could make it to Heathrow Airport so I could be with the closet relative, Jean. When I arrived, the airport was practically empty. Two people stood at the counter, one elderly man and three other people who looking worried while waiting in the gate area. A porter walked over to me and asked. It's terrible outside. "How did you make it here?" I told him, "Frightened! And on two wings and a prayer, but I made it by the grace of God." I asked him, "Can you please show me where Gate 45 is? I'm scheduled to leave for Cologne, Germany." He pointed over to my right and said, "It's over there. You might as well have a seat, love. It's going to be a long wait. I don't think you're going anywhere until this storm pass ova." I didn't realize how bad the storm was until the porter brought out a portable television to watch the BBC news reported about the storm and its severe damages. I knew my family back home would be worried for me if they watched the news. I slept in the airport. I been there for over ten hours. I looked at the flight board to see if anything had changed about my flight and it had. The attendant announced flight 735 boarding for Cologne, Germany. The plane was small and with only a few passengers. After the stewardess had us to fasten our seat belts, the captain announced over the speaker, "Ladies and gentlemen, we will experience some rough turbulence from the earlier storm. I'll fly above it." With the exception of my ears popping and the nausea we made it safe to Cologne. Thank you, Jesus, Hallelujah! I took a cab to my hotel and called John, Delroy and my parents, who had heard about the storm, to let them know I was safe.

PURNELL AND COLOGNE, GERMANY

I visited the Ford Cologne Design Center in Germany and hung out with Charles Purnell, my big brother and mentor who was there on Foreign Service Assignment. I called him "Purnell." He was one of four talented black clay modelers, along with Calvin Morrison, Charles Leaks, and Jasper Garrison, employed at the Ford Design Center in Dearborn, Michigan. He used his creative skills to work on some of my design projects that made production while we were in the Large Car Specialty Studio. Prior to coming to Ford, Purnell worked for Motown on Grand Boulevard in Detroit as a graphic artist designing those iconic album covers of the Motown Artists. Purnell shared with me since he's been on Foreign Assignment in Germany, it has been one of the highlights of his career working and exploring the European culture. He wished Ford could extend his stint from Foreign Service specialist to employee. He loved Europe. Purnell took me to his favorite pub where he frequents with coworkers and friends. Purnell introduced them to me and shared my background story which he boasted about frequently. His friends were all different ethnicities: German, Ethiopian, Nigerian, Italian, and Somalian. Before leaving Cologne, Purnell suggested that I must visit Germany's famous attraction, the Cologne Cathedral "The Dom." From a distance the Cathedral appeared as a gigantic black massive piece of architecture which one viewed for miles. Its heights appeared to be reaching past the grey clouds. As I walked through the interior of the building, it created a dark and mystical atmosphere. Also, while in Cologne, I visited my cousin Jean Louise Markray who was stationed in the military. She was on furlough for that weekend, so we had time to do a few exciting things. We did attend a Baptist church near the base. I enjoyed the service and was moved by the preacher's message. Right before he finished his sermon, I handed Jean a note and asked would it be okay for me to sing a solo? She nodded her head slowly and said "ummm, (pause) okay." I could tell she didn't quite know what to expect not to have ever heard me sing. After I finished singing "Only What You Do for Christ Will Last" there weren't any regrets, only smiles and tears of joy from my cousin and the congregation.

EMBARRASSING MOMENT
"OH MUMMY, THE LADY'S HAIR HAS FALLEN OUT"
(IT'S A BLACK WOMAN'S HAIR THANG!)

During my stay in England, I experienced one of the most comical and embarrassing things that probably could only happen to a black girl and her hair. My fiasco took place at a hair salon not too far from my job. I decided to go on my lunch hour to get my braid extensions freshened up and be back in time to make my presentation before management on the Sub B concept full-size clay model I designed. Pasty, my Jamaican friend who sung in the Angelica Voice Choir with me, was my beautician. She lived in Brixton which was twenty miles outside of London. I preferred to take the UnderGround to her house instead of driving to get my hair done. There weren't any hair salons that catered to black hair in Brentwood where I lived, so I asked Pasty if she could braid extensions into my hair. This was popular hairstyle worn by most African American females and a few of my Jamaican friends in the Angelica Voice Choir. The process involved individual strains of human hair braided three quarters way down into my hair with the ends of the hair left unbraided. There were at least one hundred individual extensions braided into my hair. I sat anywhere from five to six hours to have Pasty install them. It was worth the wait - fun, camaraderie and a beautiful hairstyle in the end. My extensions worked well for me. The style lasted three months with little maintenance; Just a once-a-month shampoo with a gentle wash and conditioning. Unfortunately, the second time, I wore these extensions and kept them in longer than I intended. I had been wearing my braids style for five months and it definitely needed to be washed. My presentation was scheduled after lunch. I remembered that I saw a hair salon not too far from my workplace. I decided to go on my lunch hour and have it washed and presentable for my presentation. When I walked in, I noticed the salon's staff and clients were white, British women. The first thing I asked the receptionist when I walked in was, "Do you service black people's hair? I'm wearing braided extensions and I would like my hair washed and blow dried." The lady said, "Yes, of course this salon is trained to do all types of hair. If you like please have a seat over to the shampoo bowl an attendant will be with you shortly, my love." It wasn't too long when the shampoo lady came and placed a black plastic covering over me so I wouldn't get wet. She proceeded to run lukewarm water and then shampooed my hair. Next, she took a small tooth comb off her tray, grabbed a handful of my extensions in her hand. She began to pull and comb with a heavy downward stroke. When I felt what she was doing, I immediately told her, "Stop ma'am! Please don't comb my extensions, you'll comb them out! I only needed you to gently shampoo and blow dry them." After she finished drying my hair, I asked to see a mirror. She started making excuses that she couldn't find a mirror. I told her never mind. I needed to head back to work for my meeting and I don't want to be late. I asked how much for the services? She smiled and said, "That will be eight pounds, my love" which is equal to ten dollars in U.S. currency. I handed her the money, gathered my coat and headed out the door of the salon towards my car.

I walked past a little boy who appeared to be seven years old. He began to tug on his mother's coat and pointed his finger down towards the sidewalk. I could hear him in the background as I got closer to my car. He spoke with a British accent, "Oh mummy, look at the lady's hair. It's fallen on the sidewalk." Out of curiosity, I was praying that he wasn't talking about me. I turned around and noticed a trail of individual black extension braids from where I was standing on the sidewalk all the way back to the front door of the salon. So embarrassing! I took my hand and felt the back of my head. Three fourths of the extension braids were on the sidewalk. I glanced down at my watch. I didn't have time to go back to the salon because I would be late for my meeting.

When I got to work, I rushed to the loo, which was the ladies restroom, looked in the mirror and tried to cover the back of my head with the few remaining extensions that were still intact on the top. It wasn't enough to cover. There was no way I would give a presentation looking this way. I looked a *hot mess*. In a panic and pushed for time, I took out the few extensions that were left, added some cold water to my natural hair, then patted and shaped my natural hair into a tiny Afro and headed to my meeting. When I walked into the studio, I sensed the strange looks on the men's faces as I passed them and made my way up front toward the clay model to begin my presentation. I tried not to concentrate or think about their reactions to my dramatic hair change from this morning when they saw me with long, flowing, twelve-inch extensions. Those extensions that were past my shoulder are now a three-inch Afro. Somehow, this black girl remained focused, more confident than ever and delivered an excellent presentation on my clay model.

GOODBYE, ENGLAND

My Foreign Service Assignment in England ended on March 15, 1989. It was time to return home to Detroit. For a going away gift, my Ford Dunton Design Center coworkers presented me with a white 1964 Mustang 3/4 scale die cast model car and a lovely pictorial book of famous England attractions. They knew I had a hobby for collecting scaled model cars so it was the perfect gift. I learned so much at Ford's Dunton Design Center to help me become a better skilled transportation designer, especially from my coworkers and mentors Joe, Ron, John Snooks and family. I reflected over my experiences in England and counted all my blessings. This black female car designer accomplished all she set out to do and more while in the United Kingdom. I met many people and established wonderful friendships. I'm thankful to Simon who acknowledged my gift to sing and invited me as a lead soloist to be a part of the choir leading solos and gospel performances throughout England and the Netherlands.

It was through my acquaintances with Simon Wallace & the Angelica Voice Choir that presented opportunities to reacquaint me with some of my hometown gospel artists who were on tour in England from the states: Fred Hammond and Commission, the "Maestro" Tommy Whitfield, my childhood friend Anita Baker, The Hawkins Singers and my favorite gospel idol songstress, Tramaine Hawkins. I never would have imagined meeting and friending Olympian Bronze medalist, Linford Christie.

A surprise farewell party was given for me by my adopted England family: the Harrison's. It was held at a lavish restaurant in London. The place was packed with all my friends I met while in England. We dined and had a wonderful fellowship. I took a lot of pictures to remind me of fond memories and the good times we shared. I told them how each one impacted my life. I'll cherish our friendship forever and promised if they ever visit the States, they are welcome to stay with me and I would show them a wonderful time.

After the party was over, I took the London UnderGround back to Brentwood. Some of my friends came, too... Delroy, his sister Sharon and brother Paul decided to join me and planned on spending the evening with me. I had already moved out of my housing complex. The Ford Company put me up in the Inn which was across the street from 1 Jason Court where I was staying. We stayed up all night, reminisced about my excursions in England, our careers, and what's it's like to live in Detroit. We sang, laughed, made future plans and ordered pizza etc. I will sincerely miss my Jamaican family, the Harrison's, my coworkers at Ford of Dunton and all the wonderful people I met who altered my life and made it brighter and better.

That morning an entourage of my friends met me at the airport. Although it was a tearful, sad, and joyful farewell, I will always be grateful to God that through my employer Ford Motor Company granted me a once in a lifetime experience.

WHAT DO YOU MEAN A BLACK GIRL CAN'T DESIGN CARS?

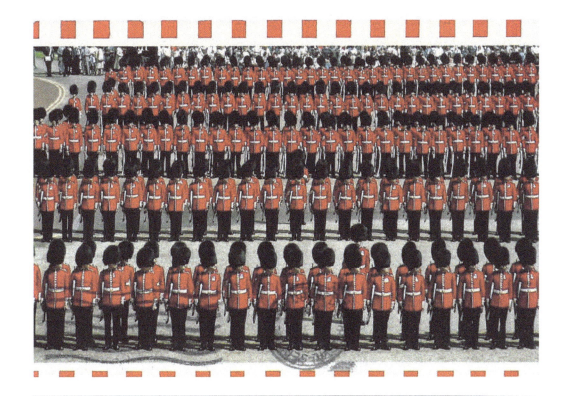

CHAPTER EIGHT
SHE EXPLORED IT

EARNEST, IT'S TIME TO EMPTY OUR NEST

When I returned from England, there was a big welcome home celebration given to me by my family. I shared all my European experiences, the things I learned and accomplished, with relatives, friends and coworkers. I went back home and lived with my parents. Although I had several things on my plate that I needed to get done, I was comfortable to return home and live with my parents. Moving out of the nest wasn't the top priority; however, my wonderful parents in an expedient, cunning and comical way pushed me out sooner than I would have thought.

One particular incident occurred when Dad went to visit his friend Rev. David Myers, who lived in the Village Square complex, apartment #1, on Santa Maria Street. It was the largest master apartment in the complex with a beautiful, furnished three-bedroom, full bath, master bed with bath, living room, dining, and kitchen. David informed Dad that he planned to move to California by the end of the week. Later that evening, my parents were in the living room watching the television. Dad mentioned to mom about David's plans to move. After Mama heard about the upcoming vacancy, she immediately got on Dad's case.

"Earnest, you mean to tell me you sat there and didn't open your mouth and mention our daughter *needs* a place? David's apartment would be perfect for Emeline! Earnest, you go back over there and tell David that Emeline is available to move in." "Right now?" Dad asked. Before I could blink, I resided at Village Square in apartment number one." I had no choice in the matter. How coincidental is it that every place I've lived has had the number "one" for my address, even when I lived in Europe at 1 Jason Court, Apt #1.

FIRST RADIO INTERVIEW 1440 WCHB
WITH DISC JOCKEY JOHN MASON

I hadn't too long returned back from England when the 1989 Ford Thunderbird made production and was awarded Motor Trend's Car of The Year. Ford profited well and must have sold several thousand vehicles because everywhere you looked, you saw Thunderbirds on the road driven by satisfied customers. I joined the list when I purchased it as my second vehicle.

After designing the Thunderbird, many doors of opportunity and special recognition began to happen for me. One exceptional moment came as my first radio interview on station 1440 WCHB "Soul Radio." John Mason, a black disc jockey, would interview me. I woke up early that morning. My radio interview was scheduled for 6:00 a.m. I sat on my living room floor in my apartment next to my stereo and waited anxiously for the phone to ring. The day before, I called family, relatives, friends and everybody, even my neighbor who lived in the apartment above me who was the warden for a women's state correctional center. I asked everybody to please have their radios on tomorrow and listen for my interview at 6:00 a.m. Finally, the phone rang. It was disc jockey John Mason!

He was as jovial and excited as I was. He made the announcement, "Good Morning Deeeeetroit! This is your host, Mason in the morning. To those of you out listening in radio land, we have on the phone with us, Drum roll please...Emeline King. She's the first African American Female Car Designer for Ford Motor Company and she designed the 1989 Thunderbird. Wow! A female that designs cars. Guess what y'all? Home girl is from…DETROIT, THE MOTOR CITY! This is groundbreaking. Emeline, tell our listening audience how you got started."

I shared with Mason that when I was about eleven years old, I loved to draw. I had a passion for cars and all types of transportation. I dreamed that one day I'd work with my father at Ford. He influenced and introduced me to the auto industry as a child and exposed me to the art culture along with a talent group of black male car designers and modelers at Ford who all became my mentors. I shared the negative responses from a few male instructors in my early school days that because I was a girl, this goal was far out of my reach. "Girls can't design cars, trucks, boats, trains and planes! You should let the boys handle this and focus on fields that cater to females. Why don't you become a nurse or secretary?" I told Mason those remarks never sat well with me. I wouldn't let their male chauvinistic ideologies deter me. I moved forward and pursued a career in transportation design.

Mason asked, "So, tell us what cars you've designed that are out on the road?" I mentioned the 1989 Ford Thunderbird and Super Coupe. I was responsible for several designed interior components which included the corporate airbag steering wheel, center console, front and rear fascia nomenclature design and the entire wheel program. Mason asked, "I heard you designed cars while you were in Europe?" I told him, "Yes, I was fortunate to do three foreign assignments in Europe for Ford. I had one of the most exciting career opportunities where I worked and lived in Turin, Italy, Brentwood, Essex, England and visited the Ford Cologne Design Center in Germany. It was wonderful to experience and learn about the different cultures and indoctrinate their method of European design. There were a lot of historical places and things I read about Europe in my history books at school growing up as a child and a student in college, but it was through my career job at Ford that I was blessed to visit and witness these wonders."

Mason said, Emeline, what do you like most about designing cars? I told Mason my biggest joy as a designer was twofold. First, the gratification of seeing my concept, which started out as a thought on a two-dimensional piece of paper then transferred into a three- dimensional clay model to a full-production vehicle. Second, the joy of seeing the vehicle I designed driven on the streets by satisfied customers. Mason asked, "What would you like to leave with our listening audience?" I would tell youth everywhere and especially little girls who aspire to go into uncharted fields or territories that's far out of the norm to 'Go for your passion! If Emeline King did it, so can you! Don't ever let anyone or anything tear down, block, stop or destroy your dream goal. God placed mentors in your life who are your *bridges of support* to help and guide you to your dream destinations.'

I DESIGNED IT, SO I BOUGHT IT

I guess not too many people can say they purchased or drove the car they designed. The Ford 1989 Thunderbird would be the second car I purchased. It was dear to my heart because I designed the interior components and the entire wheel program. It was a manual shift. I ordered it in a special paint color for the exterior: light blue metallic with silver body side molding and charcoal grey cloth seat interior. I would often get compliments on the color combinations. When the 1990 Thunderbird made production, I ended up giving the 1989 Thunderbird to my mom. She loved it and was so proud to drive the car her daughter helped to design. The third vehicle I purchased was a Red 1990 Thunderbird Super Coupe. It, too, was manual shift. Unfortunately, it started out as a bad omen but in the end turned out satisfying.

I thought it be a great idea to support black-owned businesses and purchased my vehicle from a black owned car dealership. I researched black car dealership owners which was inspiring, historical and knowledgeable for me as a black female car designer in the auto industry. I learned that the first black man to own and manufactured cars was Frederick Douglass Patterson. He owned Patterson Motors over 100 years ago. His company in the 1800s was called C. R. Patterson and Sons. In 1915, he built the Patterson Greenfield Automobile. This vehicle was quite successful being that it competed with Henry Ford's Model T. There was Homer B. Roberts who opened the first African American owned car dealership in Kansas, City in 1923. Detroit was fortunate to have Mr. Edward Davis, the first black owned franchise car dealer, Davis Motor Sales. He started out as a salesman, but because he was black, he wasn't allowed to sell cars on the showroom floor. He had to sell cars from a second-floor location. Finally, in 1976, there was former Detroit Lions football player, Mel Farr, who became the number one, first black-owned auto dealer in Oak Park, Michigan. Learning about all these trailblazers was motivating.

I was making *good* money at Ford and had saved up enough funds for a large down payment to purchase my third car, the 1990 Thunderbird Super Coupe. I located a black owned dealership to make my purchase. When I walked in the dealership, a young African American salesman greeted me at the door. I told him I was interested in purchasing the 1990 Thunderbird Super Coupe.I mentioned I worked for Ford designing cars and I helped design this car. He asked me to come to his desk so I could place my order. I told him I wanted the exterior color to be candy apple red, black interior with black leather seats and 16-inch, five spoke cast alloy aluminum wheel. Fully loaded. Because I didn't want a high car note, I handed him a ten-thousand-dollar cashier's check for my down payment. After I completed my paperwork, the salesman placed the check, along with my papers, into the folder. He informed me that he would have to hold the check for at least two days and asked me to come back Friday to finish the final paper signing.

I returned on Friday and went to the front desk to ask the receptionist to page my salesperson. She told me, yes, she would page him and to please have a seat in the lobby. While I waited, the owner of the dealership walked past me and we politely spoke to each other. He then headed toward a long flight of stairs up to his office. It took a long time before my salesman returned. He finally came with my folder in his hand. He told me, "Ms. King, I have all your paperwork here all I need is your deposit? Surprised, I mentioned to him, what are you talking about? I handed you a ten-thousand-dollar cashier's check on Wednesday for my deposit because I wanted my car note to be low. I saw you when you placed it in my folder with my paper orders. So, now you're telling me you don't have my check? I told him," Sir, you need to find my check right now or pull some kind of magic trip out of your hat! We went back and forth arguing until I had enough and asked to see the owner. The salesperson told me the owner wasn't in. I knew that wasn't true because I just saw and spoke with the owner. Since I wasn't getting anywhere with the salesman, I left him standing there looking dumbfounded and headed upstairs to the owner's office. The salesman yelled and screamed for me to stop and not to go upstairs! "He ain't there", he said. I continued up the stairs and accidentally knocked over the life-sized stand-up poster of the owner near the entrance of the steps. When I reached the top of the stairs, I knocked on the door, which was partially open. The owner told me to come in. I walked in. He was seated in a black leather chair behind his large desk. I introduced myself and explained to him what just happened and asked how he could resolve this problem. He could tell I was emotional and highly upset. He informed me that he wasn't aware that this had happened; however, he would check into the matter ASAP, locate the check and contact me. The salesman never once came up into the office while I was there.

The next day, I was at work when I received a personal phone call from the owner who explained exactly what happened to my check. He informed me that the salesman deposited my cashier's check into his own personal account which violated company policies and because of his actions, that employee was fired and no longer worked for his dealership. The owner told me he was sorry that this happened and the money would be reimbursed. Later on that day, the salesman called me at work. He never mentioned anything about the check; however, he was livid that he got fired and that I caused it. Surely, he wasn't aware that I had just gotten off the phone with his boss, the dealership owner, who told me exactly what had happened. I informed the salesman, "Maybe, if you wouldn't have taken my check, followed your company procedures for checks and not placed it in your own personal account, number one, you would still be employed. Number two, you and I wouldn't even be having this conversation, now would we? Sir, I hope you have a wonderful, fantastic and marvelous day." I politely hung up the phone. I was reimbursed and looked for another dealership.

COVER UP: DAMAGED 1990 THUNDERBIRD SC CAR DOOR

I was determined to buy a Thunderbird. Hopefully this second attempt would be more successful than that last fiasco I experienced at the black-owned dealership. I told my Dad about my bad experience with the black-owned dealership, so he decided to go with me to purchase my Thunderbird at a different car dealership. My father suggested going to the one on Telegraph Road, even though it wasn't black owned. Dad had purchased a few vehicles from there and was quite satisfied with their service. He also had a friend, Benny, a former Ford employee, who worked in that dealership's body shop. Fortunately, I was able to order and purchase my car there. Regrettably, on the day I was scheduled to pick up my car that turned out to be one gigantic, revealing and shocking disappointment.

I received a phone call that morning from the salesperson who sold me the car. He informed me that it was in and ready for me to pick up. He said I should come by the dealership around noon. We arrived at the dealership my salesman appeared nervous and told us, "Your car is almost ready. It's getting prepped and washed. The porter will bring it around in a few minutes." I was all excited. Finally, I would be driving another car I designed. We waited in the lobby. Those few minutes turned into an hour and forty-five minutes.

Dad looked at his watch and suggested we walk around to the dealership's body shop and visit his friend Benny. We stepped into the shop and noticed Benny working on a brand new red 1990 Thunderbird SC. He had just applied some Bondo (a body filler product used for automotive, marine and household repairs) to an enormous hole located in the center of the driver's side door. I had met Benny a few years before through my Dad when I purchased my first car, a 1979 red base model Mustang Capri. I asked Benny to customize my base car into a sports kit package by adding a rear spoiler and front lower fascia. I wanted it to resemble my mentor and coworker Frank Wood's Mustang Capri RS. Frank taught me how to drive a manual shift on it. (He was the only African American male who worked in the wood shop department at the Design Center.)

Benny mentioned to Dad, "Man, I would have been home by now had they not brought in this Thunderbird for me to repair. The car's door had a big hole in it. It must have got damaged when they unloaded it off the truck today. I know they wanted it finished today by noon but, there's a lot of repair work to be done. I still have to let the Bondo completely dry, then sand the surface smooth and have the door painted. It will be ready tomorrow looking good as new. I'll call the salesperson and let him know."

Benny was a master at his craft of resurfacing, so much that one would never notice the car door had been damaged. Dad told Benny, "I sure hope that's not Emeline's Thunderbird you're working on. I somehow got a strange feeling that it is. You know she helped to design it." Benny said "Oh really, congratulations." Dad told Benny, "The salesman said everything was all set, that the car was getting washed and asked us to wait in the lobby for the porter to bring it around to us. He never mentioned anything about it had been damaged earlier and was being repaired in the body shop. Benny told dad, "Now that you mentioned it Mr. King, it might be Emeline's car. I do know this was the only candy apple red 1990 Thunderbird SC with black leather seat interior with the 16 inch five-spoke cast alloy aluminum wheel delivered here today.

Both Dad and I looked at each other. We were shocked and upset. I started to wonder was this another bad sign for me to not buy a Thunderbird. We returned to the lobby. The salesman approached us in a nervous tone he mentioned to me. "I'm sorry, Emeline the car isn't quite ready, could you mind coming back tomorrow and pick it up. Dad told him "Hell naw, we won't be coming back to get that car. You might as well cancel that order *rat nah* and refund my daughter. You wasn't going to tell her the car door had been damaged and just let her drive away in it? Sir, I really should report this, but I won't. Hopefully, you learned from this big mistake." The salesman was shocked. There was nothing he could say since he was dead wrong. I'm glad Dad was led by the Spirit to go visit his friend Benny who was honest enough to inform him what really happened to the car. We left the dealership with my full refund. I couldn't believe all this misfortune for a Thunderbird? A large piece of painted sheet metal, with a variety of components and materials, placed on four wheels that I contributed to in design, all to get me from point A to point B?

My third and final attempt was at one final dealership. Oh what a blessing! No problems, surprises, delays or mishaps. I purchased my 1990 Candy Apple Red Thunderbird Super Coupe with black leather interior with 16-inch five-spoke cast alloy aluminum wheels. I drove off that dealership's parking lot one happy and satisfied "designer" customer!

CHAPTER NINE
SHE EXPERIENCED IT

SO WHEN WILL SHE BE PROMOTED?

Out of all the personal experiences I have shared in my autobiography, this chapter is the most emotional and humiliating for me. I've carried these weighted, concerning questions in my head during my entire tenure at Ford. *What hindered me from a managerial promotion? Is there something wrong that I'm not doing? Why am I not granted a fast-track managerial career path like my coworkers? When or will I ever be promoted?* It caused me to wonder when I compared myself to my coworkers, both female and male car designers who were hired after me and received positions in middle and upper management within a short span after their service dates.

My achievements, credentials, education, and design contributions as a talented transportation designer who happens to be an African American female didn't qualify me 'enough' to be selected for a promotion into middle or upper management. I've designed profitable cars for Ford. My accomplishments were recognized in media publications, radio, and television. There have been numerous one on one meetings with Human Resources, middle and upper management where I expressed concerns to them about my career path. What are the qualifications for a designer candidate to advance to the next level in management? I would always be told the same responses over and over. "Emeline, you're doing a great, fantastic job. Keep it up. Nice designs that management selected to go into production. You're the lead designer on a successful car program. Emeline you been selected to speak on our behalf and represent Ford Design. Good leadership and team work etc." So, I'm thinking…if I'm doing a fantastic job from management's perspective and they have acknowledged my design contributions and work ethic then to still not consider me a candidate was certainly confusing and contradictory. One would assume a designer who showed leadership, good work ethic, dedication, design skills, performance reviews ratings of (O) outstanding, (EP) excellent plus and (E) excellent, along with talent and experience would be a prime candidate, but it never happened in my case.

DESIGN MANAGEMENT TEAM
DIVERSE NON-REPRESENTATION

I noticed after I got hired in at Ford in 1983 that they employed a diverse group of car designers, males and females from Asian, Lebanese, Italian, Arab American, Canadian, Korean, Hispanic, Chinese and Filipino descent. They got promoted to various positions as supervisors, design managers, chief designers and directors. I had been singled out when it came time to select and promote individuals for a middle or upper management position. It was always my coworkers who benefitted and advanced up the corporate ladder. My chances for any promotion remained dormant and stunted.

Now whether it was an oversight or negligence about selecting me for a position, the proof was in the pudding as to who got promoted and the make-up of the Design Center's middle and upper management team. It was diverse, but not complete. Within my twenty-five service years at Ford, there was never the representation of an African American female car designer in a management role. I frequently met with HR and management about my career path. I also shared concern about promotions and having the same privileges as those with less seniority. So when would this African American female car designer have representation on Ford's Design Center's "diverse" managerial staff?

This was the fifty-million-dollar question that was avoided and never happened. It was improbable that I wouldn't have representation. I traveled down Ford's corporate ladder while my coworkers steadily moved up. More concrete was poured onto my glass corporate ceiling hindering my advancement.

I'm glad I had a strong support system in my parents and family. They knew what I had encountered and encouraged me. "Emeline, you are too talented and gifted to waste time worrying about how you're being treated. You can be concerned, but don't worry over it. You channel your energy on designing the cars that will one day be mass produced and recognized all over the world. God is going to bless you. Your talents will get you the recognition and open many closed doors. Your background, drive and determination are something no one can take away from you. You still will shine in darkness. You can't help but be seen and acknowledged. God's strength is with you…just keep trusting Him. You might give out, but never give up, Emeline." I took Mama's and Dad's advice and proceeded with a different outlook. My father reminded me to continue to keep a record and write down everything that I had experienced. I added it to my daily journal. I didn't know the reason behind Dad's request and how it would come in handy one day. I've always been obedient and followed my parent's advice.

MORE MERITS GIVEN RATHER THAN A MANAGERIAL PROMOTION?

Prior to my Foreign Service Assignments in England, I was at salary grade 6. I worked in the Specialty Midsize Studio where I designed interior components and the wheel program for the Ford 1990 Thunderbird and Super Coupe, which turned out successful. The car made production and was awarded Motor Trend's Car of the Year. After returning from my Foreign Assignment on December 12, 1989, I received my first promotion to salary grade 7 (rated 8.1%). Although I was thankful for my promotion, I still looked to be promoted into management after doing my Foreign Service Assignment just like my coworkers who had served a Foreign Service Assignment prior to me going over to England and was promoted into management after their return.

Unfortunately for me, there was no promotion, even though I had three Foreign Service Assignments under my belt: Italy, England and Germany. I continued to make design contributions toward successful production cars. One would assume Foreign Assignments carried some clout and would move me up the corporate ladder fast, but no. However, on July 1, 1991, I received a merit increase of 7.0% though I still held a salary grade 7. Disappointed that I didn't get promoted, I addressed my concerned with Human Resources after learning about other coworkers who returned from just one Foreign Assignment and were promoted. Shouldn't I be given the same treatment? Especially, after I completed three Foreign Service Assignments.

ONE SALARY GRADE AWAY, THEN MANAGEMENT?

It wasn't until March 16, 1993 that I was promoted to salary grade 8 (exempt). My design contributions on the 1994 Mustang turned out to be a huge success for me with high hopes of me being promoted into management. A designer had to be ranked salary grade 9 for a promotion into middle management. Finally, I was one salary grade away from being eligible. All of this came to a crashing end when Human Resources notified the change in their promotional eligibility into management. Salary Grade 9 was dropped and replaced by a new management level: LL5 and LL6 (formerly grade levels 9 and 10). Unfortunately, I remained at pay grade 8, received a few merit increases and then was transferred to the Truck Studio.

SALARY GRADES AND MERIT INCREASES

I documented everything...merits increases and promotions. This was something that my father insisted that I do from the beginning of my employment at Ford. I hired in as a general salary (GSR) pay grade level 5 and it was two years later in August 1987 when I received my first promotion to salary grade 6. After completing my first Foreign Service assignment in Dunton, England, I was promoted to grade 7. The 1989 Thunderbird made production and on July 1, 1991, I received a merit increase rate of 7.0%. Then on October 1, 1991, I received my highest increase ever, a merit increase rate 12.9%. Receiving this merit really caused me to question Human Resources on not being promoted into management especially when the maximum rate was 7% which was the highest to be given and I received 12.9%.

After successfully completing the 1994 Mustang, holding the responsibilities as lead designer and portraying managerial skills, I assumed I would be promoted into middle management, especially, after finding out that my manager made design executive. Not to mention, I worked with some male coworkers who worked on the program for just a short term and were promoted to middle management. What a slap in my face! On March 16, 1993, I received a promotion to Designer A, salary Grade 8 (exempt). From then on I received only merit increases and remained at this grade level until Ford let me go on a company involuntary separation.

EMELINE'S PROMOTIONS, MERITS INCREASES, AND SALARY GRADE LEVELS

10/24/1983	Hired in at (GSR) Salary Grade 5
8/1/1987	Promotion 7.5% Salary Grade 6
12/12/1989	Promotion 8.1% Salary Grade 7
7/1/1991	Merit Increase 7.0%
10/1/1992	Merit Increase 12.9 % (EXCEEDS THE MAXIMUM MERIT OF 7%)
3/16/1993	Promotion 8.0% Salary Grade 8 (exempt)
4/1/1994	Merit Increase 8.3% Salary Grade 8 (exempt)
4/1/1995	Merit Increase 4.6%. Salary Grade 8 (exempt)
10/24/1995	Offered Voluntary Retirement Package (12th Anniversary)
4/1/1996	Merit Increase 2.1% Salary Grade 8 (exempt)
4/1/1998	Merit Increase 4.1% Salary Grade 8 (exempt)
4/1/2001	Offered Voluntary Retirement Package (18th Anniversary)
2002 - 2006	Salary Grade 8 (exempt)
2007 - 2008	Transferred out of Design Phase to Brand Marketing Department: Program Benchmarking
FINAL STATUS	Designer A classification
JULY 30, 2008	Involuntary Company Separation

FORD DESIGN CENTER'S FEMALE TRANSPORTATION DESIGNERS

OUR DIFFERENCES STILL DIDN'T QUALIFY ME FOR MANAGEMENT

Although we shared common bonds by being female Ford employees who worked as transportation designers in a male dominant industry designing vehicles in the Design Center for the auto industry, we also had things that set us apart. The things which set us apart was more than enough to place me in the same managerial status as my colleagues. All of the female car designers who hired in after me were promoted into managerial positions. I was the only female transportation designer, and the only African American, who didn't.

Our differences occurred in our educational background, number of service years (seniority), ethnicities, design contributions that made production, program leadership, Foreign Service Assignments and designer classification (general salary grade level), upper or middle management position (design manager, chief designer or director). Being equipped and processing all these key elements would heighten a designer's movement up the corporate ladder into managerial positions; however, it wasn't the case for me, a well-qualified African American female transportation designer.

EDUCATION: WELL BALANCED AND DIVERSE

Since I had chosen to go into the field of Transportation Design, it was most important that I obtained a well-rounded and balanced education. My educational background training was diverse. Mentored by the famous African American sculptor, Mr. Oscar Graves, I graduated from the top accredited high school, university and college for the arts and transportation design. I attended Cass Technical High School in Detroit, Michigan. I attended Wayne State University in Detroit, Michigan where I received my Bachelor of Fine Arts in Industrial Design. Besides taking my full-time academics and art courses, I was enrolled in evening classes for Transportation Design, which was taught by Ford employee, Ted Finney (a program Ford established with Wayne State where students got one-on-one training with a professional designer to learn the fundamentals of transportation design in the auto industry). I was referred by my mentor Sam Mayers and enrolled in a Saturday morning transportation design course at the Center for Creative Studies in Detroit, Michigan. The course was taught by one of General Motors' top designers, Ron Sims. I shall never forget the professional teaching, training, guidance and direction that I received from Sam Mayers, a seasoned design manager at Ford.

I obtained a Bachelor of Science Degree in Transportation Design at the Art Center College of Design in Pasadena, California. Because of my prior art background experience, I was given advance standing and completed Art Center's program in 18 months. My instructors were the top experts and best in their fields of art and transportation design. In comparison to some of my colleague's education, they attended the following schools:

- One attended Art Center College of Design in Pasadena, California

- Two attended the Center for Creative Studies in Detroit, Michigan

- One attended the Cleveland School of the Arts in Cleveland, Ohio

- One attended the Ontario College of Art and Design in Ontario, Canada

SENIORITY

In 1970, the Ford Design Center hired its first female designer who was Canadian. Thirteen years later in 1983, they hired me, the first female African American car designer. It wasn't until 1987 that Ford hired a Hispanic female designer, a former General Motors designer. In 1990, a Korean female designer was hired, followed by another Hispanic and a Chinese designer. Lastly, in 1998, a Caucasian female came on board who was also a former Chrysler designer. Between the years of 1970 through 1999, there were only twelve female transportation designers at Ford, all employed at the Design Center. They were from the following races/ethnicities: one African American, one Canadian, five Caucasians, one Chinese, one Filipino, two Hispanics and one Korean. Only six were promoted into both upper and middle management. Five female designers left Ford to go work for other auto companies or pursue other interests. I acquired the most seniority with the number of Ford service years of all the other female designers with the exception of the one Canadian female designer; however, I remained the only female designer at the GSR salary level and was never promoted into management.

EMELINE'S DESIGN CONTRIBUTIONS THAT MADE PRODUCTION

- Program MN12 - Ford Thunderbird, Ford Thunderbird Super Coupe
- 1989 Thunderbird LX Wheel Program Line up:15-inch base wheel cover and 16 inch five-spoke cast alloy aluminum wheel
- 1989 Interior Components Center Console Ford Thunderbird
- 1989 Nomenclature "THUNDERBIRD SC" Design for the Ford Thunderbird Super Coupe
- 1989 Wheel & Wheel cover Program Ford Thunderbird Super Coupe
- 1990 Probe Base Wheel cover
- 1992 Ford Corporate Air Bag Steering Wheel (Used on 1993 Thunderbird, Cougar, and Mark VIII and the Mustang Mach III Concept Car Interior)
- Program SN94 1994 Mustang Fourth Generation
- Interior Small Car Specialty Mustang
- Female Oriented Design concepts incorporated in 1994 Mustang Design
- Mustang Seat Designs: Base cloth seat, Sport leather seat
- Mustang Official Pace Car Graphics, and roll bar design for the 79th Indianapolis 500 Speed Way, May 29, 1994
- 2000 Two-Seater Thunderbird interior components
- 2002 Lincoln Town Car interior components
- 2002 Stretch Lincoln Limousine Rear Luxury Package Design
- 2004 Lincoln Aviator Door Scuff Plates with featured "LINCOLN" stainless steel nomenclature design
- 2005 Ford Five Hundred/ Freestyle Production Show Cars
- 2013-2016 Lincoln MKZ Overhead Center Console

EMELINE'S LIST OF STUDIO PROGRAMS AND DESIGN CONTRIBUTIONS

Date(s)	Program/Contribution	Notes
October 1983 – August 1984	FN10, Sierra G International Studio Exterior Studio Program	
September 1984 – December 1984	Ghia Spa	Foreign Service in Turin, Italy
January 1985 – April 1985	Advance Concept Interior	
May 1985 – June 1985	Small Car Interior Studio	
July 1985 – August 1986	Specialty Midsize Exterior Studio Program MN12 Thunderbird, Wheel Program 16" Alloy Aluminum Wheel, 15" Wheel Cover	My First Car Design (1989 Thunderbird Super Coupe) Made Production My Fist Patented Wheel Cover
September 1986 – December 1986	Specialty Midsize Interior Studio Program, Corporate Airbag Steering Wheel, Interior Components Center Console	
January 1987 – August 1987	Small Car Interior Studio Program ST44 Probe Base 14" Wheel Cover	Designer on loan to studio
August 1987 – March 1989	SUB B Interior/Exterior	Foreign Service – Dunton, England
April 1989 – December 1990	Mustang Interior	

June 1989 – July 1989	Small Car Interior 1993 Probe 15" Wheel Patent Design	Designer on loan to studio
July 1989 – December 1989	Midsize Specialty Car Interior and 1994 MN12 Thunderbird	Designer on loan to studio
January 1990 – March 1990	Small Car Interior	
April 1989 – December 1990	Mustang Interior SN95 Ford Corporate Airbag Steering Wheel	
January 1990 – December 1990	Mustang Interior Studio Program – Mach III Concept Car	
January 1991 – December 1993	SN95 Mustang and SN95 Mustang Interior	Co-located Team Danau Technical Center
January 1994 – December 1994	Truck Studio Ranger Program	
January 1995 – April 1997	Transit Truck	
October 25, 1995	12th Anniversary	Offered Voluntary Retirement
April 1997 – March 1999	M205 Thunderbird Two-Seater Convertible	
2000	FN10 Lincoln Town Car – Stretch Limousine Luxury Package	
2001	15th Anniversary – DN101	Offered Voluntary

	FN45 Program	Retirement
2007	Brand Marketing Department: Program Benchmarking	Transferred out of Design Phase
July 30, 2008		Involuntary Company Separation

MIDSIZE LUXURY INTERIOR STUDIO

I left the Truck Studio in 1997 and transferred to the Small Car Specialty Studio. I stayed in that studio from April 1997 until March 30, 1999, where I continued to design concepts that made production. I was assigned to work on the M205 program, the 2000 Thunderbird convertible hard top two-seater, another one of Ford's iconic vehicles. It was exciting to make design contributions toward the interior and exterior. Learning about the Thunderbird's history gave me insight on maintaining the Thunderbird brand image when it came to design.

2000 THUNDERBIRD TWO-SEATER M205 GOES HOLLYWOOD

One big, successful milestone for the 2000 Thunderbird occurred when the James Bond movie "Ice Castle" made its debut. I wanted to go see it because the Ford Thunderbird was in it. One scene shows a tangerine colored two-door 2000 Thunderbird driving up to the ice castles. The driver's side door opens and out steps actress Halle Berry wearing a sharp, black leather two-piece suit. I felt proud that I was a part of the team that designed that vehicle.

MIDSIZE LUXURY INTERIOR
FN10 LINCOLN TOWN CAR INTERIOR
STRETCH LIMO LUXURY PACKAGE

After I left the Small Car Specialty Studio, I transferred to the Midsize Luxury Studio and then onto the Large Car Luxury Studio where several design production contributions for the FN10 Lincoln Town Car were designed. My responsibility was to design the "rear seat luxury package" for the stretch Lincoln Town Car Limousine. The stretch limo Lincoln Town car interior luxury package was exciting to work on I was responsible for designing the fold down tray and rear center seat console.

For this program I spent the majority of my time directing several design components at an outside vendor shop where they customized stretch limousines. I had to design and oversee the development of several interior components for the rear seat luxury package which involved modifying the back of the front seats to contain a designed fold down tray made out of a mahogany wood. The rear seat center console depicted a cup/napkin/pen holder set and other small luxury amenities.

2004 LINCOLN AVIATOR INTERIOR DOOR SCUFF SILL PLATES WITH FEATURED NOMENCLATURE DESIGN

Influenced by the monogram method, I thought it would be a great idea to incorporate the Lincoln's name on the interior door scuff sill plate. It was an embossed raised graphic stainless steel metal plate design. When you opened the door and looked down, you would see the signature nomenclature design brand name 'Lincoln' embossed on the silver brushed finished plate, a design theme currently used on Lincoln's today. It can be seen on the 2002 Lincoln MKZ, and also was used on Ford Lincoln vehicle models between 2013 and 2016.

I also contributed in design to other Ford production vehicles:

- FREESTYLE PRODUCTION SHOW CAR (2003 NAIAS)

- 2005 FORD FIVE HUNDRED: Interior Components

FOREIGN SERVICE ASSIGNMENTS

Prior to all the females who hired in at Ford after me, I had already designed some cars that made production and had served three Foreign Service Assignment stints. My first Foreign Service Assignment was for three months (August 1984 until December 1984) in Ford's Ghia Studio in Turin, Italy. Even after I returned home from my second Foreign Service Assignment at Ford of Europe's Design Research and Engineering Center in Essex, England and the Ford Design Center in Cologne, Germany (December 1987 through December 1989), there was no change in my salary grade status and no promotion.

PUBLIC RELATIONS

I was involved with several Ford public relation events where I was selected to do public speaking and design presentation on Ford products. I made design contributions on behalf of Ford management at major design events including the 1994 national conference for the Industrial Designers of America (IDSA), 1994 North American International Auto Show (NAIAS), the 1994 Mustang Blitz's Market Research event, AT&T Engineers Week, Wake Forest University in Winston Salem, North Carolina and the University of Michigan in Ann Arbor, Michigan. It was at the request from my former alma mater, Art Center in Pasadena, California, that I was the commencement speaker for the graduating class of 1995.

AWARDS

- Dollars and $ense Fastrak Award – 1992

- Spirit of Detroit Award – May 20, 1993

- Spirit of Ford Sculpture Contest Winner – October 22, 1998

MULTIMEDIA COVERAGE

- Ebony Magazine

- Essence Magazine

- Smithsonian

- Executive Female

- Dollars & $ense

- Road & Track

- Michigan Chronicle

- Chicago Tribune

- WCHB AM 1440 Radio

- CBS Morning Show – September 1991

- Good Morning America – January 1994

- North American International Auto Show

DESIGN CENTER FEMALE DESIGNERS GET PROMOTED

Three female designers (Canadian, Caucasian and Filipino) who came from Chrysler made upper management at the director level. Three females (Chinese, Hispanic and Korean) who came from General Motors made middle management as design managers. My one goal and remaining regret is that I was never granted a promotion into management, even after 24.9 years of service at the Ford Design Center. The only reward for all of my numerous successful achievements and accomplishments was more merit increases that affected my salary grade level. I started out with a salary grade 5 and ended my tenure with a salary grade 8 (exempt), Designer A classification. Unfortunately, the worst devastation of my career happened on July 30, 2008. I became the only female transportation designer to be given an involuntary company separation. It hurt, but it didn't crush me. I rose up from my misfortune, dusted myself off, jumped in my ride, took another detour and drove toward a better, brighter and promising future destination.

DESIGN CENTER'S FEMALE DESIGNER'S CAMARADERIE

On one occasion, the top female design director over global trim and color, hosted a going away dinner at a restaurant in Royal Oak, Michigan. It was planned for one of the visiting Asian female designers who worked in the color and trim department at the Design Center. She was on Foreign Service Assignment and would be returning home to Japan. The director invited a few of the female designers, modelers, engineers who worked at the Design Center to the event. It was a beautiful affair. We all had a chance to socialize and learn something new, personal and exciting about each other that we didn't know outside of our work environment at Ford.

The top female director also showed her hospitality on another social occasion and invited us to her beautiful home. I thought it was commendable that all of us chose this unique field within the auto industry to design cars at Ford. I admired and looked up to the director, especially for her successful career path. She had reached one of the highest positions for a female designer at Ford Design Center, next to becoming the president of design. When I first hired in, I would have loved to have been mentored under her wings and guidance. I'm thankful God had rams in the bushes for me through my special mentor, Sam, the black modelers and co-workers at Ford, and my father who was there to lead and guide me as I traveled through a dark and uncertain bumpy road.

SIMILAR CAREERS, DIFFERENT PROMOTIONAL OUTCOME

Mimi Vandermolen, the top female design executive at Ford as director over Global Color and Trim, reached the highest milestone for a female in the auto industry at

Ford's Design Center. Our career paths were identical and we shared similarities since we both were *firsts* as female transportation designers. We set the road maps for other females to follow. I was the first African American female to study transportation and graduate from the Art Center School of Design in Pasadena, California. She was the first woman to study industrial design at the Ontario's College of Art and Design.

Photo by Dan Murray

Female reporters queue up to take a spin in the new 1993 Ford Probe, a car Ford marketers expect will strongly appeal to women.

committee also provides a speaker's bureau so employees can talk to professional and civic groups. And a training videotape on how to sell effectively to female customers was developed and distributed to dealerships, with the help of the committee.

Burns said there is no one item that "fits" the women's market. "There has been a sales effort to understand what it is women are looking for," she said. "But in many ways, it's just like what men want. When we design a product that fits women, we will satisfy men also."

Emeline King, product designer, Ford North American Design, said Ford designers are spending more time now considering the specific needs of women drivers.

"Many of these needs are based on simple physical differences between men and women," said King. "Women are proportionately shorter in the legs than men and have longer torsos. By designing as we do at Ford, for the fifth to 95th percentile of the population, we are able to satisfy a very large audience."

King said women will enjoy the Probe's soft interior and its ergonomically driven cockpit, with components and instruments located in well-organized, functional groups oriented toward the driver. The Probe also has seats that conform to the body and provide consistent support along the back, seat and thighs.

I worked on the 1994 Mustang. She worked on the redesign of the 1974 Mustang II exterior and interior and the 1979 Granada. After being promoted in 1979 to foreign specialist, she led the interior team on the Taurus 1986 family sedan. In 1987, she was promoted to the position of design executive for small cars, overseeing interior and exterior design developments in North American, a first for a woman in the automotive industry. I had recently finished designing the corporate wheel interior components for the MN12 1989 Thunderbird/Thunderbird SC, 1989-wheel program for the MN12 Thunderbird and a patented 15-inch base wheel cover. After seeing how successful my wheel program turned out, it was at her request that I go on loan to her studio and help design the base Probe 15-inch base wheel cover for her ST44 program. It was an honor to have been asked to work on her program.

 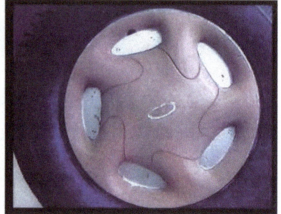

We both were lead interior designers for successful design programs from start to finish. She was over the 1993 Ford Probe program[3]. I was over the 1994 Ford Mustang. We both incorporated from a female view and prospective certain design components into our vehicles that would cater specifically to the female buying market. We both had experienced Foreign Service Assignments. Our accomplishments were recognized by management. Over my career span, I received merit and salary increases instead of promotions into design specialist, design manager, chief designer and director. When I compared the list of our similarities and accomplishments in design, I questioned, "Ummm, why haven't I gotten promoted?"

SAME PROJECT, SAME RESPONSIBILITIES
MUSTANG MACH III CONCEPT CAR

When it came time for promotions amongst the group of diverse male designers and me, there were several occurrences which lead me to believe male chauvinism existed in the auto design industry. Females are better off placed in an interior design studio designing interiors versus holding a management leadership position making authoritative decisions. Before I left for my second Foreign Service Assignment in England in 1988, two coworkers, both Caucasian males, returned from the same Foreign Service Assignment and were promoted to design managers in 1987 and the other in 1989. It occurred again in the Small Car Specialty Interior Studio. I worked on the same program with another designer. We basically performed identical roles of following the development of the 1994 Mustang Mach III concept car, but it wasn't until our design manager got transferred to another studio program that he was replaced by my coworker who was promoted in 1990 to design manager over the Mach III program.

Although I remained at a designer general salary grade level throughout my involvement on the 1994 Mustang Mach III Concept Car from January 1990 until December 1990. It was rewarding to be the designer selected by management to represent them on their behalf whenever I traveled and made numerous press release presentations. I spoke on the design development process for the Mustang Mach III concept vehicle at various public events. I traveled to Denver, Colorado in September 1993 to present the Mach III at the Denver International Airport opening.

There was a beautiful display of aircraft carriers with a stealth plane on board to serve as a backdrop for the Mach III, while I talked about how it was designed. In June 1993, I spoke at the Society of Women Engineers convention (SWE) in Chicago, Illinois and on April 4, 1993, In July 1993, I spoke for the SN95 long lead process at the Dearborn Proving Grounds in Dearborn, Michigan.

AFRICAN AMERICAN MALE DESIGNERS
ACHIEVEMENTS IN MANAGEMENT

There were a total of twelve black male designers who hired in from 1956 through 2000, six of whom made it into middle and upper management. Prior to my hiring in 1983, only two African American male car designers were a part of Ford Design Center's management staff. McKinley Thompson, historically the first African American male transportation designer in the auto industry, was hired by Ford in September 1956 and promoted to manager of the Appearance Development and Feasibility Design Modeling Department in 1976. He retired in 1984, a year after I hired in. It was an honor to meet him in that short time. The second designer to make management was my mentor, Sam Mayers, who hired in 1966, and was later promoted to Design Manager. He was a veteran of thirteen years. Another designer who hired in 1967, was Nehemiah Amaker, a General Salary Role (GSR) designer who retired in 1998. If one could bet the next African American designer to move into a managerial position based on seniority, I probably would have been next in line.

In 1984, another African American made design specialist. One more hired in 1985 and later was promoted to design manager. Another male who was hired in 1985, was promoted to design manager in December 1999 and then to Chief Designer in 2000. Finally, another male designer made chief designer in 2000. I remained at designer status General Salary Role.

RANGER TRUCK EXTERIOR STUDIO:
EMOTIONAL, LOW PERFORMANCE RATING

After completing the SN95 Mustang Program, I got transferred to the Ranger Truck Exterior Studio in January 1994 and was there until December 1994. My experience in that studio was a real emotional blow, starting with the transfer over to truck instead of a promotion for my involvement on the 94 Mustang. Second, what took place prior to my move in December of 1993 and what occurred after, I believe caused me to miss my chance to make management due to an unfairly rated low performance review.

There were two Caucasian, general salary level male designers assigned to work on the Ranger truck program with me, one of whom worked with me previously on the SN95 Mustang project. Our manager was an African American male hired in 1985, two years after I was hired. He was promoted to design manager in December 1993, a milestone accomplishment as the third black design manager in middle management. In January of 1994, he was appointed manager of the Ranger Truck Exterior Studio.

My manager arranged for me to take the training course: *Introduction to Computer Aided Design*. I would later use this new technique along with my skills of 2D concept sketching and rendering towards the Ranger Program. I can't recall if the other designers had taken this course prior to my transfer to this studio. The training course was a challenge and required the majority of my time away from the studio. I spent hours after work to become efficient with this new system of designing. My manager was well skilled with this program. Eventually, I was able to comprehend and apply it. After I completed the course, each designer in the studio was given their performance reviews. I received my lowest performance review ever…satisfactory minus (SM)! I was placed on probation and transferred out to another truck studio, International Transit from January 1995 until December 1996.

The two Caucasian male coworkers received managerial promotions. Personally, I don't know what they were rated, but I'm assuming they had to have been rated high with possibly, an excellent plus (EP) or outstanding (O) or something *special* to get promoted into middle management.

I was hurt, embarrassed and disappointed with my rating. I shared what I'd experienced with Sam, my mentor. He informed me on several occasions as a design manager that he advised, helped and directed those who may have needed extra assistance. In the end, it benefitted the designer, strengthen their design skills and better equipped them to apply new technologies which resulted in high performances ratings. Sam was a talented, gifted transportation designer who mentored many African American designers at Ford, other companies and practically anybody who aspired a career in transportation design throughout the auto industry. I remembered many hours spent down in Sam's basement as he advised me as a young aspiring female transportation designer. He showed me rendering techniques, transportation design and all what is needed to be a well-accomplished designer.

On one occasion, Sam shared how a Ford African American male designer who recently got promoted came to him for his assistance and advice on being a design manager. Sam informed me about a cultural bond that existed between male and female designers of the same ethnicities. They looked out for each other and helped one another. Now whether it was done through mentoring, some kind of buddy system, or just friendly camaraderie, in the end, this bonding helped many designers to improve or solve any problem they faced. It helped expedite their flight up the corporate ladder into management. Sam suggested, "Wezzy, the mire fact that you were both African American, and a talented car designer, there was no reason or excuse why you received a low rating or even was set up to fail.

Between the years of 1993 through 2002, there was an influx of promotions for designers into middle and upper management. The majority of male designers at the Design Center achieved levels from design manager, chief designer to director. Thirteen male designers, all of different ethnicities, were promoted into both middle and upper management: four chief designers and nine design managers. They hired in after me. Some even worked in the same studio and on the same programs and projects with me. I was happy for my colleagues who were selected for high achievements in their careers. I looked forward to the day when management would select me. I thought my pre- and post-accomplishments would have a proven leadership role. One can only imagine how I felt.

MY CLAIM TO GLORY: THE 1994 MUSTANG

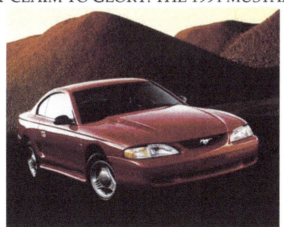

I was in the Small Car Specialty Studio when I made an appointment to talk with one of Design Center's executives. Prior meetings with HR and management indicated that my design contributions on Ford products which made production, my leadership skills, foreign service stints, my seniority and salary grade level wasn't enough to promote me into management. I needed to know exactly what more did I need to achieve or do? I thought my track record had proven that I was capable and qualified. So what does management looks for in a designer to consider them for managerial?

I shared my thoughts and concerns with the design executive. He suggested, "Emeline, I will tell you what you lack and what management looks for. You need to be on a "hot" program where you're recognized as the "lead designer" for that program and responsible for following the program from start to finish. Management needs to relate a face or designer's name with that program. That's how you get promoted. That's how you're in the loop of things." I listened and seriously gave thought to what he told me. I thanked him for such honest advice because in all of my meetings with management, I never was privy to this information. I told my design executive, "Yes, that sounds like something I want to and could accomplish but, the problem is I'm never the designer who gets selected to work on or even be considered for 'hot' programs." He suggested there might be something coming down the pipeline and he would keep me in mind. I left his office and strongly considered what he said. I was determined to work on the next hot program. If HR and Management wasn't coming down the mountain to choose Emeline for their next big, hot project, then certainly I would hike myself up there and ask.

I prayed about it. I strongly believed God heard my request and granted it. Fortunately, my opportunity came sooner than I thought…just a week later. It was during our Monday morning staff meeting when my manager informed the studio about Ford's marketing department and upper management's plans for a new 1994 Mustang design project: a totally revamped design of the American iconic car, the 1964 Mustang. It would debut in January 1994 at the North American International Auto Show (NAIAS) held at Cobo Hall in Downtown Detroit. SN95 would be the program's code name for the 1994 Mustang. He listed the Mustang's objectives and discussed in detail what would be involved with the program. He concluded the meeting with saying it was going to be a historic and hot program. Bingo! I sat there thinking, "Hallelujah, that's all I needed to hear". Today would be the right time and my moment to work on an exciting, hot car program. It's my opportunity to gain management recognition and possible a promotion based off of my design executive's advice.

After the meeting, I approached my manager and informed him that I would like the opportunity to work on the SN95 Mustang special program. He informed me that they needed a skeleton work team of designers to just "start the project off" in its beginning phase and would later select other designers to come on board and finish the project. They would be assigned to work in an offsite facility, the Roush Warehouse in Allen Park, Michigan. I immediately let him know I was interested with one exception. I wanted to follow and stay on the SN95 program from concept to finished production, or basically until the vehicle rolls off the assembly line into the dealership showrooms for the public to purchase.

As a female designer, I had something I wanted to contribute to this design project, especially designing from a female perspective. This vehicle would tap into the female market more and increase sales for the Mustang, something that probably hadn't been considered or top priority for the SN95 program. I definitely wanted to see the project through. Thank you, Jesus, my prayers were answered and I was assigned to work on the SN95 Mustang program.

The SN95 team relocated to the Roush Warehouse in January 1990 which was converted into the Danau Technical Center Design Center Studio in Allen Park, Michigan. I never imagined my design contributions and leadership role on the SN95 project would be my catalyst for unlimited opportunities and more exposure of my talents. I was the only female designer assigned to work on the interior. The majority of the male designers worked on the exterior. It was important prior to the sketching and theme selection phase of the program to familiarize the design team, management, and marketing with the design history behind the Mustang.

In order for one to know what the future design of the SN94 Mustang would look like, it was important to show pictorially where the history of the Mustang had been. I organized and displayed a series of 8 ft. x 5 ft. image boards that included pictorial images of the Ford Mustang's exterior and interiors arranged in chronological order from year 1964 to the current model year. It showed all the Mustang's design clues which supported the brand although they had been modified down through the years. Three design clues in particular were the C-scoop in the side door panels, the three-bar rear taillight design and the galloping horse graphic emblem depicted in the front honeycomb grille pattern instead of the blue Ford oval.

With more assignments being added to complete the program from management, I was given more responsibilities which resulted in me taking on designing for both the interior and some exterior components. I worked effectively with other design departments like in fabrication where my father worked. On several occasions, I had to go check on the status of a Mustang part. I watched him take part in making molds for both the interior and exterior fiberglass body. As the lead designer, teamwork is always the top priority when it comes to working with the various departments: design studio, engineering; fabrication shops: plaster, metal, wood, paint, and marketing. With clear, precise directions and good timing, each department is given time to complete the various elements of the vehicle to meet one's deadlines. In the end, teamwork produced an accomplished team which crafted a functional fiberglass show model designed on time for any scheduled and last-minute reviews where management needed it *yesterday*.

INTERIOR DESIGN 1994 MUSTANG

There were a lot of interior design components for which I was responsible: the instrument panel, cluster graphics, door panels, headliner, steering wheel, center console, and seat program (the base cloth and sport leather high series). I worked closely with modelers on the development of the design concepts for both the door and instrument panel, incorporating user friendly hardware and other interior trim components like the headliner and flooring. I was accountable for designing the seat program. I coincided with the color and trim department on the selection of fabrics for the seats and the door trim, etc. The Engineered seat packaging was needed to design for seat comfort and excellent ergonomic enhanced features. The seat appearance represented quality fabric material for the base and sports model vehicles. Market research surveys were used to test for seat comfort levels and ratings on the seat's design appearance. I followed the design and worked closely with Lear seat suppliers to develop and manufacture underneath seat structure and selection of the best foam density. There was much involved not only on the design side of the Mustang, but on the manufacturing side, too. It required visits to vendors, dye shops, and plants (in Saline and Chesterfield, Michigan), to check quality and approve parts like dye molds and gaps for the Mustang interior and exterior components.

The whole Mustang interior cockpit theme was designed to create a friendly and inviting sporty environment and give one the feeling of being in the comfort of their home. Special attention was given on the doors to be designed using soft touch feel buttons and control knobs. These elements, including the paint texture, were all designed with the female buying market in mind. It was important as a female designer to incorporate elements that would cater specifically to women's needs and concerns within the automobile like the ease of entry and exiting the vehicle in a dress, short skirt, long evening gown, coat or high heels. I designed the door handles, shift knob, radio control buttons and steering wheel to have a smooth, soft touch with rounded edges so upon usage they wouldn't break a fingernail, snag a pair of stockings, rip a skirt, break a heel or get their clothes caught in the pedal. It was important to have a secure place to store a purse and select the right type of seat fabric material that wouldn't cause friction from different clothing material upon contact from the occupant. The seat fabric texture and surface needed to prevent packages or a purse from sliding forward and off the seat onto the floor when the vehicle came to a sudden stop.

The brand marketing department for decades considered the image of the Mustang as "the ultimate male macho machine", but that image changed and was improved once I came on board designing from a female perspective with a touch of "feminine elegance."

THE OFFICIAL PACE CAR
78TH INDIANAPOLIS MOTOR SPEEDWAY INDY 500

**1994 OFFICIAL
PACE CAR UNVEILING
December 29, 1993**

When the 1994 convertible top Mustang was selected as the pace car for the 78th Indianapolis Motor Speedway Indy 500, I designed the exterior car graphics and did design modifications for the roll bar. Ford flew me and one of my coworkers down to Indianapolis where we worked together and applied the finished design stencil graphics to the official pace car. We toured the famous racetrack which was breath taking and visited the Indianapolis Motor Speedway Museum which was filled with historic race cars from the past to present. There was a Mustang Pace Car press release party we attended. Since I had been on this program, I had now served in the capacity of a design manager. Internally, I worked my way up from being on the skeleton team to lead designer following both the Mustang SN95 interior and exterior. I'm glad I followed my design executive's advice and did not throw in the towel or gave up. With determination and commitment I became the face of the 1994 Mustang.

WHAT DO YOU MEAN A BLACK GIRL CAN'T DESIGN CARS?

ABUNDANCE OF BLESSINGS FALL ON ME

Cover Story: FACES BEHIND THE NEW FORD MUSTANG

The hottest new car for 1994 is? You guessed it — the all-new Ford Mustang. It's the car's first major revision since the Mustang created an American frenzy when it was introduced to the public at the New York World's Fair in 1964.

After 30 years, Ford has recaptured the style of the original pony car, infused it with modern technology, to create a car that attracts the young and old, men and women alike and has "muscle car" enthusiasts honking their horns.

The '94 Ford Mustang, which went on sale in December, hopes to rekindle the nostalgia that resulted in 263,434 sales in '64 and more than one million between '65 and '66.

Behind the $700 million dollar project are African-American men and women who were instrumental in the planning, design and construction of the new vehicle. These are the people whose contributions rarely receive attention, although you may spend everyday of your life driving around in their craftsmanship.

Their employer, the Ford Motor Company, is one of the most integrated corporations. African-Americans make up 16% of the 325,333 persons employed by the automotive giant.

Some of the African-Americans who played a major role in the development of the new Mustang offer their thoughts on the new car....

In our cover stories "African Americans On Wheels" will feature ranking executives employed by the auto industry; as well as, engineers, designers, and electricians. In future issues, we will feature Roy Roberts, general manager of GMC Truck; Jerry Florence, vice president of Marketing at Nissan; Elliot Hall, vice president at Ford; and many others.

EMELINE KING, leader of the Interior Design Team for the New Mustang, says "it's history that makes this car unique." King's task was to change history by taking a once muscular car and making it attractive enough for women. King became intrigued with Mustangs when she first saw one at the age of 13 at a California auto show.

LOU CALLAWAY, Plant Manager says, "I basically get the same excitement when I look at the new one, as I did when I first saw one in '64." Callaway was in industrial relations at Ford when the first Mustang was built.

I might not have gotten a managerial promotion after my success with the SN95 1994 Mustang but that didn't stop the magnitude of interior and exterior exposure and recognition I received for work well done. I was featured in numerous news media, print publications, and magazines ranging from *Ebony, Essence, Smithsonian, Executive Female, Michigan Chronicle, Road &Track, The Chicago Tribune, The Washington Post,* etc.

Quotes From Mustang People

BUD MAGALDI
Mustang Design Manager

Where Were You (When You First Saw a Mustang)?

"I first saw one in California. I was studying design at the Art Center in Los Angeles. We all heard about it, we were all studying design, so we went to a dealership for a look – and we couldn't get near the cars. Just as quick as they would come in they were being sold, the convertibles especially. The first one I saw was poppy red with a red interior."

What Do You Think of the '94 Mustang?

"If you really analyze the car, there's an awful lot of the 1964 1/2 and 1965 car in there. Just look at the new car, the way it was done with the character lines on the body side, the horses and the long hood. Yet, it's contemporary. When we talked with Mustang owners they kept telling us that we should capture the heritage of the original Mustangs. And if there was one element that was brought up again and again it was that the design should be American. We also kept the design simple and avoided hang-on stuff. We didn't use any tapes or decals. All of our graphics – the horses, the bars, the GT symbol – are three-dimensional."

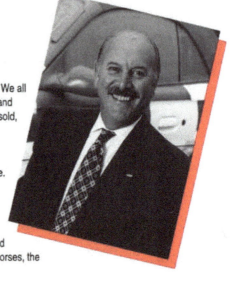

EMELINE KING
Mustang Interior Designer

Where Were You (When You First Saw a Mustang)?

"It was at an auto show in California years back. They showed various types of Mustangs. That was the first time I really noticed one with the emblem. I was about 13."

What Do You Think of the '94 Mustang?

"I researched the entire history of Mustang interior design, beginning with the original car, and we incorporated a lot of the historical features, such as the double-pod cockpit theme. By having a history, the Mustang allowed us to go back and feed on the good points. Its history makes this car unique."

"We also focused on good ergonomics – such as locating the radio up high so you could reach it easier. The entire upper area of the dashboard has been darkened to cut down on glare."

"All the buttons and knobs have a soft feel to them. We also treated the instrument panel and the doors as a unit. They flow into one another."

These articles acknowledged and wrote about my role as female lead designer for the Mustang interior design. "A talented female designer who beat the odds." I interviewed with WCHB 1440AM radio station and via satellite with the television shows CBS Morning Show and Good Morning America about my involvement as a female designer on the 1994 Mustang. There were speeches and demonstrations I gave on the design process of the 1994 Mustang at various events (see appendix). I was presented with several awards and acknowledgements for my design work leadership involvement with the 1994 Mustang. I was the recipient of the Dollars and $ense FASTRAK AWARD by Donald C. Walker Publisher held in Atlanta, Georgia. I was featured in their 1992 National Black Magazine *Dollar and $ense*. I shall never forget how proud I was when my own hometown Detroit awarded me with the Spirit of Detroit Award presented by Detroit City Council in May 20,1993.

SHOWERED WITH BLESSINGS

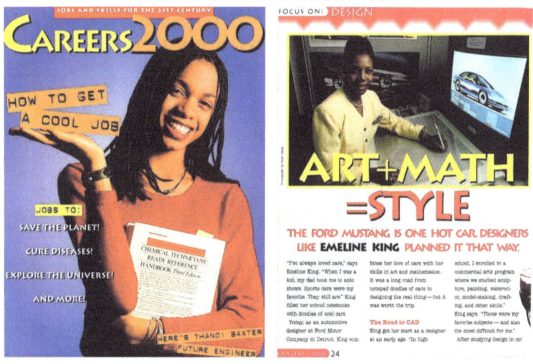

Every one of my blessings had a snowball effect…they kept increasing and coming. Because of my career as a black female car designer for Ford, I served as a Career Day speaker throughout Detroit Public Schools (DPS) and was special guest speaker at my former school, Keidan Elementary. That's where my mom worked as a paraprofessional, so she was able to attend this event with me. I don't know who was more excited about this special day, me or her. I showed demonstrations to the students on how to draw and render a car, then gave each one of them an autographed car sketch. I enjoyed the looks on their faces seeing something for which they had not been exposed. I shared my background journey with the students and all the things it encompassed to follow one's dream; catch it and how to turn it into a reality. When I was growing up, I attended those same institutes of learning. My career as a Female Transportation Designer designing cars at Ford could not have happened if it wasn't for my father's influence, the exposure, my determination and several role models. I instilled in the students they can accomplish anything in life. The sky isn't the limit to your ambition and goals. *You're equipped to go far beyond* and I expected them to reach higher. I especially told the young ladies that it was important to never let your gender or anyone destroy your dreams. Stay focused and committed.

Wikipedia even acknowledged recognition for my design contributions toward the fourth generation, 1994 Ford Mustang interior[4]. With my faith in God along with the talents and gifts he gave me, and strong will power, there were many doors of unlimited opportunities and blessings that poured out for me "during and after". I worked on the 1994 Mustang. I realized me not getting a managerial promotion from management for my work done on the 1994 Mustang was only a mustard seed (which is the smallest grain seed) compared to all the blessings that God had in store for me.

ESSENCE MAGAZINE DEBUT

I was grateful for the amount of coverage and exposure I received for my role in the 1994 interior Mustang design (see appendix). I appeared twice in *Essence Magazine*[5]. For the Essence photo shoot featured in the Essence Special Issue, it was shot in the International Studio, which was sentimental for me because it was behind that famous blue door and the first studio I worked in after I was hired at Ford. I wore my purple two-piece suit and rocked brown colored twisted braids styled up in a French roll. For my photo shoot, the photographer had me sit inside Ford's new concept car, the Mach III, which had a slate gray color interior with a bright lime green exterior. Several years later, Ford held a private auction at the Design Center and auctioned off some of its vintage concept vehicles of which included the Mustang Mach III. A famous Hollywood late night talk show host celebrity who was an ardent car collector bought the green colored Mach III.

I also did some design work on the Mach III. Ford selected me to attend a few Mach III publicity events where the car was on display and I served as the design representative for Ford giving presentations on the Mach III concept car. Three trips included: the SWE Convention held in Chicago, Illinois, Denver, Colorado for the opening of the Denver International Airport and the Sears Point Raceway in Sonoma, California for the Mach III Media Day. When the magazine came out, I was featured on pages 118-119 in a full color page spread. For a keepsake gift, Mark, my boyfriend Donn's brother, worked in a frame shop and beautifully framed the article. I added it to my wall collection of success.

EBONY MAGAZINE DEBUT

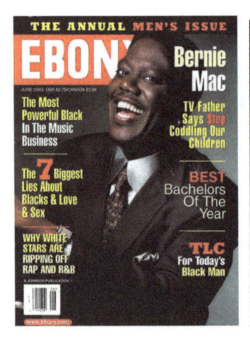 

I always admired the beautiful, classy, and talented African American lady who was in charge of Design Center special events. She reminded me of actress Halle Berry. Her staff also worked with Ford World Headquarters public relations department. Her office was located near the Design Center's mahogany row where the Design Center President and other executive's offices were. I was overwhelmed with joy when she informed me that both Ebony and Essence magazines wanted to interview me and do a photo shoot on me and the 1994 Mustang. Ebony magazine was honoring their 100-year anniversary issue. The photo shoot would be featured in Ebony Salutes Ford Motor Company & Black America: A 100-YEAR ADVENTURE and the Annual Men's Issue in *Ebony* (Vol LVIII, Number 8, June 2003, Page 45).

This was my second time being featured in Ebony Magazine. I was photographed by Ebony in the Design Center's Showroom. This place brought back fond memories when Dad brought me here as a little bright eyed, excited and curious little seven-year-old little girl to the Ford Design Center's employee Christmas party. I used some of my early Thunderbird concept sketches and renderings for props and displayed them on top of a silver 2000 convertible two-seater Thunderbird. I wore my red two-piece suit. I made a dramatic change to my hair. I had it cut off and wore a nice, cropped hairstyle.

DOLLAR AND $ENSE FASTRAK AWARD

I was so elated when Linda Lee from Ford's World Headquarters Public Relations Department forwarded a letter to me from Donald C. Walker of *Dollar and $ense Magazine*. The letter read, "Congratulations! It is with great pleasure that I inform you that the editorial board of Dollars & $ense Magazine has selected you as the recipient of our annual FASTRAK Award. As recipient of this prestigious honor, you will be presented your award at an elegant black-tie awards banquet during the spectacular weekend of events recognizing America's Best & Brightest Young Business Professional Men and Women, August 14-15, 1992 at Atlanta's Peachtree Hotel." The Dollars and $ense Fastrak Award recognized individuals in the business sector who had made successful, outstanding accomplishments.

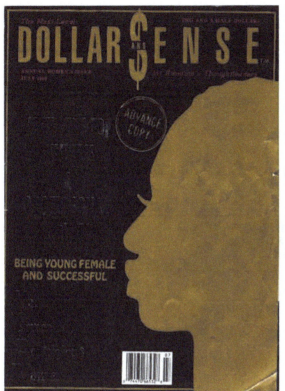

My mother and sister, Evelyn, accompanied me to Atlanta. We stayed at the Peachtree Hotel. Yvette, my hairstylist, did my hair in a wet set wave pattern and added some eighteen-inch hair tracks for length. Dollars and $ense requested that all recipients wear white apparel. I wore a beautiful white two-piece suit that I purchased from Winkleman's store for the evening ceremony. After we got dressed, it was time to go downstairs to the ceremony.

We took the elevator down to the banquet hall. We got on the elevator and to my surprise, standing poised and quiet in the back was the world-renowned neurosurgeon from Johns Hopkins Medical Center in Baltimore, Maryland, Dr. Ben Carson. He was the keynote speaker and an honorary chairperson for the evening's awards ceremony. A native of Detroit, he was known for the first successful operation to separate conjoined twins. It was funny… my mom, an avid admirer of successful people, especially those who overcame adversities and made something out of their lives, wouldn't miss the chance to meet Dr. Carson, but instead as a proud mother boosted and talked about her daughter's accomplishments! "Dr. Carson, I would like for you to meet my daughter, Emeline King. She's the first black female transportation designer at Ford. She helped designed the Mustang." He congratulated me and invited us to his book signing for "Gentle Hands" when we returned to Detroit. I told him we would be honored to attend.

The room was filled with at least 500 people of which 50 were Fastrak Award recipients. The hall was beautifully decorated in white. The dinner was delicious and I had a chance to mingle with the other recipients and learned about their success. It was an honor when they called my name and I walked up to the podium to receive my award, a trophy in the shape of a seven-inch black triangular shaped marble with the inscription: FASTRAK AWARD presented to Emeline King by Donald C. Walker Publisher Atlanta, 1992, The National Black Magazine *Dollar and Sense*. I returned back to my table as everyone complimented me on achievement, my attire and hair. My mother and sister were proud of me. I was humbled. It was a lovely affair.

CBS MORNING SHOW AND GOOD MORNING AMERICA

I was on vacation with my boyfriend Donn when I received a phone call on Thursday morning from Ford's Public Relations department. A representative told me that the television show, "Good Morning America" wanted to do an interview with me. It would be scheduled for Monday, the week of the 1994 North American International Auto Show. Ford's representative gave me a heads up on what questions I should be prepared to answer when asked by the host of Good Morning America during the interview. Mainly, it would center around my role as lead interior designer for the Mustang and how the vehicle was designed to be a female-friendly oriented vehicle with women in mind.

Ford's representative told me Ford would send a limousine to pick me up at my house on Monday around 7:30 a.m. I was elated! I could hardly wait to get off the phone. I called my family and told them the news. Then informed Yvette, my hair stylist and booked my hair appointment for my interview. I trusted her to come up with something fabulous and unique for this event. The day of the Good Morning America interview, I wore a red two-piece suit. Yvette buckle styled my hair, a wave pattern reminiscent of a roaring 1920s coif. I wore hazel contact lenses and a black leather three quarter length coat with black fox trimmed collar. I sat and waited anxiously by my window looking for the black stretch limousine to turn onto my street. When the limo pulled in front of my house, a Caucasian male chauffeur parked, got out the car, proceeded up the walkway and knocked on my door. I opened it. He asked me, "Hello, ma'am. Are you Emeline King? I'm here to drive you to Cobo Hall for your interview with Good Morning America." He opened the rear door for me to get in. I asked him would he mind taking a photo of me in front of the limousine. This was a Kodak moment that I would cherish and did not want to ever forget. On the way to Cobo Hall Exhibition Center, I struck up casual conversation with him and told him about my background and interest in how I became a car designer. The driver was impressed and congratulated me on my accomplishments.

Wow! I felt like a celebrity. I don't think a stretch limousine ever rode down my neighborhood street, especially in the 'hood. When I arrived at Cobo Hall to the area where the interview took place, the camera crew with their lights and cameras were set up in front of a bright polished red two-door convertible top 1994 Mustang. It was my prop for my interview and demonstration. A makeup artist powdered my face so I wouldn't appear shiny on camera. Once I was miked, I was ready to go. Two co-host reporters from the Good Morning America Show were there on set with me to interview. The host would interview me via satellite. He asked me to explain what some of the design features on the Mustang were that I designed to make the car more appealing to the female market. I talked about the Mustang being a female-oriented car and how ergonomics was the key factor in designing the car. Ergonomics is the ability to design products for a workplace environment around people. Surveys were done to get input from the female market on what they would look for in a car, including concerns and improvements. All interior components needed to be user-friendly and meet their needs. Each control button on the instrument panel and door needed a soft touch feel to the surface. Several interior components were designed with smooth, round edges to prevent snagging a good pair of stockings or causing a tear in one's apparel while entering or exiting the vehicle. Both interior and exterior door handle shapes were designed so when one pulled the handle, it wouldn't injure or break a finger nail. The seat's shape and fabric material were designed with soft but firm foam padding and shaped to give comfort like sitting on your favorite living room sofa. I designed the interior to allow a person wearing a skirt or dress to not have a problem or any difficultly in entering or exiting the vehicle. Finally, the Mustang car remained macho with lots of horsepower and poise. Its image was never compromised. I just wanted to 'rev it up a notch or two' by adding some feminine elegance design features to complement its appearance which would cater specifically to the female market. The Mustang was aggressive, but still elegant. I compared it to the man who wore a well-tailored suit and complemented it with the right designer tie and handkerchief. A women in a dress isn't complete without her designer brand accessories: matching hat, purse, jewelry and shoes. Overall, the dual cockpit theme created a warm, inviting, safe, ergonomic environment. All of my family, relatives and friends who watched me on television were proud. Every VCR in our house was set to record my interview that day.

NORTH AMERICAN INTERNATIONAL AUTO SHOW
1989 THUNDERBIRD DEBUT

I always looked forward to going to the North American International Auto Show (NAIAS) with my dad, another one of our favorite daddy daughter annual social outings. Prior to being hired at Ford, I would attend these events as the anticipated and inspired public spectator in awe of all the wonderful car products and concept vehicles. There was representation from every car company displayed at the Auto Show. It wasn't until after I hired in at Ford as a transportation designer that I began to see the cars and trucks somewhat different - more than a large piece of sheet metal on top of four wheels. I was more appreciative as a professional car designer who was part of a team of designers that created these magnificent Auto Show vehicles from concept to production. They all began in the creative minds of the designer.

I was aware of the behind the scene events that took place prior to the pony and whistle show. It took a lot of time, effort and design to build these production and concept vehicles for the entire world to see at these Auto Shows. Mom and I attended the Auto Show Pre-Charity event when the following cars made their debuts: 1989 Thunderbird, 1990 Thunderbird, 2000 two-seater convertible. I was honored to have made design contributions to some iconic Ford products.

We enjoyed the evening dressed up in our elegant, after five attire. We strolled around, watched the displays, and mingled amongst the crowd. I introduced mom to one of my former managers when I worked on the 1990 Thunderbird, Ted Finney, who was also my former instructor at Wayne State. He taught me *Introduction to Transportation Design*. There was also another former manager, Mark Conforzi, who I worked with on the Mustang and M205 two-seater Thunderbird. There were other people in the auto industry we ran into who all had pleasant things to say about me as a designer. It was a lovely evening. I don't know who was blushing with pride more: my mom about me and what I'd accomplished or me seeing the cars I had worked on.

2000 Thunderbird (MN205) Two-seater Hardtop Convertible

National Mustang Day
Thursday, December 9, 1993

NORTH AMERICAN INTERNATIONAL AUTO SHOW
1994 MUSTANG DEBUT

It was a gratifying moment for me when the 1994 Ford Mustang debuted at the North American International Auto Show (NAIAS) held at Cobo Hall, the iconic pony car that I followed through in design from start to finish. The grand opening began with the Friday Pre-Charity premier night. It was an extravagant affair. Everyone was in attendance from the auto industry, both private and public businesses, from local and national dignitaries to Who's Who in Detroit. Every Ford design department, suppliers, manufacturers and divisions who had a role in the design of the Mustang were present.

The place was filled with men and women elegantly dressed in formal attire, sipping on champagne, admiring the cars on display. I wore a lovely, red evening gown with gold trim from Lord and Taylor's. Donn wore a well-tailored black tuxedo. Everyone looked fabulous. We spent the evening socializing with the people, and taking photographs with the new Mustang, and other concept and production cars.

THE SPIRIT OF DETROIT AWARD
MOTOWN LEGEND MUSICIAN THOMAS 'BEANS' BOWLES

Although I have received much recognition and accolades over the years that I've worked for Ford, the one that caught me off guard was when I was recognized by my own city. The Detroit City Council awarded me the Spirit of Detroit Award for my contributions made toward the 1994 Mustang. This award, presented by Detroit's City Council, is given to a person, event or organization for an outstanding achievement or service. I had received so many awards on behalf of my contribution to the Mustang, I could hardly keep up. I don't recall being notified by Ford's PR department about this event. I'm sure I must have gotten some kind of notification to attend. Anyway, the ceremony was going to take place on a Tuesday afternoon on Detroit's Belle Isle, and I needed to be present.

On that day, I arrived for the affair and noticed a few of Detroit dignitaries seated on stage including Brenda M. Scott, the president of the Detroit City Council. There were several people seated in the audience. I decided to sit in the first row next to one gentleman whom I had the pleasure of meeting the night before at one of Henry Ford College's big band concert: Mr. Thomas 'Beans' Bowles, who played the Barry saxophone along with my boyfriend Donn who played the trumpet. After the concert, Donn introduced me to Mr. Bowles. He was a tall, light skinned bony looking man. Mr. Thomas 'Beans' Bowles, a Motown musician, was known to have played the Barry saxophone and flute on several Motown hits with such artists as Marvin Gaye and the Supremes. He shared with us his musical career and offered some musical wisdom and advice. We escorted him to his car and asked if he wouldn't mind taking a picture with us. Being a musician myself, I thought it was an honor just being in the presence of such a great living legend. We enjoyed making his acquaintance and thanked him.

Mr. Thomas "Beans" Bowles, Emeline and Donn Johnson

The program was about to start, so the council president approached the podium with greetings and congratulated all those who were being honored. She read the bio about the first recipients for the award who happened to be Mr. Thomas 'Beans' Bowles. Everybody applauded as he walked up to receive his award. As I sat there wondering *where on the program I was going to make a presentation about the Mustang*. It was strange that the only information Ford's PR told me was to attend. Next, I heard my name called and the president of the council read my bio and what I had accomplished on the Mustang. She then asked me to come up to the podium. She stated how proud she was to have a fine product from Detroit, the first African American female car designer, a native Detroiter, who designs cars for Ford. "You are a positive role model for the city of Detroit through your accomplishments with the 1994 Mustang." I was totally surprised to be honored with the Spirit of Detroit Award! I never would have expected that to happen to me. When I got home I added my award to my growing collection of awards on my display wall of success and accomplishments. My family was overjoyed when I shared the news with them.

PUBLIC SPEAKING COMES NATURAL

It was during and after I worked on the SN95 1994 Mustang project that I continued to be blessed with invites to appear as guest speaker to make presentations at various organizations and events for Ford. On one occasion, I gave a presentation about the design process of the Mustang and the effects of ergonomics and the female buyer to a group of marketing students at Michigan State University in Ann, Arbor MI. It was held in one of the lecture halls on campus. Art Berry, a coworker who worked in the front office at the Design Center, the only black in his department, volunteered to drive me. During our ride up there, Art asked if I ever got nervous speaking before an audience. I told him, "No. Out of all the times I spoke on Ford's behalf, I never had a problem speaking before an audience, no matter the size. I owed my strong speaking skills to my parents who exposed me to great speakers, lecturers and the opportunities to speak in church. I often practiced my presentations before my family and church which built self-assurance to speak at various church events like Women's Day, Career Day, banquets, concerts, and prayer breakfasts. I would be invited to speak at women conferences, commencements and Career Day for Detroit Public Schools. As a vocalist and musician, I've sung and performed my instrument before several large audiences all of which developed, strengthened my skills and increased my confidence level. I told Art after I was hired, Ford offered a Dale Carnegie course to all its employees. Jokingly, I probably could have saved the company lots of money by having them practice their speeches before my family or church congregation.

I learned through experience, the key to public speaking is to first know your subject or topic well. Second, know the type of audience you will address. You don't want to appear confused, distracted or don't know what you're talking about. Be prepared so the delivery won't sound nervous. Know your audience level. You don't want to talk over their heads and get some strange reactions or looks from your audience or lose their attention. My family always gave me constructive criticism which built my confidence. To overcome any fear and have an idea what the audience would see and hear, I practiced my speeches, as well as sung and played my horn in front of the mirror or recorded myself.

My biggest influence and motivation came from my father. He always spoke with confidence. He once told me he could sell a person an empty peanut shell knowing that there wasn't a peanut inside. Dad was a Baptist preacher. I learned so much from watching him stand in the pulpit on Sunday and deliver to his congregation encouraging, motivating, educational, compelling, captivating, and soul winning convicting sermons. Dad had several pastors and minister friends of whom I met and was influenced by when it came to their styles of preaching, speaking, or lecturing. One of the greatest orators/preacher/pastor who always left an audience and me spellbound, a man who I looked up to as my spiritual mentor, was Rev. Dr. Frederick G. Sampson. Just to stand in his presence and listen to his delivery of sermons, sermonettes, lectures or casual talks always left a lasting impression. I was fortunate through my father to have met and listened to so many great, talented, skilled men and women of the cloth and other lecturers that their public speaking skills were bound to rub off on me.

EXPERIENCING JOB HARASSMENT

The first time I encountered sexual harassment on the job occurred while I was in International Studio in the Design Center. I was the newest employee and had been on the job for a month when the middle-aged Caucasian man who worked in the engineering department located at the far end of the International Studio introduced himself to me. As time went on, he developed a bad habit to make frequent stops by my desk. I felt uncomfortable every time he came around because of his subject language. He would start off with a friendly, casual conversation. "Emeline, how are you doing today?" My reply to him was "I'm fine." The conversation would always be short and brief while I continued to work on my assignments. He would stand near my cubicle and talk about the weather, current events, the studio program, etc. So far, not a problem, but then his conversation switched and turned personal.

He'd spoke of his "young" girlfriend and how after they were intimate, she'd crawl out of his bed onto the floor, sit in a fetal position in the corner and not say a word to him. He didn't understand her reason for not talking or letting him touch her and wanted to know why this always happened to him. Whoa! I was shocked and surprised. I didn't appreciate him revealing his personal and intimate business to me. He noticed I wasn't interested as I continued to engage myself in my work. I totally ignored him. He got the message and said, "Well, goodbye Emeline, I guess I'll get back to my work."

The following day, we had our studio staff meeting and that particular engineer was present. I was given a new assignment by my manager to start a full-size tape rendering of my concept theme sketch for the FN10 Town Car exterior program. After the meeting, I had to stop by the engineering department to pick up a FN10 packaged drawing. I returned to my cubicle and then grabbed my sketch from off my desk with a couple of supplies to begin my tape drawing: an assortment of black tape, a stapler and a ruler. I headed out onto the studio floor to start my full-size tape drawing and rendering. Before I could step out of my cubicle, there he was standing in my cubicle. He stated that tonight he would have his girlfriend swing naked from the chandelier…maybe that will get her to communicate with him. He mentioned, "By the way…Emeline, you're a sexy black woman. What should I do to get her to be comfortable and open up to me?" Him asking me that provocative question was the final straw. I had had enough of his explicit sexist mannerisms and was ready to lash out with the words to tell him, "Don't ever come by my cubicle anymore! I'm uncomfortable with your sexual language." Unaware to me, my coworker, a Caucasian female clay modeler who worked in our studio, happened to be seated in the cubicle next to me. She stood up and angrily spoke to him, "I heard your conversation and what you told Emeline! That's blatant sexual harassment on the job! I could report you to HR for using that type of language around here and being disrespectful toward Emeline." The look on his face was priceless. His complexion turned red and he immediately stormed out of the area.

She told me his subject manner and the frequent stops to my desk to tell me about his personal encounters were totally uncalled for and a form of sexual harassment on the job. "Emeline, if he comes back over here, you report him to HR. He'll be written up and fired!" She had been on the job for a couple of years and was one of two talented female clay modelers at Ford. I thanked her for coming to my rescue and sharing that information. From that day on, I never had that problem of him stopping by or coming near my desk area. Whenever I saw him in the studio, his *only* form of communication to me was a quick hand wave from a far, far away distance.

STEREOTYPING: FEMALES DESIGN INTERIORS
LEAVE THE EXTERIOR MUSCLE CARS TO THE MALES

After I hired in at Ford, I was placed and worked in an exterior studio designing car exteriors. I noticed over time my placement changed. I was put in more interior studios designing interiors than exteriors. I addressed this interest to HR and management because I'm a female designer; I shouldn't be limited to only designing car interiors but have opportunities to design car exteriors. I wondered if Human Resources or management favored auto industry design gender stereotyping where male designers are considered better at designing the car's exterior and placed there because exteriors are tough, rugged, hard and possess an outdoor environment feel. Females are considered best at designing the car interiors because they can relate to the softer, friendly, domestic environment feel. Each gender was placed in their specific lane. "Leave the *macho muscle* car exteriors for the males to design and the "soft oriented" interiors up to the female designer."

During my early childhood I faced with having to listen to a few male instructors who tried to steer me towards the *feminine* occupations. Their belief was that a female wasn't capable of drawing cars and later in my professional design career, trying to compete and survive in this tough male dominated industry was challenging. My skills and talent proved that I could draw, design cars and maintain my place. My background trained me efficiently to design both the car's exterior and interior. During my interviews with Ford and other auto companies, I presented a portfolio which consisted of both interior and exterior concepts, sketches, renderings and 3D models with the majority being exterior. I didn't want my career as a female transportation designer to be viewed as capable of only designing "interiors", a stereotype label I would not accept. I preferred to design the whole car, inside and out. Had I never spoken up about my capabilities, interest and what I could offer as a female designer, I'd probably be stuck designing interiors for the rest of my career years at Ford.

I FOLLOWED YOU, NOW IT'S TIME TO MOVE

A shocking and misunderstanding incident occurred while I was assigned to the Large Car Specialty Exterior Studio to work on the 1990 MN12 Thunderbird SC exterior program. It was getting close to lunchtime and I decided to go to Fairlane Mall in Dearborn, not too far from the Design Center. After enjoying my lunch, I had thirty minutes left before I need to return to work. I took a few minutes to try on a pair of shoes in one of the shops. On the other side of the shops display window, I thought I saw a man who appeared to be watching me. I couldn't tell exactly who it was, only that he was tall and his face was slightly hidden underneath a large wide brimmed hat. I made my purchase and headed back to the Design Center. I was a minute late getting back to the studio. It wasn't too long before the studio's design executive who was on Foreign Assignment here asked me to come to his office. I hadn't the slightest clue as to what he wanted. I walked into the office. He looked at his watch and informed me, "You're late getting back from lunch. I happened to have followed you." I thought to myself, "That must have been the person I saw at the mall." Wow! That's some strange, weird news to me. I told him, "Yes, I was a minute late. That time you spent following me was uncalled for and unprofessional."

Afterwards, he handed me my performance review along with a small 3x5 white envelope and told me I was being transferred to an interior studio. Just hearing the words transfer and interior, I don't know what came over me but I started to cry and the first thing came to my mind was why I was being transferred? Was being late the reason? Was I being punished and sent over to an interior studio? I knew I wasn't ready to leave this studio. I enjoyed designing exteriors for the MN12 and the whole wheel program. I had made some good design contributions that went into production. He noticed how emotional I was so he left and asked my manager to come to the office to speak to me. I could only focus on his last statement that I was being transferred to an "interior" studio. When they returned it was my manager who explained to me. "Emeline, you've done an excellent job on the MN12 and the program is finished. You've been promoted and it's time to move to another studio for your next assignment. You should be happy. Look in your envelope." To my surprise, I hadn't realized the small envelope I was holding acknowledged I had been promoted to Salary Grade 7 and had received an excellent performance review rating.

GIVE DADDY A HUG

While in Turin, Italy on a Foreign Service Assignment working in the Ghia Studio, I had the pleasure of spending time with a few of my coworkers after work. They were friendly and helpful in showing me some of the famous sites and attractions in Italy. My coworkers, both Italian males, asked me if I didn't have plans for the evening would I like to go to an Italian nightclub with them and see some more of the city?" I told them, "Yes." One of them offered to pick me up around seven o'clock. He drove a little white two-door compact, manual Fiat and because of his height, he appeared cramped and uncomfortable behind the wheel. It was a beautiful night. When we drove up to the place, it didn't have the slightest appearance of a night club but an old-looking, dark grayish stoned structure with large, wooden doors that stood over eight feet in height. The building was located on a narrow cobblestone street. He managed to find a place to park. There wasn't a name located on the building. The inside was packed with young Italian men and women. I was the only African American female. That evening, we enjoyed fine Italian cuisine with vino and lots of dancing. I enjoyed trying to converse with the Italians with my limited Italian vocabulary and using my "How to speak Italian book." We had a great time. The evening went by fast. It was getting late, so I asked my coworker to take me home. When I got to my apartment, I looked at my watch it was 5:00 in the morning. I would only get three hours of sleep before it would be time for me to get up and go to work. I went straight to bed.

That morning, my coworkers and I all made it to work on time. The rest of the coworkers hadn't arrived yet. I sat at my desk before getting up to work on my full-size tape rendering of a two-seater sport car called the *Advancee*. I knew it wouldn't be too long before those three hours of sleep caught up with me. My eyes lids got heavy. I started to yawn. I tried hard not to fall asleep, but my lack of sleep gave in. I laid my head down on the desk and *Kaboom!* I was out. I don't know how long I had been asleep but the loud sound from my coworker snoring immediately woke me up. When I looked to my left, he had his feet crossed and propped on top of the desk. His arms were folded behind his head with his mouth wide open. I glanced over to my right; the other male designer was knocked out, face down with both arms stretched out on top of his desk. All of sudden, from a distance I heard the design executive call my name. "Emeline, I need to see you in my office right now!" From the tone of his voice, I sensed something was wrong. I said to myself, "Man, I shouldn't have stayed out so late.

When I walked in the office, the executive immediately got up from behind his desk walked toward me and yelled, "Emeline, I saw you sleeping on the job! Do you know what my boss would do to me, if I was caught sleeping on the job? I'd get fired!" Tears started rolling down my cheeks. I started to cry. I told him I was sorry. I stayed out too late last night with my co-workers and I only had three hours of sleep. It took a toll on me. I promised this would never ever happen again. "Please, I hope you won't let this one incident affect or end my Foreign Assignment and stay here in Italy."

All I could visualize at that moment was Ford putting me on a plane and sending my butt back home to the states, *"via coach, ASAP!"* This would be a total embarrassment and stain for my Ford career not to mention a huge disappointment to me and my family. He saw how upsetting this was for me. He asked me to calm down and told me, "Please stop crying. You're not in trouble. Just don't let your personal life affect your career. "Now come over here and give daddy a hug." I was stunned to hear his ending request. So not knowing if he was telling the truth about this incident not being placed in my record, or me getting fired or sent home, I did it.

SUGAR DADDY

My second Foreign Service Assignment was at Ford of Dunton Design Center in the UK. I had been in England for about a week. I was at home in my apartment and had just settled in from getting familiar with this new transition as a foreign service specialist, traveling to and from my workplace, meeting my coworkers and getting accustomed to my new assignment. I laid in bed thinking about how I wanted to spend my time learning as much as I could about designing cars in the UK. I was excited about being in England and looked forward to my new career adventure.

It was 11:00 p.m. when the phone rang. There was a five-hour time difference between Detroit and England. I expected it to be my parents who I had just spoken to just about twice a week at that time. To my surprise, it was a disturbing phone call from back in the States. The baritone voice said, "Hello Emmaline, this is Pastor". There was only one person in the world that mispronounced and addressed me by that name. I told him, "I'm fine" and asked "How are you? Is there something wrong?" I never would have imagined receiving a phone call from this person. He told me, "No, no" and that he had to call me because there are a lot of things on his mind that he needed to get off his chest. At that moment, I wondered what it could be. He stated, "Well... it started that

Sunday he heard me sing a solo while I was in the choir stand. My church was invited over to celebrate one of his pastoral anniversaries. He mentioned after I finished singing and returned to my seat that I accidentally touched his shoulder when he was seated in the pulpit. He told me, "Emmaline, since that touch, I have not been the same. It went through me." He knew he had a wife, and even had me sing at their wedding, but he would be whatever I wanted him to be, my sugar daddy, lover or whatever I tell him to be. He mentioned that he wanted to tell my father, who was just in his office on Sunday, how he felt about me. His church asked him what he wanted for his anniversary. "I thought about having them send me to England for my vacation to be with you." This was far too much information. I nearly fell out the bed. He goes on to mention whenever my church comes over to use his church's baptismal pool, he would be on the lookout from the pulpit just to see me walk through the doors and down the side aisle dressed in my blue fox fur hat and coat.

After hearing his words, I was shocked! I couldn't believe the things that were spurring from his mouth! This man was well in his late fifties. I was twenty-one at the time. I was totally unaware about his feelings and didn't have a clue to what was going through his mind. He continued to tell me about that time I came over to the house to talk confidentially with him about the reversed "Dear Jane letter" I had just received from my boyfriend who was in the military. He decided to break up with me via letter and I was hurt over this. This pastor told me he wanted to confess his feelings and everything that day to me after read the letter that my boyfriend sent. He wanted to tell me that my boyfriend had moved on and that I should move on, too. He said I needed a real man in my life and not a boy. After he finished with his infatuated feelings, I had the courage to tell him, "I never felt that way about you, pastor, and I never will. I always respected you as my spiritual leader and advisor, someone I confided in and talked to but only on a spiritual level. Nothing more and nothing less. I can't believe you spoke to me like that and made me feel so uncomfortable. I glad you didn't tell my father because you probably wouldn't have any fingers or arms left to dial this number." I told him, "This isn't normal for you. I'm gonna pray for you. Have a nice day and take care of yourself. Goodbye." Just as soon as I hung up the phone, I frantically dialed my sister Am, and then we did a three-way call to get my mother on the phone. I told them everything he said to me. I don't know what was going on his head, but there was something definitely wrong. I was upset and frightened but my mom and Am were there on the phone to calm me down and assured me not to worry. "Everything's going to be fine." They would handle it. I don't know what the dynamic duo did or said but two things for certain; he never called me again and by the time I returned home from my foreign assignment in England, that case was sealed and shut. Now as far as him wanting to reveal his feelings for me publicly, it remained silently between him and the good Lord.

KNOCK, KNOCK WHO'S THERE?
'N' WORD, GO BACK HOME!

While away on foreign assignment in another country I never would have imagined being called the "N" word. I was the only African American female who lived in my apartment complex at 1 Jason Court. Quite often, when I went out in the small town, I rarely saw another African American female in Brentwood, England. Everyone I met while doing my daily activities like going shopping, getting petrol (gas), going to the bank, dining out or even at my workplace, always treated me kind, friendly and with respect.

One night while in my kitchen cooking spaghetti, I heard a faint *Knock! Knock! Knock!* at my front door followed by a scratching noise coming through the keyhole. I asked, "Who was it?" A male's voice with a British accent said "Niggar, you need to go back home to your own country." I ran back to the kitchen grab a long knife from off the table and stuck it in the keyhole and said, "Whoever you are, if you don't get the hell away from my door, you're gonna be the one who won't make it back home." That startled me a little because I never had an incident like that to ever happen at my door while in England.

The only other strange incident to occur at my door was when "the Bobbie", which is the slang name for a British police officer, knocked on my door and asked for Emeline King. He told me he was from customs and needed to see my work documents, papers and verification of my Foreign Service status. I didn't know my time had expired so quickly and I stood the chance of being deported immediately back to the States. I had been working well over a year and I was still listed as a Foreign Service "specialist" instead of Foreign Service "employee." In order to stay in the UK my status would either have to be renewed or extended to "foreign service employee."

I told him, "I'm sorry I wasn't aware about the expiration date". Ford handled all of my paperwork. I told him first thing in the morning, I would inform my Foreign Service advisor at work about this matter. I'm sure he would get it resolved. That morning I immediately spoke with my Foreign Service advisor the about the visit from the local authorities and the obscene name caller at my door. My advisor apologized for what I had experienced. Concerned for my safety he promised to take care of both of these serious matters for me.

"NIP HER IN THE BUD"

After spending a year in the Ranger Truck studio, in December 1994, I was assigned to another truck program, the International Truck Studio and worked on the Transit Truck Program designing vehicles for England. I stayed in Transit Truck from January 5, 1995 to April 1997. It was during my performance review from the design executive who was on foreign assignment from England that revealed to me what his and management's opinions were of me.

I was still receiving invitations to speak about my Ford career and recognition on the success of the 1994 Mustang while in the Transit Truck Studio. I received an invitation letter and phone call from Smithsonian Magazine to come serve on a panel of designers at the Geneva Switzerland Auto Show. *Smithsonian*[6] was the first magazine to feature me in their February 1984 issue on page 78.

I was excited about the invitation to represent Ford and an opportunity to attend the Geneva Auto Show in Switzerland. I went and informed my design executive about the letter. That didn't sit well with him at all from how he responded to me. "Enough of this! I'm going to have to nip all this in the bud." My design executive must have pulled some strings because the *Smithsonian* request was not met and I wasn't allowed to go.

A couple of months later, this same design executive provided my performance review. It revealed and exposed true feelings about me. The conference room was small by the time you walked in, you were out. I sat down in the chair on the opposite side of the desk from my design executive while I listened as he read my performance review aloud. After he finished, I asked him to please hand me the performance review so I could read it for myself. He handed me the paper. I noticed all the ratings had satisfactory (S) which in no way reflected the quality of my work performance on the transit truck program. I told him I disagreed with his ratings and that I would write a rebuttal because my work doesn't come close or represent the rating that he gave me. I looked him straight in his eyes and asked, "Why would you give me a low unsatisfactory rating when you know it doesn't reflect my work?" At that moment my question must have hit a nerve. It was like what mama told me, "Throw a rock in a pack of dogs. The one that barks the loudest is the one that's hit and hurt." He jumped up out of his chair and banged down hard on the desk with both fists and replied, "Because nobody wants you on their bloody team! Whenever your name come ups in our meetings…" He took his hand and swiped it across the desk. "…Everybody just passes your name by. They… don't… like… you!"

I was hurt and alarmed from his remarks and there was no way in hell I was going to give him the pleasure or satisfaction of letting him know or see how devastated I was from his comments. It did, however, show me his true colors. So, with a straight poker face, I smiled and told him, "Please excuse me, I need to go to the restroom. I'll be right back." I left immediately and headed straight to the ladies restroom in the basement. I found an empty stall and wailed like a baby.

The same female modeler who helped me with the harassing engineer happened to come in and asked me what was wrong. I told her what had just occurred. She empathized with me; after which I pulled my self together and returned back to the room. I collected my performance review paper from off the desk. I thanked him for giving me my performance review and for exposing his true feelings about me and how I'm viewed. I smiled and politely left the room. I knew in my heart God allowed me to see this man's true feelings and revealed the things which had been said about me behind closed doors that I wasn't aware of. Although the meeting turned out more personal toward me than business, I decided I would not let the visiting executive's words or his satisfactory (S) performance rating destroy my work ethics and character. I stayed in the Transit Truck Studio for a week and then was transferred. I still continued to uphold my standards as a talented transportation designer designing profitable cars for the auto industry and being respectful to those who may not ever return the favor.

STRIKE THREE, SHE'S OUT!

On October 24, 1995, I celebrated my 12th Anniversary at Ford. It was a reality check. A curved ball was thrown at me when I was offered a "voluntary retirement package." Deeply concerned why I would be offered a voluntary retirement package during an early part of my career at Ford, I scheduled an appointment with Human Resources to find out the reason for this action. I was informed there could only be one of three reasons a designer would be offered a voluntary retirement package. First, a voluntary retirement package is given to an employee who had less than ten years with the company. Second, it was given to any employee who was 50 years of age or older and the third reason was if the company felt the employee had reached the furthest they could go within the company, they may be offered this option.

Well, after hearing Human Resources' reasons, the first two answers were clearly bogus to me. Number one, I was nowhere near the age of 50 at the time. Number two, I was only 38 with twelve years of service, not ten. Number three, analyzing all three reasons made me realize this could be a sign that the company wanted the first African American female transportation designer out. What made matters worse for me was on my 18th anniversary, which occurred on April 1, 2001, I was offered my second voluntary retirement package. Both packages were "voluntary" and I had a choice in the matter and right to reject both offers and still remained employed at Ford. Too bad that wasn't the case on July 30, 2008. By then, I wasn't so fortunate. My fate was sealed shut and I was given an "*involuntary* company separation." There wasn't a choice in the matter; just like they say in baseball, *Strike three. You're out!*

MY CHANCE FOR PROMOTION BACKFIRED

I felt really proud of what I had accomplished on the SN95 program; it was a success. The SN95 collocated team moved back to the Design Center and the new production 1994 Mustangs were available in dealerships for purchase. Another milestone in my career had been accomplished. Kudos for following good advice from my design executive. I acquired much exposure both internally and externally by working on this program more than I ever could imagined from media, print, radio, PR events etc. I gained name recognition through a hot program.

Management was now aware and informed of Emeline King, a black female car designer whose face, design contributions and leadership were connected to a major successful car project: SN95 1994 Ford Mustang. Finally...did my design contributions and work ethnics on the Mustang project pave my way to my golden ticket into management? Unfortunately, it wasn't too long before my expectations for a managerial promotion came crumbling down after I witnessed some fortunate changes amongst my colleagues who worked on the SN95 design team.

It was 11:30 a.m.; time for my lunch break. I decided to dine at the Coney Island restaurant located in the strip mall on Ford Road. I ordered a Greek salad and a glass of orange juice. I enjoyed my lunch and was excited about the direction my career was headed. It was soon time for me to go back to work. I left the restaurant and proceeded toward the parking lot where my truck was parked. Suddenly, my attention was drawn to this brand new, 1994 shiny red, convertible top Mustang driven recklessly by a Caucasian man. He yelled out, "YEEEEEEAH!" with one arm up in the air in celebration of some kind of joyful event. I stood there and watched him drive sporadically back and forth. Suddenly he applied the brakes, *SCREEEEECH!* raced the motor, *brum...brummm...brummmm...* and exited out of the lot. I felt a sudden tightness in stomach. I realized it was my coworker who had worked on the SN95 project with me. I was over the Mustang interior and he followed the exterior. He later transferred out of the studio to work on a different car program before the Mustang program had ended. I wondered what caused him to be that excited. When I got back to work, there was a memo placed on my desk. It announced the 1993 personnel changes and the managerial positions were effective immediately. Happy for my colleagues, I noticed it included names of people who worked on the SN94 Mustang program with me. At the top of the list was my manager's name; he had been promoted to design executive. There were several other appointees from management, the marketing division, engineering and design who received promotions. I searched for *my* name but it was nowhere to be found. As I read down the list of names, there was another name which stood out - my coworker who I had just seen in the parking lot was promoted to design manager.

Was that the reason for his behavior? I would have thought for certain I would had been listed and promoted to design manager. I was crushed after seeing the names of all who worked on the SN95 1994 Mustang with me had received their promotions. My manager walked over to my desk. He noticed me reading the memo and asked, "Emeline, could you please come with me to my office. I have your performance review. I thought, "Well, maybe I jumped to conclusions about not seeing my name listed on the memo. Maybe my manager would be the one to inform me of my promotion, especially, since we worked together on the same SN95 program. He knew how involved I had been as the only designer left on the SN95 team who followed and worked on the program from concept start to production end.

My manager handed me a manila envelope. I opened it and took out the 8x10 sheet of paper. I read it and saw nothing pertaining to a managerial promotion, only about three of four listed assignments and how I was rated. A performance review rating of excellent (E) was written by each Mustang assignment I had responsibility for during my time on the program. Shocked! The ratings didn't reflect anywhere near my level of work. I shared with him the list of responsibilities that I was involved in and contributed to support my reason for a higher rating of outstanding (O). I informed him that I went to management at the very introduction of the program with a special request to work on an iconic vehicle, the Ford Mustang. I believed the SN95 Mustang project was going to be exciting and a challenging program and now with the effects and increase of the female market pouring revenue into the car buying industry, I knew I had something to offer especially coming from a female designer's way of thinking. I wanted to be a part of the SN95 design team and contribute towards this iconic, macho, muscle machine and be in it for the long haul from start to finish. I was grateful when they granted my request.

My role as lead interior designer for the Mustang carried much responsibility and showcased my leadership abilities. I worked closely and followed through with all departments in the Design Center: design, modeling, engineering, marketing, graphics, metal, paint, fabrication, color and trim in the development of the Mustang. There were numerous visits where I traveled to the manufacturer plants in Saline and Chesterfield, Michigan. I visited tier one suppliers: Lear seating and met with vendors to give direction on the design models, check the quality, approval and signed off on the die models and other interior and exterior Mustang components. Management trusted and selected me as lead interior designer to represent and participated on their behalf in Mustang Blitz's. I traveled to several states along with marketing reps, design managers and executives to introduce the Mustang to the press, Mustang club owners, universities, and the general public. I attended events like Auto Shows, news media and print where I spoke in behalf of Ford management about the design process and branding of the Mustang plus countless Public Relations affairs through media, radio, television where I gave interviews. I had total involvement with the SN95 Mustang program from start concept design, modeling, manufacturing, marketing, finish production into dealership showrooms. My performance review ratings should reflect what and how I contributed to this program. Based upon my leadership abilities, teamwork and designs that I contributed to the Mustang program, it could only signify two end results for me: an outstanding (O) performance review and managerial promotion.

After successfully completing all the responsibilities I was assigned to do on the SN95 program, I deserved nothing less than an (O) outstanding. My manager said he was sorry but (O) outstanding performance reviews are given only to executives. After that statement, I knew there was no chance for my ratings to be changed. I shared with him my thoughts about what I read on the memo and that I should have been rewarded, too, for my contributions just like my coworkers who worked with me on the SN95. Knowing it took teamwork and that upper and middle management were mire reflections of the hard work, talent, skills and efforts of their subordinates: SN95 design team members made it possible to successfully complete an outstanding job for an iconic American car.

I acknowledged my manager for his hard work, commitment to be on the program from start to finish, his leadership, talent and skill towards the SN95 program which had paid off for him. I extended my hand and congratulated him on his new promotion to "design executive." Before leaving I thanked him for giving me my performance review and I would like for my rebuttal to go into my record. It was a pleasure to work with him on the SN95 from the beginning to completion. I returned to my cubicle desk, wrote my rebuttal and waited for my next assignment.

After I served as the lead interior designer for the SN95 1994 Mustang program, I would have thought for certain I'd be promoted to manager, just like my manager, who was promoted to design executive right after working on the SN95 1994 Mustang with me. Unfortunately, there was another male designer who hadn't even stayed on long enough to finish the program who was promoted to design manager in 1993. There was no promotion for me, only an overall performance review rating of excellent plus (EP), not even an outstanding (O) evaluation rating for the hard work I contributed to the Mustang program.

THE SPIRIT OF FORD DESIGN CONTEST

Ford sponsored a design contest which was open to all the designers in the Design Center. The project assignment was to design a 3D sculptured piece, using the media of your choice. The key objective for the sculptured piece would be to enhance visitor trust, confidence in and respect for Ford Motor Company products and services through experimental demonstration of Ford's excellence in design, engineering, manufacturing and customer service. The winner of the contest would have a replica made of their winning sculptured piece. It would be placed outside in front of the Ford multimedia center near the entrance. The 50,000 square foot Ford multimedia center building was located on Village Road directly across from the Henry Ford Museum. It is reminiscent of Ford's renowned Rotunda, remodeled to coincide with Ford's future product design objectives.

My entry design was influenced by "The Spirit of Detroit", Detroit's famous iconic sculpture located in front of the Coleman A. Young Municipal Center in Downtown Detroit and the handy works of my mentor, Mr. Oscar Graves. The Spirit of Detroit's bronze statue stood 16 feet tall. The green patina colored, crossed-legged man represented the spirit of man. Mounted inside of its right hand stood three figurines of a family representing humanity and extending their hands up to the sky for divine direction. In the other hand rested a golden orb signifying the deity. Using the contents of the Spirit of Detroit, I referenced and modeled my sculpture in the format of a polished metal ten-inch-tall figurine standing at a forty-five-degree angle. One arm was stretched out and pointed toward the sky. The other handheld a circle in the shape of a tire with all the names of the Ford brands: Ford, Mercury, Lincoln, Jaguar, and Land Rover, engraved in a circular pattern on it. The sculpture was base mounted on an oval shaped piece of mahogany wood. I worked with tech designers in the computer aid design studio and multimedia to construct a video that showed a mechanical animation replica of a sixteen feet tall figurine in front of a building. The Ford brand wheel rotated back and forth from one hand to the other. It signified the Spirit of Ford's new direction in the auto industry as one united family continuously growing and moving toward unlimited design possibilities.

My presentation was held on October 21, 1998 before a panel of three judges: a Caucasian male and female from the marketing division, along with the president of the Design Center. I spoke passionately, informative and was convincing about my entry. I even had designed engineering drawings on how my design would be manufactured. When I finished, I could tell from their facial expressions that my presentation made a strong, lasting impression on them. I was well dressed that day, tailored in a baby blue, two-piece peplum suit. After my presentation, I headed back to the studio. I passed by some of my coworkers in the hallway with their entries. They ranged from a variety of materials: wire framed, glass, plastic, and cement. There were even two coworkers who struggled carrying their overly decorated tree stump!

I was notified the following week by the committee to come back. They needed to meet with me. The lady over the contest told me, "Congratulations on winning the contest. Emeline, you had the best, most innovative sculpture piece of all the entries, but because we had so many designers to enter the contest, and we wouldn't want to hurt their feelings, it might be a good suggestion not to mention that you won the contest." Regrettably, my winning Spirit of Ford sculpture project never got off the ground, nor was there any notice, memo or announcement about the results of the contest, especially the designer who had won. I was even more shocked when the lady who headed the contest went behind her desk to hand me my prize. Instead of receiving recognition on paper and having my design built she presented me that day, for my hard work and the winning design, with a blue monogrammed Ford baseball cap...*really?!*

MY GRATITUDE: FORD DESIGN CENTER AFRICAN AMERICAN MALE TRANSPORTATION DESIGNERS AND MODELERS

Charlie Leak, Sam Mayers, George Rogers, Emeline, Melvin Edwards, Charles Purnell, and Calvin Morrison

Although I remained the only African American female transportation designer at the Ford Design Center throughout my twenty-five years of service, words can't measure the amount of gratitude and appreciation I felt to be a part of an elite talented group of African American male transportation designers who designed cars at the Ford Design Center. These early forerunners were my pioneer heroes. McKinley Thompson, Sam Mayers, Nehemiah Amaker, Derek McCullough (London, England) and Michael Burton. They each paved the way for me and several others. After I began my journey of designing cars, I was blessed to work with the following designer colleagues who came after me. They were my multi bridges of support, encouragement, and strength. I held the highest level of respect for my Ford design brothers who made design contributions for vehicles on the road today. They are the gifted, talented men who were my role models: Dennis Moses, Mike Ellis, Aaron Walker, Kenneth Hill, Tobias Francis, Earl Lucas and Michael Boyd. This journey would not have been complete without the esteemed recognition of other African American male designers from other companies within the auto industry who were influential like Edward Blanford, Fred Edwards, Stephen Franklin, Ralph Gilles, Dennis Hughley, Garth Newberry, Arthur Pryde, Michael Reynolds, Edward Welburn and Hugh Wilson. With all due respect to my beautiful, talented African American sisters who came along and traveled down the path of uncharted waters with me, they, too busted through that glass ceiling and excelled as accomplished, African American female transportation designers in the auto industry: Marietta Kearney (General Motors) and Crystal Windham (General Motors), Donna Burton (Chrysler) and Veronica Moses.

MY BRIDGES OF SUPPORT
CLAY MODELERS/FABRICATION/ADMINISTRATION

I could not have become an accomplished designer had it not been for my "bridges of support". I know none of my design projects could have flourished into 3D existence successfully without assistance from my coworkers who used their skills and crafts to work on my design contributions. I didn't walk alone on my design journey. I'm especially grateful for all my African American brothers and a sister who worked in the various design departments. They each were my strong mentors and supporters: the clay modelers – Calvin Morrison, Charles Purnell, Charles Leak, George Rogers, Jasper Garrison, Andy Walker and Melvin Edwards, both of whom were clay technicians. I also acknowledged my "bridges of support" in the Design Center's fabrication departments: Frank Woods and Larry Hawthorne from the wood shop, Tom Jones (trim shop), Julius Herron (metal shop), Rev. David Ramsey and Al Poole (paint shop), my father, Rev. Earnest O. King, Sr. (plaster), Ernie Trailer, Joe French, and Ray Nightingale and William "Bill" Bownman (engineering), Art Berry and Richard Porter (administration), Bennie Bailey and Diane Fox (PR, special design events).

HISTORY OF FORD DESIGN CENTER
AFRICAN AMERICAN MALE TRANSPORTATION DESIGNERS
(Listed in Service Years by Chronological Order)

McKinley Thompson	First African American Male Transportation Designer; hired September 1956; First African American enrolled in the prestigious Art Center College of Design in Pasadena, CA; promoted to manager of appearance development and feasibility design modeling department in 1976; retired in 1984
Sam Mayers	Hired in at Ford in 1966 as design manager; retired in December 1999
Nehemiah Amaker	Hired in at Ford in 1967 as general salary role designer; retired in 1998
Derek McCullough	Worked at Ford then left to work in Europe
Michael Burton	Worked at Ford 1978-1980; also worked at Chrysler and General Motors

HISTORY OF FORD DESIGN CENTER AFRICAN AMERICAN TRANSPORTATION DESIGNERS

Emeline King	First African American Female Transportation Designer; hired October 24, 1983; general salary role designer; involuntary company separation 2008
Dennis Moses	Hired in at Ford in September 1984 as design specialist; general salary role designer
Mike Ellis	Hired in at Ford in 1985; design manager December 1999; chief designer 2000;
Aaron Walker	Hired in at Ford in 1989 as general salary role designer
Kenneth Hill	Hired in at Ford from General Motors in 1995 as design manager; involuntary company separation in 2008
Tobias Francis	Hired in at Ford in June 1999 as general salary role designer
Earl Lucas	Hired in at Ford in May 1999; chief designer in 2000
Michael Boyd	Contract designer; involuntary company separation 2008

CASS TECH ALUMNI: PRESTON THOMAS TUCKER
DESIGN INNOVATOR IN THE AUTOMOTIVE INDUSTRY

How amazed was I when I learned some famous male transportation designers were Cass Tech Alumni. These trailblazers made design contributions in the auto industry plus we shared common backgrounds and interests. Let's start with Preston Thomas Tucker, an American automobile entrepreneur who grew up outside Detroit in the suburb of Lincoln Park, Michigan. First learning to drive at age 11, Tucker was obsessed with automobiles from an early age. At the age of 16, Preston Tucker began purchasing late model automobiles, repairing/refurbishing them and selling them for profit. He attended Cass Technical High School in Detroit. He is most remembered for his Tucker 1948 sedan, initially nicknamed the "Tucker Torpedo", which introduced many features that have since become widely used in modern cars. Those features include a rear engine, rear drive configuration, headlamps that turned with the front wheels. The most recognizable feature of the Tucker '48 was a third directional headlight (known as the "Cyclops Eye") which was located in the center of the front of the vehicle[7].

CASS TECH ALUMNI: JOHN DELOREAN
ENGINEER INVENTOR IN THE AUTOMOTIVE INDUSTRY

John Zachary DeLorean was born in Detroit, Michigan and attended Detroit's public grade schools before he was accepted into Cass Technical High School, a technical high school for Detroit's honor students, where he had signed up for the electrical curriculum. DeLorean found the Cass experience exhilarating and he excelled at his studies. DeLorean was an American engineer inventor and executive in the U.S. automobile industry. He worked at General Motors and was widely known as the founder of the DeLorean Motor Company (DMC)[8].

In the mid -1970's, the DMC designed a prototype two-seater sports car with gull-wing doors. The production model, called the DM12, was released in 1981. Known as the DeLorean, it is perhaps what he is best known for today. His design was featured in the 1985 film *Back to the Future*[9].

TRANSPORTATION DESIGNER WHO INSPIRED ME: SYD MEAD

Besides having my father, I had my coworker Sam and childhood mentor and sculptor, Oscar Graves, as my greatest teachers who inspired me. It was the American industrial designer and neofuturistic concept artist Syd Mead whose contributions in both automotive and science fiction films influenced and was my solace of inspiration. I admired his style and the creative futuristic masterpieces he graced on paper. He opened the door to every designer and exposed what the future of design elements looked like. His illustrations took me back to my childhood days of being infatuated about the futuristic concepts, space stations, vehicles and gadgets, etc. from my favorite television shows: *The Jetsons, Lost in Space and Star Trek*. His abilities to create and illustrate, in my opinion, could be compared to what Michelangelo's hand and paint brush was to the Sistine Chapel, the creative mindset composition of Diego Rivera's mural depicting the birth, emergency, bureaucracy and struggles of the auto industry in Detroit and the skilled marble architectural design of the Taj Mahal.

In 1959, Mead was employed with Ford Motor Company in Dearborn, Michigan. He worked in the Advanced Styling Studio from 1960 to 1961. After leaving Ford, he ventured into illustrating books and catalogues for other product companies. He launched Syd Mead, Inc. in Detroit. He was widely known for his design for science fiction films such as Star Trek, The Movie, Blade Runner, TRON, 2010, Short Circuit, Aliens, Time Cop, Johnny Mnemonic, Mission Impossible and Elysium. What a coincidence after reading his biography to learn that we shared a few things in common. Both our fathers were Baptist ministers and exposed us to art culture. At an early age, Syd's father read him magazines about Buck Rogers and Flash Gordon that peaked his interest in science fiction, just like my father who introduced me to the arts and transportation design in the auto industry. These experiences ignited my interest to want to design cars for Ford. Both Syd and I started drawing at an early age and attended the prestigious Art Center College of Design, in Pasadena, California. Syd Mead was in his own league and unique category as depicted through his God-given talent, futuristic illustrations and concepts which he contributed successfully both in automotive, industrial design and in the science fiction film industry. I chose an unchartered path for a female African American transportation designer in a male dominant auto industry. We both worked at the Ford Design Center and left our design footprint.

If there was a category given for the most creative futuristic designer, eighth wonder of the world in design, it would befall Syd and his ability to hold back the curtains, illustrate what the future would be in design and leave every designer in awe. Not only did I admire Syd Mead's imaginable concepts, illustrations of futuristic modes of transportation, interior and exterior architecture, products, technology and fashion etc., but I found his masterpieces fascinating, especially how he depicted his background illustration renderings of different cultures of people. There were even images of African American men and women adorned in futuristic costumes and apparels. I believe God broke the mold when he created Syd Mead's creative style. I would imagine every designer including myself wished they could come close to emulate his styling technique and come up with the most creative concept designs. However, it never hurt to look, observe, digest, and learn from his illustrations[10].

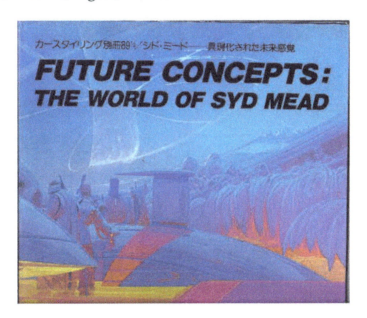

To keep abreast on car design within the industry, I subscribed to *Car Styling*. The car designers '*Holy Grail*' which was filled with all types of information, photos, and illustrations about car design. I was so elated when received my special edition of *Car Styling* on Syd Mead: FUTURE CONCEPTS: THE WORLD OF SYD MEAD in the mail. I had the pleasure to meet Syd Mead at a designer's gathering during my year at Art Center. Syd lived in Pasadena, California. I was spell bound just to stand on the same ground in his presence. He was a small, petite, introverted individual. I mustered up enough nerve to tell him how much I admired meeting someone of his unique acclaimed caliber. There probably never will be another designer as great, gifted and talented as Syd Mead to ever come along on this planet; the greatest futuristic designer of all times[11].

TRANSPORTATION DESIGNERS WHO INSPIRED ME: LUIGI COLANI

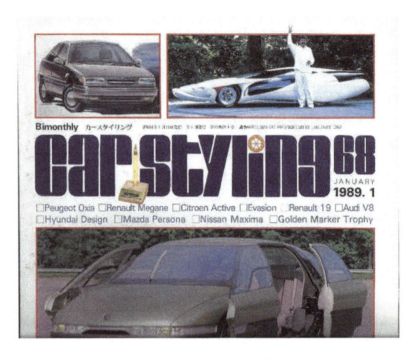

There were a few male transportation designers who inspired me during my career at Design Center, both Luigi Colani, and Syd Mead. It was their ability to challenge the norm and the courage to venture off onto a different path and create unique design concepts. During my time at Ford, I met the famous transportation designer Luigi Colani from Berne, Switzerland. I read an article in the book, *Car Styling,* and was enlightened on how he incorporated nature's shapes into his concept vehicles. I had been at the Ford Design Center for a year when Jack Telnack, our design president, invited Mr. Colani to the Design Center to display some of his concept vehicles and gave a lecture to all the designers. It was exciting because he brought some of his futuristic concept vehicles which all resembled some form of nature depicted on wheels.

They were all drivable concept vehicles displayed in white and lined up at the entrance to the Design Center.

One concept that caught my attention was Colani's transport and concept truck UTAH 12 design which was inspired by the dragonfly and featured a "bug eyed cab" that reminded me of the head of a dragonfly. It must have stood over eight feet in height. His concepts were heavily impacted by nature. Each concept vehicle resembled a series of white continuous flowing, stretch, futuristic, cloud-shaped, sheets of plastic that were molded into a drivable concept vehicles. The lecture was interesting and held in the Design Center's showroom. Mr. Colani spoke for approximately forty-five minutes on his usage of the elements to design his concepts. He then took out his black magic marker and gave a demo. He drew the shape of a large human femur bone on a white drawing pad and talked about how he had something to start with to design it to become whatever the creative mind chose. He was influenced by nature's shapes and the world was full of unlimited choices that he could incorporate into unique and beautiful designs. That basically was it.

After the lecture was over, everyone started to clear the showroom and head back to their studios. I personally wanted to meet Mr. Colani, so I walked over to the stage and approached him. He was a tall, slender man of at least six feet tall. I introduced myself to him and told him I was a newly hired designer at Ford who admired the concept vehicles he brought and was inspired from his lecture. I also asked him if he didn't mind, could I please have the drawing he used for the demo? He kindly tore off the drawing from off the 18x24' easel pad and gave it to me. With a Swedish accent, he glanced down over his glasses, and said to me, "Lady Designer, set no boundaries to design. Go beyond your mind. Don't be afraid to explore, learn and apply nature."

FIRSTS TO CLEAR THE PATH: BESSIE COLEMAN

I've always been inspired by those who were firsts. They had the courage to start out on an unchartered path, not knowing the journey wouldn't be traveled alone because they opened the roads and cleared the way for other to follow. Born to a family of sharecroppers in Texas, Coleman went into the cotton fields at a young age while also studying in a small, segregated school and then went on to attend one term of college at Langston University. She developed an early interest in flying, but African Americans, Native Americans, and women had no flight training opportunities in the United States, so she saved up money and obtained a sponsorship to go to France for flight school.

Bessie Coleman was an early, American civil aviator. She was the first woman of African American descent, and also the first Native American descendant to hold a pilot's license. Because flying schools in the United States denied her entry, she taught herself French and moved to France, earning her license from France's well known Caudron Brother's School of Aviation (*Federation Aeronautique Internationale* on June 15, 1921) in just seven months[12].

FIRSTS TO CLEAR THE PATH: MAE JEMISON

I admired Mae Jamison for her courage because outside from television and in the real world, there were no female astronauts. She was a pioneer who entered a field that was male dominated. Space was far from the normal career for women to enter. Although she faced and was steered to go into fields more suitable for females, she stood her ground. A school located in Detroit, Michigan is named in her honor, Jemison Mae C. Elementary School.

Mae Jemison is an American physician and NASA astronaut. She became the first American women to travel in space when she served as a mission specialist aboard the Space Shuttle Endeavor. Jemison knew from a young age that she wanted to study science and one day go into space. The television show *Star Trek* and, in particular, African American actress, Nichelle Nichols' portrayal of Lieutenant Uhura, further stroked her interest in space. Jemison enjoyed studying nature and human physiology, using her observations to learn more about science. Although her mother encouraged her and both parents were supported of her interests in science, she did not always see the same support from her teachers. When Jemison told a kindergarten teacher that she wanted to be a scientist when she grew up, the teacher assumed she meant she wanted to be a nurse. Seeing a lack of female astronauts during the Apollo mission also frustrated Jemison. She later recalled, "Everybody was thrilled about space, but I remember being really, really irritated that there were no women astronauts[13].

MY TRAILBLAZERS: THE BUFFALO SOLDIERS

To celebrate Black History Month, a historic event took place at the Ford Engineering EEE Building. It was hosted by my coworker and friend, Karen Walker, who also was a member of the Ford African American Network (FAAN). She invited me to attend this special program honoring members of the Buffalo Soldiers (Detroit Chapter). The Buffalo Soldiers served in the western United States from 1867 to 1896. They were all African American servicemen from the 9th and 10th Calvary regiments of U. S. Army[14].

The Buffalo Soldiers main tasks were to help control the Native Americans of the Plains, capture cattle rustlers, thieves, protect settlers, stagecoaches, wagon trains and railroad crews along the Western front. They also protected the National Parks. The nickname, Buffalo Soldiers, was given to them from the Native American tribes they encountered in the Indian Wars because of their dark, kinky curly textured hair which resembled the fur of the buffalo[15]. It was an honor to meet the members dressed in uniform and view their memorabilia displays. Although theses trailblazers faithfully served in the military, they still faced and experienced blatant racism and discrimination. They were not provided with the best of equipment. It still was a segregated infantry division, although they were fighting on the battlefield in the West, while at home, African American men, women and children were being lynched, segregated and persecuted in the East[16]. I admire their courage, determination and the fact that they earned the reputation of faithful courageous servants. I also admire their mode of transportation since they traveled on horseback.

WE SHARED SOMETHING IN COMMON
THE MONTFORD POINT MARINES

Robert Middleton, Joe Burrell, Andrew Evans, Edsel Stallings, Calvin Morrison

You never know who knows whom or the history behind their story. I was fortunate through two of my mentor friends, Calvin Morrison and Robert Middleton II, National Commandant, to be introduced to an historic group of black military servicemen, the famous Montford Point Marines. They were America's first black recruits to be inducted into the United States Marine Corps during World War II. My coworker, Calvin Morrison, invited me to attend the Montford Point Marines Annual National Heritage Military Banquet, where the legendary World War II black Marines, Joe Burrell, Edsel Stallings and Andrew Evans were being honored.

Calvin Morrison was a veteran Marine and member of the Black Pilots of America (BPA). He was a licensed pilot, instructor and owned his own Cessna 172 plane. A talented artist and the first African American male "master clay modeler" at Ford, he worked on the interior components for the 1989 Thunderbird project I designed while in the International Studio, plus a few of my other design projects. My other friend, Robert B. Middleton II, was in attendance at the military banquet. Robert is the National Commandant of the Montford Point Marines of America. At the age of five, Robert saw a black Marine wearing the uniform with the red NCO stripe running down his blue trousers, which is what inspired him to become a Marine himself[17].

Both Robert and Calvin were loyal, decorated veterans who not only introduced me to the Montford Point Marines but shared my automotive career accomplishments at Ford.

We were all elated to meet each other. I got a chance to talk to them and hear stories from this phenomenal group of African American servicemen. I learned that the Montford Point Marines got their name from the base where they trained – Camp Montford Point North Caroline (1942-1949). Camp Montford Point was a segregated training site for African American Marine recruits. For the following seven years, the camp remained open until it became desegregated. It took faith in God, courage and strength of character to beat the odds that the world set before the Montford Point Marines while they served in the military and even upon returning home.

Their heroic stories, trials and victories won brought tears of both joy and sorrow after hearing all the things they had to encounter and endure: discrimination and racism in its purest form while on and off the battlefield. These men were true military heroes. In 2012, Congress awarded them with the Congressional Gold Medal, the highest award that can be given to a civilian by Congress. One of the things that the Montford Point Marines shared in common with me, Robert and Calvin was that we were all firsts in our fields – trailblazers in the military and in the auto industry, which opened doors for many others to follow. Meeting the Montford Point Marines enlightened me to see that what I struggled with at Ford with regards to a managerial position never measured or even compared to their challenges and what they faced. Their career journey gave me more determination to fly higher beyond the sky. Before the banquet ended, I had us all take a photo together. Edsel Stallings asked if I would send him a copy of the photos. When I asked him for his address, what a coincidence to find out that we lived in the same neighborhood!

Edsel Stallings and Emeline

WALID, I NEVER KNEW I INSPIRED YOU

When I look back over my career at Ford, I never realized who I had influenced or what effect I had as a female transportation designer in their lives. I remember the time I debuted my first gospel solo concert at my church, Mt. Calvary Baptist. My father was the pastor and my biggest supporter. Dad posted a flyer about my upcoming event for that weekend, Sunday July 8, 1990, near the main entrance on the Design Center employee's bulletin board. I noticed it when I left work that Friday.

On the day of the concert, after I sung my last song, I thanked everyone for coming and acknowledged my guests and visitors. There was a couple seated in the audience. The man stood up. I had never seen him before. He stated how much he and his lady friend enjoyed my concert performance and didn't know I was a multi-talented young lady. He introduced himself as Walid Saba. He had recently gotten hired in 1989 as a transportation designer at the Ford Design Center. He asked if I didn't mind, he would like to share something special that happened to him. He looked at me, pointed and said, "Emeline, it's because of you that I was inspired to become a car designer." He told the congregation, who were all African Americans, how he once read an article in the *Smithsonian* magazine (February 1984, Volume 14, Issue 11, page 78). He saw the picture of an African American girl named Emeline King, who went to the Art Center and was a transportation designer for Ford. Seeing the picture of me in that article motivated him to enroll at Art Center and pursue a career in transportation design, then ended up working at the same place with me. After Walid spoke, there wasn't a dry eye in the audience. We took photos and I introduced him to my family. I told him it was a pleasure and a great honor to have met him too. What a surprise, Walid. I never knew.

INCARCERATED BUT INSPIRED TO RISE: THE EBONY MAN ARTICLE

On another occasion, my boyfriend Donn and I were invited to a friend's house for a Fourth of July get together. Donn was in the kitchen having a conversation with his friend's brother who mentioned that while incarcerated, he was inspired after reading the August 1992 issue of Ebony Man (EM). The article featured a black female car designer named Emeline King from Detroit who designed the Ford 1994 Mustang. When Donn shared this news with me, I realized that it doesn't matter where you are on your highway of life's journeys, there will always a female transportation designer for Ford that was documented through media print. It was even made available in the penal institution to inspire that individual to take a step in a new direction toward a brighter, better and more promising future.

INSPIRED:
JAMES FLOYD, 87 YEARS OLD

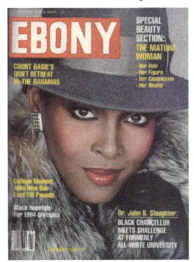

For years, 87-year-old Mr. James Floyd, a former black supervisor for the Detroit Free Press, kept on his living room mantle one of his pride processions: an article in *EBONY magazine* about Emeline King, the first African American Car Designer for Ford Motor Company. One day, Mr. Floyd's granddaughter, Michelle Williams, my oldest brother Earnest Jr.'s girlfriend, came to visit and noticed the article on his mantle. After hearing Mr. Floyd proudly boast to Michelle about this black female car designer who designed cars for Ford, Michelle informed her grandfather of her acquaintance for years with the young lady in the article. At first, he didn't believe Michelle knew me but she finally convinced her grandfather that she knew me because Emeline was her boyfriend's sister and we all grew up and played together on Quincy Street. Also, Michelle and her grandmother Mrs. Russell, lived across the street and were good neighbors to the King family. Down through the years, Michelle kept abreast and knew of all my many accomplishments. Unfortunately, I never got a chance to meet Mr. Floyd, but I was touched to hear he cared enough to have kept the article about me on his mantle. When Mr. James Floyd passed away at the age of 87, it was at the request of Michelle that I sang at his homegoing service. It was a cherished honor.

YOU'RE NEVER TOO OLD TO BE RESPECTED: MOTHER LOIS HOLDEN, MY 110-YEAR-OLD NEIGHBOR

I'm grateful my family grew up in the type of neighborhood where there were good, caring neighbors who mentored, respected and looked out for each other. One lady in particular was Miss Russell, my neighbor on Quincy Street who held the highest respect for both my parents and all the King children. It was in the early 1960s growing up on Quincy Street where only the well-behaved children in our neighborhood were the ones Mama allowed us to play with. One of them was Michelle, the granddaughter to Miss Russell and Mr. James Floyd, whom my parents highly respected. She lived across the street from our house and next door to her granddaughter. My brothers, sisters and I always referred to her as, "Miss Russell, the nice lady across the street." She always kept an eye on us as we played outdoors. My big brother, Earnest Jr. was her favorite little spark of sunshine. If the King children needed a scolding or a kind word of encouragement, as a neighbor, she made it her business to step up to the plate.

Miss Russell was a Motown recording gospel artist. She sung with the Heavenly Chanters and the Gospel Stars on the Motown Label and toured with the Motown Revue. One day, she informed my mother that she needed someone to play some chords on the piano for her. We owned a piano in our home since my mother was the pianist for her church, Antietam Baptist Church. She suggested my sister Am. Mama felt that this would be a good opportunity for Miss Russell to mentor an aspiring upcoming young gospel musician. As the years passed, my family stayed closely connected to Miss Russell. She and my Dad had a special bond. After her former church dissolved, my father took her in as a member of our church.

Mother Lois (Russell) Holden was born on February 3, 1910, two years after the Ford Model T was built. It was the first Sunday in February 2019. We celebrated her 109th birthday at my church, Mt. Calvary Baptist Church. Everybody was there to show her much love: all of the Mt. Calvary members, my family, Mother Holden's family, her special son whom she adored, John, who was Caucasian, with his lovely wife Dawn. Mother Lois (Russell) Holden had raised him from the age of two. State Representative, Issac Robinson, presented the State of Michigan award to commemorate her 109th birthday. Her niece, Cerita, on behalf of the Detroit City Council, presented the Spirit of Detroit Award. Both Mother (Russell) Holden and I held something in common - we both were recipients of the Spirit of Detroit award. There was a resolution read in her honor from the Council of Baptist Pastors of Detroit and Vicinity where the honorable Dr. Dee Dee Coleman served as president. Media representatives from the Detroit News, Free Press, Michigan Chronicle, Shot News and WDIV Channel 4 captured and recorded this historic event.

It was during her interview with the media press where Michelle, my father and I sat in on and listened with admiration as she shared her life story, career, love for God and her family. She gave special recognition and love for the King family. She watched each one of the King children grow up and didn't mind chastising them. She was proud being neighbors to the King family. She praised my parents on how well they raised their children and brought them up in a Christian home environment to groom them to be successful obedient children. She wasn't afraid to let everyone in the room know that my father was a well-respected man in the neighborhood and how she *"loved her Pastor!"* She knew of all our accomplishments. I was totally surprised when she mentioned my success as being, "A black female car designer for Ford." What an amazing talented woman of God to acknowledge her cherished memories of us.

Mother Lois (Russell) Holden turned 110 on Monday, February 3, 2020. That first Sunday, Mt. Calvary was blessed to give our oldest member, Mother Lois (Russell) Holden, another extravagant celebration dinner party at our church. Her family was present along with local and state representatives who presented her with awards which acknowledged the oldest living person in Wayne County. Having a caring neighbor like Mother Lois (Russell) Holden when my siblings and I were growing up taught me how a person's true character never changes; how you were raised and what you accomplished in life can influence someone no matter how young or old they are.

You never know who is watching or looking out for you. Thank you, Mother Lois (Russell) Holden, for being, *"My special neighbor who cared."*

CHAPTER TEN
SHE DID IT

"THINK POSITIVE"
COLLECT YOUR ACCOMPLISHMENTS

There came a time when I was at a low point about where my career path at Ford was heading. I focused on the negative things I had been through and was going through, rather than the multitude of positive things I had accomplished. Would the day ever come for me when I would not be passed over for a promotion into management? I was the last player left on the bench as I watched my coworkers, the male designers and every female designer who got hired in after me, get promoted into both middle and upper management all from different ethnic backgrounds: Caucasian, Asian, Hispanic, Filipino, Italian, Chinese, Korean, and African American males. I thought: *Could it be that an African American female isn't good enough to have a place in the management team of Corporate America's Design Center no matter how successful her design contributions were*? For years of being the only African American female transportation designer, I just got tired of *never* being considered or selected, knowing my appointment would complete the fabric of a 'diverse' management team representation at the Design Center.

I knew I was destined to design cars and had made major design contributions. I always strived my best to make my talents and gifts better, yet it was always a struggle trying to reach one simple goal of being promoted into management. Even after I demonstrated numerous successful design production projects, along with my leadership abilities and having the most seniority, this plight seemed unpalatable. I recalled a special conversation with my friend Donn who suggested that I take a step back and just focus my attention on the positive things I had achieved. He was aware of everything that I accomplished at Ford and all the things that were obstacles in my path that I was trying to achieve. He advised me to collect every printed material that featured me as Ford's female African American transportation designer, along with every successful design project, award, letter of recognition, etc. and bind it in a book: "Emeline's Portfolio of Accomplishments." Donn told me, "Up until now, you really haven't seen your total impact and value by just focusing on minor obstacles. "Emeline, your portfolio of accomplishments documents all you have completed and achieved so far in your career at Ford. It's the total proven track record of even far more greater things to come. Your roadmap is evidence to what is possible for every little girl or female who aspires to design cars one day."

🇬🇧 Moving the dream forward, a Ford U.K. designer compares hard design and engineering points on a large air-brushed rendering.

Throughout my years at the Design Center, I kept every article on all my successful accomplishments. So I took his advice and assembled magazines, newspaper articles, television and radio interviews, speeches, awards, recognition letters, etc. that I had been featured in and placed them chronological order in several binders. I never realized how much material I had collected down through the years. It was overwhelming! My mom even went and laminated many of my articles that she had kept over time to go into the binder. I achieved so much that my positive accomplishments outweighed all of the negative roadblocks by a landslide.

Wow! I never took time to see the whole picture and all I had already accomplished at Ford in one setting. I'm thankful Donn Johnson, this phenomenal musician and educator, suggested that I make a portfolio collection of my life at Ford documented in print accomplishments. In addition, Donn informed me, "Emeline, you'll never know the full scope or how much your life's career and what you've accomplished had and will forever impact and touch others. *Ms. Trailblazer,* you might not at this moment have a few letters of the alphabet behind your name to represent a managerial title, but it can never measure up to your design production works that have gained recognition and exposure both internally and externally. Your strong determination helped you to fulfill your childhood dream. You never gave up and most importantly, you have earned and designed your place in history."

A LETTER TO MY EMPLOYER
WILLIAM CLAY FORD JR.

By January 2002, I had already celebrated my 19th anniversary. While my service years at Ford increased, my chances for promotion into management still remained stagnant compared to how the other male and female transportation designer coworkers continued to flourish. I continued to meet with HR and management for guidance, feedback and direction on my career path and opportunities for a promotion into management. I shared my feelings with my Dad who always been supportive. He encouraged me, "Emeline, keep doing your best. Write everything down. Don't get discouraged and don't give up. God hasn't forgotten about you." He suggested, "Since you haven't made progress up to this point in this goal you've been trying for several years to achieve, why not write a certified letter to Mr. William Clay Ford, Jr. and address your concerns to him? Tell him about your background and what you've accomplished. Just let him know how you feel and how you've been treated. What do you have to lose, Emeline? Everybody breathes the same air."

So I took Dad's advice and sent a registered letter to Mr. Ford. I informed him about the things my father told me to say. To my surprise, two weeks later I received an email from Mr. Ford's office that a person from Human Resources had been assigned to check into this matter. Unfortunately, nothing was resolved, but I was still determined not to throw in my towel.

DISAPPOINTED DETOUR:
OUT OF DESIGN TO BRAND MARKETING

January 7, 2007 is a day that I won't forget. I never imagined the day would come when my world of "designing cars" sailed over the cliff. My manager informed me of my next assignment in the marketing side of the company. I would be moving out of the Design Center's design studios and transferred to the brand marketing studio. In my opinion, this transfer was shattering.

I sensed Ford was trying to oust me and limit my design creativity. Brand marketing was on the opposite side of the spectrum compared to a designer's love and skills to create profitable design concepts and production vehicles, a process where I was most experienced, efficient and contributing at the Design Center. My transfer over to brand marketing would seal my fate to not be able to design cars for Ford Motor Company Design Center. This was more disappointing than not receiving a managerial promotion. I wasted no time in discussing my transfer with both my manager and Human Resources. Yes, it made me mad as hell that I no longer worked as a designer but would have to succumb my skills to secretarial data entry, paperwork, ordering competitive cars for research and development, making comparison charts, and setting up displays for reviews. None of these assignments involved much artistry or creativity. I looked back on what it all took for me to get to this point in my career - the education, sacrifices and skills that prepared me for my transportation journey. I would rather apply them in design.

This was a huge disappointment to end up analyzing competitive vehicles instead of creating them. Even more devastating to me was that I was never transferred back to my design area in the Design Center to *design cars*, my one and only passion. Don't get me wrong. I respected brand marketing and never had a problem with learning new and different genres but working in the Design Center's design studios, I was surrounded and embedded in a creative design environment. I enjoyed contributing to every car and truck program. I got satisfaction from designing and seeing my selected two-dimensional design concepts evolved into three-dimensional mass produced and profitable Ford vehicles.

"THEY DID YOU A FAVOR, POSTER CHILD"

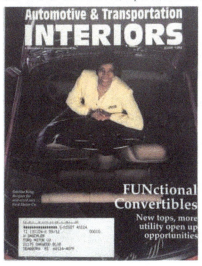

Workplace diversity sensitivity was being implemented at the Design Center. The Human Resources department incorporated a new department to address these issues. They even hired an African American female to head the diversity department. Well, it was about time! I immediately scheduled a meeting with her thinking maybe she could relate to what I had experienced by us both being black females. Maybe she had the solution to solve my problems as an African American female in Corporate America and the barriers that hindered my path from movement up the corporate ladder.

I shared my work history at Ford, my big transfer out of design over to brand marketing and the numerous times I was passed over for a managerial promotion. I even brought in my book collection of Ford accomplishments and achievements to show her, of which she was amazed and astonished. She mentioned diversity in the workplace was high on the radar scale and the Design Center has dealt with it by offering diversity training for its employees plus middle and upper management. She stated that she would like to arrange another meeting with Design Center's management. Maybe this time my concerns would finally be resolved. Unfortunately, the meeting turned out unproductive.

I went back to meet with the diversity representative one more time and she shared her feedback and overview. She concluded it in one statement: "Girl, you're nothing but Ford's poster child." She went on to say, "They've done you a really big favor with all your media exposure in magazines and newspapers and flying you all over the place to represent this company." You're not the only black who this has happened to." It was quite emotional for me after hearing those comments. She told me, "You're stressed out. Maybe you need counseling? I could arrange for you to get some counseling right now. Your medical insurance allows you three free sessions." Well, I never expected she'd say the answer to my concern was counseling. After hearing that statement, my mind reflected on what Daddy had been telling me throughout my entire career at Ford. "Emeline, don't worry over or about *anything*. God's gonna work it out for you." His plans for you are far bigger and greater than man's. I told the diversity representative, "Please don't get me wrong; I'm not stressed out. I'm concerned about what can be done about how I've been passed over. I'm always open for sound advice and direction." I attended a couple of the free sessions where I expressed to the therapist what I had experienced as a black female car designer dealing with the barriers that existed within Corporate America. I knew it wasn't going to be easy for a black female in a male dominant field, but I was there for the fight. My upbringing, educational background, support groups and mentors prepared me for these challenges. I only wished I could have a spot and move up the corporate ladder like other ethnic (both male and female) designers. I was well qualified but maybe in the mindset of corporate America "well qualified, is not enough."

After counseling, I involved myself with other black organizations within Ford. I continued to surround myself with mentors for their support and direction, my family for encouragement and strength, with my total faith and trust in God that He would guide, direct and bring me through.

THE FORD AFRICAN AMERICAN NETWORK (FAAN)

The Ford African American Network (FAAN) is an organization made up of African American Ford employees. They address several African American issues and concerns plus host events, and workshops that are informative, educational and motivating. They often brought in well-known black guest keynote speakers in various business, entertainment, social and political fields to enlighten and share their career paths. On several occasions, I had the pleasure of meeting and talking with some highly successful people: Julian Bond, Travis Smiley, Diana Carolyn, Susan Taylor and the top black male CEO executives at Ford.

Earlier that year, I attended a symposium given by FAAN. The event took place at Ford's World Headquarters' auditorium. The room was filled with Ford employees and on stage was a panel of men and women from one of the business management sectors. The commentator for the evening approached the podium and asked everyone to turn their attention toward the table which contained a clear half glass of water. She posed a question to the audience, "Who can tell me if this glass of water which I hold in my hand half-filled or half empty?" Several employees in the audience shouted out their answers, but there was only one answer from a black man seated next to me that stuck with me the most. He replied, "It all depends on your situation at hand and how you see it!" I took his strong answer into consideration and compared it to how I looked at my entire career path at Ford.

I analyzed and weighed everything I had experienced and accomplished at Ford's Design Center. How did I view my overall career at Ford? Was I seeing my life at Ford as a glass half-filled with disappointments, barriers, let downs, pass over's for promotions, and a non-managerial status? No! My eyes were opened. The glass represented my successful career path at Ford half-filled with accomplished design concepts that made production. The other half of empty space represented a cleared, positive pathway, guide and road map that I had set for every male or female after me to follow.

DR. FREDERICK G. SAMPSON: MY SPIRITUAL MENTOR

After my last meeting with the diversity department of Human Resources about this situation, I decided to place my mountain of disparity in God's hands. It was too high for me to climb and fight. I never wavered in faith. I knew God hadn't brought me this far to let my gifts, talents and goals not be fulfilled, recognized and rewarded. I didn't want to waste any more time and energy about a position in management and being transferred out of the design phase into brand marketing. I remembered what Dr. Frederick G. Sampson, my spiritual and intellectual mentor who I deeply admired, told me at one of my father's pastoral anniversary banquets where he was the guest speaker. He and I engaged in conversation about my Ford achievements and challenges. Dr. Sampson always encouraged me with his spiritual advice that helped me address and solve my own concerns. He had a way of using the simplest phrases, anecdotes, biblical scriptures, poems and stories of his own personal experiences to compare, address and solve problems.

I always found it captivating to be in his presence as I sat and listened to the sound of his authoritative, baritone voice as he spoke to me in a medieval English dialect. One of his favorite poems which he often quoted was "Harlem" by Langston Hughes.

That poem motivated me to not let my dream just sit and lay dormant or become dried up and wither away. Dr. Sampson told me, "Don't allow the cluttered debris to cloud your focal point. It can all be blown away. You have been equipped with all the tools needed to overcome whatever is set before you, even with being passed over several times for a promotion into management." He told me whenever I felt discouraged about what I was going through on my job to "hang onto hope". He told me to keep on pushing when it felt like I was slipping into despair. "Grab a hold of hope, hang on tight, pull yourself up and make your mark in the pages of history. Don't look back, you've made it!"

Mom, Dr. Frederick G. Sampson, Kyla Williams (niece), Emeline, Brianna Torrence (niece)

P.U.S.H.

Praying to God for strength and direction enabled me to get through a lot of tough times and situations on my job. It kept me centered and focused on what I was destined to do, which was to design cars. When I looked over my career at Ford, the one *main thing* I always did was pray until something happened. It was just one of several things that both Dr. Sampson and my parents told me to rely upon. I recalled a conversation one evening with Dr. Sampson and his words to me were to "keep on pushing". Those three words inspired me to never give up on whatever I set out to accomplish. Outside of designing cars, my second love was in music. Both design and music kept me balanced. Music has always been a part of my life vocally and instrumentally. In my spare time, this was a great opportunity to work on my other gift. I recorded my first CD project and wrote an inspired song entitled P.U.S.H. I used the word "push" as an acronym which stands for "pray until something happens".

I asked Donn to produce my CD project. His expertise in music and as a musician was perfect as he scored, arranged and played the instruments on my CD project. Donn and I spent numerous hours in the pre-production stage to avoid unnecessary time spent in the studio because time equals money. Donn arranged my studio sessions to be recorded at one of his musician friend's studio. Kevin, who was Irish and a professionally skilled engineer, mixed the music for my CD. I used my design skills for the CD cover and had it packaged and manufactured through World Class Tapes Company in Ann Arbor, Michigan.

My first CD project was a success with great support and demand. Although I never made management, I still remained devoted to my job and continued making design contributions that went into production. All my praying was not in vain, especially when I pushed - prayed until something happened.

SHE DID IT

October 24, 1983 is the day I hired in at Ford and walked down the long, white corridor hall at the Ford Design Center. I stopped in front of the blue door that first day aroused by my curiosity at age seven while attending Dad's employee Christmas party and questionied 'what was behind it?' Disappointed, I wanted to go behind that blue door, but Dad told me I couldn't enter because I was a visitor and didn't have access. Well, today I am a Ford employee with an ID badge and complete access as a Ford transportation designer assigned to work at the Design Center's International Studio. I had to take in a deep breath and exhale for a moment…because I was now a part of an elite, talented group of men who designed cars that my father had once told me about.

My childhood dream was fulfilled. I was designing cars for Ford with my father!

Emeline with 1994 Ford Mustang

Dad with 1979 Fiberglass Model   Dad at the Design Center with 1979 Ford Mustang

Please be my guest, hop in the front seat, and take a ride with me on this journey. Buckle up and fast forward twenty-five years later. Never would I have imagined that on Friday, July 31, 2008 at 3:30 p.m. that I would be escorted out of the Ford Design Center brand marketing department by my supervisor and a security guard. I was given involuntary company separation with 24.9 years of service. I wish they could have waited a few months; then, I would have had twenty-five service years. I left carrying only the few personal belongings I was able to fit into a 12x12 brown cardboard box. Embarrassed! Devastated.

Throughout my entire Ford career, I was determined to break through the cement ceiling that hindered so many African Americans, particularly women, from achieving design goals and a managerial position in a male-dominated auto industry. For this poster child who graced the covers of numerous magazines, represented Ford, and designed cars that satisfied the buying public and was profitable for the company was now a clear, white 18x20 inch blank poster. It was time to shift gears and push the pedal to the metal. Full speed ahead. Today, would be my final exit. Goodbye blue door.

EPILOGUE

The one good thing about my journey is it didn't come to a dead end but detoured toward higher and more promising adventures. Although my job classification as a transportation designer who designed vehicles for Ford ended once I walked out of the blue door at the Design Center on Friday July 31, 2008, it didn't close or lock the door on my abilities as a designer who is capable of designing anything. I knew there would be unlimited possibilities and opportunities waiting for me that outnumbered the infinite stars in the sky. I'm grateful to have shared my story with you. May it encourage and enlighten all who traveled or are traveling on a dark and uncharted road. I left the high beams on for you. I never gave up. I overcame adversities, roadblocks, and setbacks and accomplished much in design as the first African American female transportation designer for Ford. I fulfilled my dream's passion.

I'm proud to have designed, worked and represented an amazing organization like Ford Motor Company. Throughout my career at Ford, I designed production cars that made their presence on the road and have carried into the future. Yes, after all I overcame, achieved, accomplished and broke through that cement corporate ceiling. I believe after reading my autobiography, it will be inspirational and motivational for every little girl and boy to go far beyond where my footsteps have been. They now have a roadmap they can follow. That road has been cleared and paved. Thank you, Ford Motor Company for being my springboard to heights I never would have achieved in a design career.

ACKNOWLEDGEMENTS

To every mentor, my gratitude for you because you served as my multi-constructed bridges that guided me across to conquer every dream and challenge I faced. I'm thankful throughout my entire career at Ford for the unwavering love and support of my father and mother who encouraged me. "Emeline, you might give out, but don't ever give up!"

To my sisters, brothers, relatives, church families, friends, instructors and Ford coworkers, you were the "premium gasoline" in my tank that kept me running throughout my career journey.

To my publisher, Dr. De'Andrea Matthews, founder and CEO of Claire Aldin Publications, my many thanks to you because you were God sent. Your role in my body chassis of life served as the four wheels that enabled me to travel and reach a final destination in publication. Through your guidance and expertise, my two-dimensional childhood dream of designing cars at Ford with my father was manifested into a three-dimensional autobiographical book. I pray my autobiographical journey will impact all who are determined to venture out, take the "keys of their dreams" and turn the ignition to accomplish every goal and succeed.

Finally, I never would have accomplished becoming the first female African American transportation designer at Ford and have worked with my father without God's blessings, directions and guidance.

To God be the glory for all the things He has done in Emeline's life.

What do you mean a black girl can't design cars?

Emeline King, she did it.

APPENDIX

ACHIEVEMENTS AND ACCOMPLISHMENTS IN MEDIA & PRINT

Emeline King's list of accomplishments in media and print that occurred during and after the 1994 Mustang project:

Source	Date	Notes	Title	Author
Smithsonian	February 1984	Volume 14, Issue 11, Page 78	Tomorrow's Cars Taking Shape Now in Pasadena	Ellen Ruppel Shell
Ebony	January 1984	Volume 39, Number 3, Page 84	Black Auto Designers: Talented Few Help Shape the Future for Ford	
The Executive Female	May/June 1985	Volume VIII, Number 3, Page 39		
Michigan Chronicle	September 5, 1987		Business in the Black: Auto Designer Heads Overseas	
Ebony: The Annual Men's Issue	June 2003	Volume LVIII, Number 8, Page 45	Ebony Salutes Ford Motor Company & Black America: A 100-Year Adventure	

Dollars and $ense	November 1992	Pages 7-8	America's Best and Brightest: 1992 Tribute Highlights	
Dollars and $ense	Winter Edition	Page 17	Black Auto Designers & Engineers	
Career Focus	September 1991	Volume 4, Number 4, Page 61	Childhood Dream Becomes Reality for Young Engineer	Freida Curtindale
Detroit Metropolitan Woman	July 1992	Volume 2, Number 7, Page 23	Auto Designers Consider Women's Needs	
Ebony Man (EM)	August 1992	Volume 7, Number 10, Page 37	Black Automobile Designers Though Still Relatively Few in Number, They're Drawing Attention by Drawing Well	

Publication	Date	Volume/Page	Title	Author
YSB	November 1992	Volume 2, Number 3, Page 26	What's Going On? Did You Know	Lori Dodson
American Woman	December 1992	Volume 4, Number 6, Page 54	Muscle Building	
Frontline	October/November 1993	Volume 2, Number 6, Page 25	Design Center Ford Cars and Trucks: From Concept to Reality	
Cosmopolitan	February 1993	Volume 214, Number 2, Page 171	Moving On from an Entry Level Job	Linda Stern
Road & Track Special Series: Guide to the New 1994 Ford Mustang	February 1, 1994	Page 42	Mustang Style Capturing the Essence of America's Favorite Pony Car	John Lamm
Motor Trend	January 1994	Volume 46, Number 1, Page 18	MT Car of the Year Paces Indy 500	Daniel Charles Ross
Motor Trend		Page 50	The Power of Ideas At The Wheel	
Upscale	February 1994	Page 61		

Automotive & Transportation		Page 118	Front Cover Functional Convertibles	
Essence	November 1994	Volume 25, Number 7, Page 118	Rollin with a King	John Russell
Essence	November 1997	Page 160	Lifestyle Road Scholars	
Career 2000		Page 24	The Ford Mustang Is One Hot Car: Designers Like Emeline King Planned It That Way	
Washington Post	1993		King Retooled The Mustang into the Hottest Car of the Year	
LVC Lately	Winter 1999	Issue 6		
WCHB 1440			Radio Interview	John Mason
CBS Morning Show	1994		North American International Auto Show	
Good Morning America Design	1994		North American International Auto Show	

ADDITIONAL MEDIA CONTRIBUTIONS

11/17/1991	New York, PA	Women Are No Longer Just Taking a Back Seat in the Car Industry
4/26/1992	The Gwinnett Daily News	Auto Designer Predicts Shape of Future Cars
6/12/1992	The Atlanta Journal	Ford Hires Young Guns to Fire Up New Mustang
7/9/1992	Automotive Weekly	Women Behind The Wheels: She's Hard at Work with Ford's New Mustang Team
9/1992	Minority Business News USA	
1/6/1992	Michigan Chronicle	Ford Edition: Auto Design Has a lot to Offer
11/9/1993	Drivetime Extra (Winston Salem)	Elegant Muscle
12/26/1993	The Washington Post	Business Section: A Makeover with Muscle
1/30/1994	Chicago Tribune Women's News	New Breed Enters the Male World of Cars by Design
3/9/1994	Las Vegas Review Journal Living	Women Playing Larger Role in Designing Cars
11/15/2020 until 1/9/2022	Detroit Institute of Arts	Detroit Style: Car Design in the Motor City 1950-2020

FORD CORPORATE PUBLIC RELATIONS EVENTS

Presentations on the Design Development Process of the 1994 Mustang and MACH III Concept Car

10/1993	Mustang Blitz '94	Winston Salem and Greensboro, North Carolina
9/1993	1994 Ford Mustang Launch	Solvang, California
9/1994	The World Press Institute	Dearborn Inn, Dearborn, Michigan
5/29/1994	1994 Mustang Official Pace Car Graphics/Roll Bar	78th Indianapolis 500 Speedway, Indianapolis, Indiana
9/1993	MACH III - Denver International Airport opening	Denver, Colorado
7/1993	SN95 Long Lead Process	Dearborn Proving Grounds, Dearborn, Michigan
6/1993	MACH III – SWE Convention	Chicago, Illinois
4/1993	MACH III Media Day	Sears Point Raceway, Sonoma, California

FORD CORPORATE PUBLIC RELATIONS EVENTS

Presentations on the Design Development Process of the 1994 Mustang

Women's Marketing

8/1993	American Driver and Traffic Safety Education Association (ADTSEA)	Troy, Michigan
4/1993	University of Michigan – Marketing Students	Ann Arbor, Michigan
4/1993	Take Your Child to Work Day Ford Design Center	Dearborn, Michigan

1989 Foreign Service Assignments: Sub B Compact
Full-size Clay Dinoc Models
Ford Design Center - Essex, England

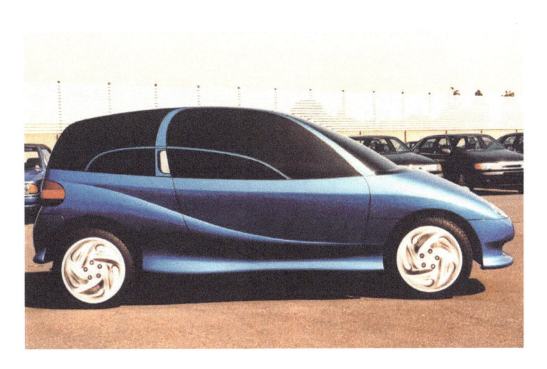

1989 Foreign Service Assignments: Sub B Compact
3/4 Split Clay Dinoc Models, Concept Sketch
Ford Design Center - Essex, England

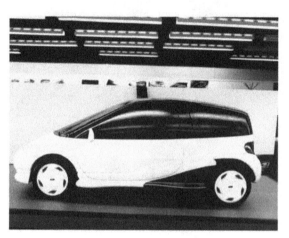

1989 Foreign Service Assignments: Sub B Compact
Canson Rendering Concepts
Ford Design Center - Essex, England

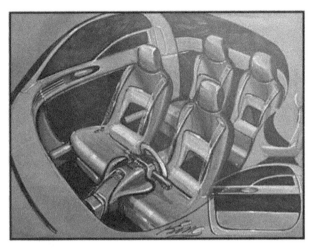

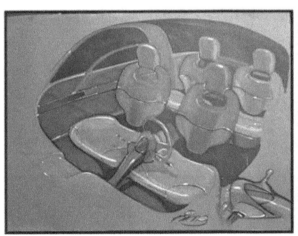

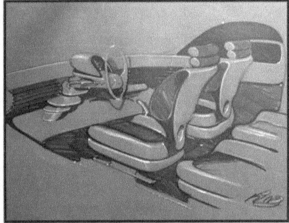

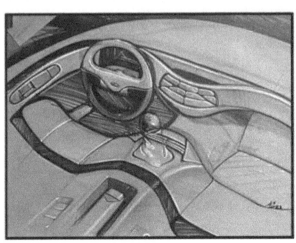

Mustang Studio Design Center
1990 Mustang MACH III Theme Renderings

Roush Off-Site Studio 1994 Mustang Official Pace Car

1994 Mustang Celebration
Ford World Headquarters - Dearborn, Michigan

Emeline with Sir Mack Rice and Tracey Bush, Ford co-worker

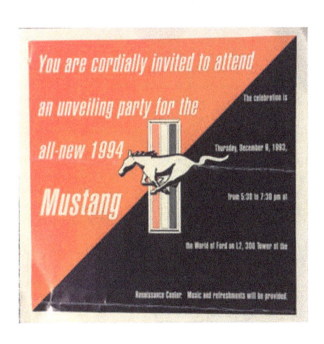

Sing-a-long performance with Sir Mack Rice, composer of Mustang Sally, with me and Tracey Bush

Mustang Studio Design Center
1990 Mustang MACH III Concept Vehicle

Small Car Exterior MN205 Studio
2002 Ford Thunderbird Two-Seater Convertible Hard Top

Small Car Exterior MN205 Studio
2002 Ford Thunderbird Interior Seats and Door Trim Concepts

Small Car Exterior MN205 Studio
2002 Thunderbird Hard Top Convertible Two-Seater Concepts

SN97 Mustang Exterior Concept - Small Car Studio
SN95 Center Console Concepts - Mustang Interior Studio

D197 Interior Door Trim - Mid-size Luxury Studio

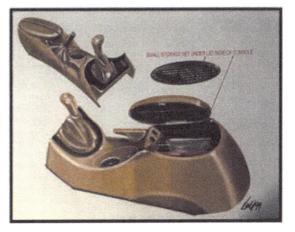
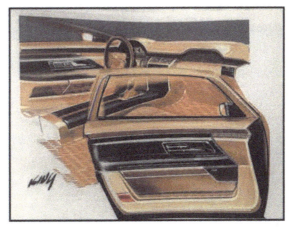

Future Two-Seater Sports Car with Interior Trim Concepts

Future Ford Model T Roadster and Interior Trim Sketch Concepts

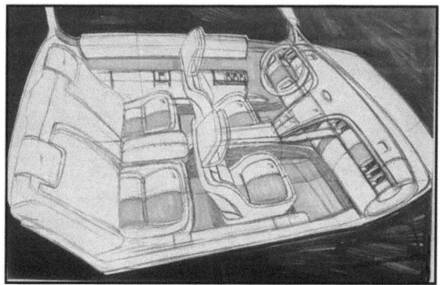

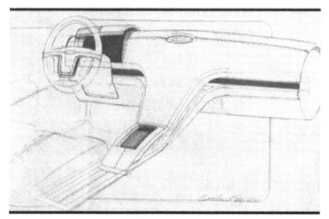

Jill of All Trades Acrylic Paintings

Bourbon Street Beats

Jill of All Trades Acrylic Paintings

Georgia On My Mind

Jill of All Trades Acrylic Paintings

R.E.S.P.E.C.T.

Soul

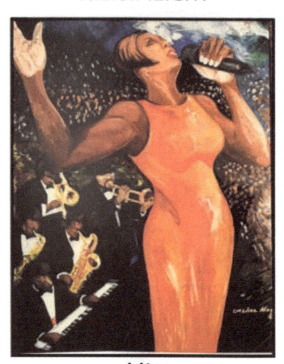
Misty

Madonna and Child

Jill of All Trades Acrylic Paintings

Meling Take Five
presentation to Rodney Whitaker, Jazz Bassist

Eboni Eyes

Donn's Favorite Things

Jill of All Trades Celebrity Acrylic Paintings

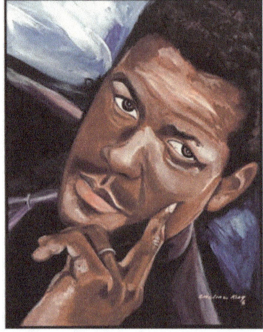

Jill of All Trades Acrylic Paintings

First Lady (Mama) Mrs. Emogene King

The Family That Prays Together Stays Together

Adoration & Praise

I Got Music In Me
Emeline's Concert Performances at Mt. Calvary Baptist Church

Mt. Olive Baptist Church

Front Row: Sidney Holmes (musician), Isaac Prince (musician), Emeline, Dad, Mom
Back Row: (background singers) Hollis Anderson, Evelyn "Am" (musician), Ida Abbington, Eugenia "Kizzy", Pierre Radney

I Bet You Can't Play That Sax, Lenny Girl

Pic 1- Dad playing his tenor sax
Pic 2 - Emeline with Mr. Bobby Barnes
Pic 3 - Emeline's saxophone instructors Mr. John Garland and Mr. Bobbie Barnes

Emeline's alto saxophone, Ms. Purple Priscilla
and soprano saxophone, Ms. Song of Solomon

Mt. Calvary Baptist Church Music Department

Emeline (alto sax), Evelyn "Am" (minister of music, organ)
Saxophone Tribute to Mom and Dad at their Pastoral Anniversary

2010 Winner of Detroit Stars Singing Competition

Contestant winner announced; Emeline pictured with contest judges

Emeline's solo performance of "Summer Time"
Comerica Bank Grand Prize

2010 Detroit Stars Singing Competition Winner

Emeline performs The National Anthem at Comerica Park
during the National Negro League Weekend

Comerica Park with Mom and Dad

I Got Music In Me
Emeline's Concert Performances at Davison Missionary Baptist Church

Evelyn "Am", Shamiah Jackson (makeup artist), Emeline, Eugenia "Kizzy",
Davison's Pastor Dr. David Yarber, Jr. and First Lady Wren Yarber

I Got Music In Me
Emeline's Concert Performances at Davison Missionary Baptist Church

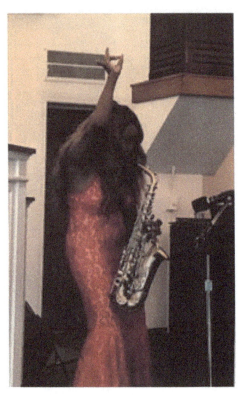

Special Presentation of a beautiful floral bouquet designed by my sister Eugenia "Kizzy"

Emeline, Dad and Eugenia "Kizzy"

You're Never Too Old to be Respected
Mother Holden - My 110 year-old Neighbor

The Rev. Earnest O. King Sr. right, holds the hand of "Mother" Lois Holden while King's daughter Emeline King presents Holden with flowers, and John Awrey of Brighton, left, who was raised by Holden, smiles.
ROBIN BUCKSON, THE DETROIT NEWS

Mt. Calvary Baptist Church Birthday Celebration for Mother Holden
From the top: Evelyn, Eugenia, Mother Holden, Emeline
Middle Row: Earnest, Jr. Errol David, Dad and Michelle Williams (granddaughter)
Bottom Row: Mother Holden's Family - John Awrey (son), Emeline, Dawn Awrey (daughter-in-law)

The King Family

Earnestine (Tine), Earnest (Dad), Emeline, Errol David (Bobbie), Emogene (Mama), Evelyn (Am), Eugenia (Kizzy), Earnest, Jr. (Brother)

Designer Perspectives
Detroit Style: Car Design in the Motor City
1950-2020

"My favorite medium is clay. I like the feel of clay. I like the smell of clay. Working with clay, you're able to take a two-dimensional sketch and have that transferred into a three-dimensional shape."
https://www.dia.org

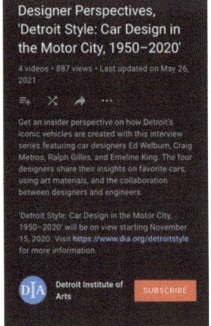

REFERENCES

1. Michigan Chronicle. *Auto Designer Heads Overseas.* September 5, 1987.
2. Gupta, Tanya. BBC News. *Great Storm 1987: The Day 18 People Were Killed.*
3. http://www.core77.com./posys/39532/Mimi-Vandermolen-the-Ergonomics-Genius-Behind-Fords-"Rounded-Edge-Revolution"
4. en.wikipedia.org/wiki/Ford_Mustang_(fourth_generation).
5. Russell, John. Essence Magazine. *Rollin' With a King.* November 1994. Volume 25, Number 7, p. 118.
6. Ruppel, Ellen Shell. Smithsonian. *Tomorrow's cars is taking shape now in Pasadena: Automobile makers around the world look to California's Art Center College of Design for the People to Lead Them into the Future.* February 1984. Volume 14, Issue 11, p.78.
7. en.wikipedia.org/wiki/Preston_Tucker
8. detroithistorical.org
9. en.wikipedia.org/wiki/DMC_DeLorean
10. www.imdb.com/name/nm0574927/
11. en.wikipedia.org/wiki/SydMead
12. www.biography.com/explorer/bessie-coleman
13. en.m.wikipedia.org/wiki/Mae_jemison.org
14. https://www.nps.gov/articles/buffalso-soldiers.htm
15. en.m.wikipedia.org/wiki/buffalo_soldiers.org
16. www.history.com/topic/westward-expansion/buffalo
17. www.google.com/amp/s/www.wxyz.com/news/person-of-the-week/robert-middleton-is-honoring-the-legacy-of-the-montford-point-marines%3f_amp=true

ABOUT THE AUTHOR

As a "Jill of all trades," Emeline King is a prodigy of the fine arts. Going 'against the grain', Emeline kept her mind on her dream: designing cars for Ford Motor Company with her father. Despite being told what "Girls can and should do," Emeline relentlessly chased her dream despite the societal views of her time. Emeline earned a Bachelor of Fine Arts in Industrial Design from Wayne State University, along with a Bachelor of Science in Transportation Design from Art Center College of Design in Pasadena, California and a certificate in graphic design from Specs Howard School of Media Arts.

Emeline joined the design team at Ford Motor Company in 1983. Tearing down racial and gender barriers, this opportunity earned Emeline the distinction of being the first African American female car designer for Ford Motor Company. To date, Emeline still holds this honor. Emeline's concept designs did not go unnoticed. She has earned several accolades, along with being featured in a variety of news media print, radio and television ads: *Smithsonian, Road & Track, Motor Trend, Ebony, Essence, Ebony Man, The Washington Post* and *The Michigan Chronicle,* to name a few. Emeline was the recipient of the first Annual Fast Trak Award from *Dollars and Sense* Magazine.

Emeline's God-given gifts are multi-dimensional. Not being restricted to her professional car design career, Emeline operates heavily in several forms of fine arts. Gifted to sing and play several musical instruments, Emeline was the winner of the 2010 Detroit's All-Stars Singing Competition hosted by Comerica Bank and 107.5 Kiss FM Radio. She's had the distinct honor of performing the national anthem at Comerica Park during the National Negro League Baseball All-Stars Game. Emeline sings with the Gospel Music Workshop of America (GMWA): Detroit Chapter and The Kenneth Wilson Chorale. Emeline produced her first hip-hop gospel CD entitled, "W. W. J. D. (What Would Jesus Do)" which was featured at her first solo gospel concert. Having rendered inspirational, soul-stirring performances on local, national and international platforms, Emeline continues to pursue her musical career, collaborating vocally and instrumentally on upcoming performances and album projects.

Emeline freelances as a graphic art designer. Her hobbies include acrylic portraits/abstract paintings, caricatures and sculpturing. The owner of King Enterprises, LLC, Emeline is a Zumba and group fitness instructor. Emeline works with the youth at her church and designs stage props and costumes for various stage plays.

Emeline currently works as a substitute teacher for Detroit Public Schools system and other local districts. As a motivational speaker, Emeline enjoys mentoring and encouraging youth by telling them that *"Opportunity is unlimited — regardless of your gender. Don't be afraid to 'plunge and soar' into uncharted waters. Rely strongly upon God for His direction. Pray for wisdom and understanding. He will send the right people and mentors in your life to be bridges over troubled waters to nurture, help and assist you to carry your dreams over to reality."*

Emeline's father always told her, "Lenny Girl, everybody has a story in them." Adhering to her father's words of wisdom, Emeline is now adding 'author' to her extensive resume. Emeline is currently working on two projects: designing illustrations for *But Emeline's a Girl, She Draws Cars, Too?* which is the children's book version of her autobiography, *What Do You Mean A Black Girl Can't Design Cars? Emeline King, She Did It!* She is also working on her father's upcoming book release. Emeline endeavors to have her children's book distributed in every educational facility.

Born and raised in Detroit, Michigan, Emeline is the proud daughter of Reverend Earnest O. King, Sr. and Mrs. Emogene King. A member of Mt. Calvary Baptist Church where her father serves as pastor, Emeline serves as choir directress for Mt. Calvary, as well as directress for the Calvary District Association Voices of Calvary and Davison Missionary Baptist Church.

"God has given me multi-dimensional talents and gifts for which I'm truly grateful. My gift of thanks to God is to use each one to its fullest for His glory, my inner self satisfaction and mankind's entertainment."

~Emeline King

CPSIA information can be obtained
at www.ICGtesting.com
Printed in the USA
BVHW021548140123
656278BV00002B/6